Eternal Treasures:
TEACHING YOUR CHILD
at HOME

by Cheryl Swope and Rachel Whiting

Thoughts About Eternal Treasures: Teaching Your Child at Home

Eternal Treasures, the new book from LCMS School Ministry, is a resource for parents, pastors, congregations, and schools to nurture the next generation in Christ and in all that is good, true, and beautiful. Cheryl Swope, Rachel Whiting, and their many contributors provide readers with a guide to Lutheran home education that will be useful and edifying for those beyond the homeschool community. More than a mere "how-to," *Eternal Treasures* delves into the *what* and *why* of education among Christians, dispels misunderstandings about home education, and shows what is lost to future generations, including the children we love, when Christian catechesis and strong academics are missing from our educational approaches. If you have ever said, "I want to do everything I can to help my children remain in the Christian faith," this book is for you.

Rev. Paul J. Cain
Headmaster, Martin Luther Grammar School, Sheridan, Wyoming
Permanent board member, Consortium for Classical Lutheran Education

This book will be helpful for every Christian homeschool parent, not only Lutheran Christians. I appreciate the emphasis on the Church Year and the Divine Service for order and comfort. *Eternal Treasures* will become an easy reference, as we seek to provide our children with a strong sense of routine and purpose to our days.

Karen Craig
Homeschooling mother, author of *Matin Latin* Series

Eternal Treasures provides a holistic approach to the Christian parent's responsibilities of education and nurture of children. As a new parent, I truly appreciate this shared wisdom of experienced parents who are bold and intentional in the choices they make for their children's education.

Andrew Bates
Director of Programming, WorldwideKFUO.org

In *Eternal Treasures*, Cheryl and Rachel aptly and eloquently call us to consider our vocation as the educators of our children. As with any vocation, the devil, the world, and our sinful nature war against that which is of God. *Eternal Treasures* reminds us to stand boldly as forgiven sinners and take up the blessed task before us. The collective writers point readers to the truth of the Gospel, even as they address the need for right use of the Law, as we daily live out our vocation as our children's educators. *Eternal Treasures* is practical, uplifting, and inspirational. Whether we are parents or those supporting parents in their teaching vocation, *Eternal Treasures* will encourage and equip us.

Jocelyn Benson
Head Teacher, Wittenberg Academy

This is an excellent homeschooling resource written from the perspective of Lutheran Church—Missouri Synod members. With countless testimonials on real issues that face the first-time homeschooler as well as those who have been at it a long time, the lists of useful resources and ways to acquire them are invaluable. "How to" pointers are everywhere, with the encouragement that comes both from good experiences and failure. Especially appreciated is the constant theme of God's Word and Sacraments as indispensable to the Christian life.

David Mommens
Parish pastor, St. John's Lutheran Church, Columbia City, Indiana

Lutheran families may consider a plethora of options related to the education of their children. *Eternal Treasures: Teaching Your Child at Home* is the definitive resource for Lutheran families who are seeking to establish a quality learning experience in their homes for their children. *Eternal Treasures* addresses the why, what, and how of home education with useful resources and numerous testimonials. It is a "must have" for families involved in home education.

Terry L. Schmidt
Director of Schools, Lutheran Church Missouri Synod

Cover design by Erica Schwan. Pelican image from a chasuble photographed by Todd Whiting.

Printed in the United States of America
First Printing, 2015

ISBN-13:978-1517270155   ISBN-10:1517270154

For our eternal treasures
Michael, Michelle, Owen, Ella, Ava, and Livia

and for yours

Thou, like the pelican to feed her brood,
Didst pierce Thyself to give us living food;
Thy blood, O Lord, one drop has pow'r to win
Forgiveness for our world and all its sin.

— *Thee We Adore, O Hidden Savior*
(Lutheran Service Book, 640:3)

Contents

ACKNOWLEDGMENTS

On behalf of all Lutheran homeschooling families, we thank the Rev. Dr. Matthew Harrison for generously sharing your thoughts in this book's foreword. As parents and teachers, no greater task awaits us than to give our children sound Christian teaching for this life and for the life to come. Your steadfast leadership gives all of us the courage to press on.

We thank the Lutheran Church—Missouri Synod (LCMS) School Ministry for providing the vision and the means to propel this book to creation. We especially thank Terry Schmidt for your exuberant support, Susan Green for your patient assistance, and Matt Bergholt for faithfully attending every group meeting on this project!

We thank all who helped from within the LCMS in other areas: Pam Nielsen, Anna Karsten, Erica Schwan, and the other talented, creative behind-the-scenes involved in formatting, communications, and marketing. To Jennifer Duffy, a special thanks for keeping everything organized. You made all of the meetings enjoyable! Thank you to all those in the LCMS Executive Offices: Rachel Asburry, Kim Vieker, and the Rev. Dr. Jon Vieker. We appreciate your work in seeing this book to completion.

We thank the pastors and headmasters of all Lutheran day schools willing to open your doors to homeschoolers. We thank especially the schools featured within this book. We hope that your warm welcome will become a model, as we mutually serve one another to embrace the common cause of Christian education for our baptized children.

For the creation of this book's index, we thank Kelly Rottmann at *customindexing.com*. Your professionalism and prayers calmed our nervous deadline days, and your flexibility allowed this resource to have an index, even while you celebrated the graduation of your oldest homeschooled student!

Thank you to all of our early proofreaders and reviewers. We especially thank the Rev. David Mommens, Jocelyn Benson, Sarah

Koehneke, Susan Knowles, and Karen Craig for your close readings, suggestions, and insights.

We thank Jennifer Farrior, our initial copy editor, who worked tirelessly through revisions and re-organizations, all the way until Easter Sunday when your water broke to announce the arrival of your third child!

Thank you to our final copy editor, the Rev. Charles Henrickson. Armed with unwavering doctrine, expansive knowledge, and a mighty red pen, your thorough examination of the final copy gave us just what we needed.

We thank ALL of our contributors. The voices are too numerous to name, so we highlight those who provided large, original works to *Eternal Treasures*: the Rev. Erik Rottmann and his wife Kelly, the Rev. Arthur Rickman and his wife Deaconess Eva, the Rev. Paul Cain, the Rev. Christian Tiews, Deaconess Mary Moerbe, Todd Whiting, Nicole Manners, Melinda Heine, Holly Scheer, Susan Knowles, Sarah Koehneke, Rachel Pollock, Sara Scheler, and Michelle Swope. Thank you to everyone who contributed!

To our families: we thank our parents for always cheering us on and for helping to care for our children, as we worked on this book. We thank Joseph, Michael, and Michelle Swope, for your ongoing encouragement, love, and support throughout Cheryl's efforts on this project. To Todd, Owen, Ella, Ava, and Livia Whiting, your kind sacrifice and gracious forbearance with Rachel's writing are greatly appreciated. Thank you to both families for being vulnerable enough to share your stories, so this book could be "real."

Last, but certainly not least, we thank our own pastors — the Rev. Charles Henrickson, the Rev. Kent Schaaf, and the Rev. Jeffrey Ware — for your work in catechesis which continues to bless our families to this very day.

Western Civilization is entering a true dark age. The so-called "Dark Ages," named for the decline of learning with the demise of Rome and the disappearing vestiges of classical antiquity until the renaissance, was for all its challenges and egregious abuses an age of faith. Western culture — and the broad swath of the world that it most affects via governments, entertainment, and education — is leaping into a black hole, the likes of which never shall have been experienced in human history. It shall be an age of radical rejection of faith, because the progressivists, the political and ideological liberals, have decisively abandoned classical liberalism and the unique contributions to the world from the ancient and Christian West.

The ancients knew of natural law. The Bible teaches natural law and its concurrence with revealed law (Romans 1). The fathers of the American Constitution knew natural law and that a democratic republic based upon natural law would not stand should the *vox populi* supplant natural law. Hermann Sasse saw a nightmare unfolding in the face of National Socialism. The same could be written of the scourge of Communism in the twentieth century and of the radical Islamic state today. But does the following paragraph have any more appropriate target than our own government even now?

> The Caesar cult in its manifold forms, the deification of the state, is one great form of the defection from the idea of the state. There are also other possibilities of such defection. The government can forget and neglect its tasks. When it no longer distinguishes between right and wrong, when its courts are no longer governed by the strict desire for justice, but by special interests, when government no longer has the courage to exercise its law, fails to exercise its duties, undermines its own legal order, when it weakens through its family law parental

authority and the estate of marriage, then it ceases to be
governing authority.[1]

Sasse specifically included the issues of education in a courageous blast
in 1936.

> The lie is the death of man, his temporal and his eternal death.
> The lie kills nations. The most powerful nations of the world
> have been laid waste because of their lies. History knows of no
> more unsettling sight than the judgment rendered upon the
> people of an advanced culture who have rejected the truth
> and are swallowed upon in a sea of lies. Where this happens,
> as in the case of declining pagan antiquity, religion and law,
> poetry and philosophy, life in marriage and family, in the state
> and society — in short, one sphere of life after another falls
> sacrifice to the power and curse of the lie. Where man can no
> longer bear the truth, he cannot live without the lie. Where
> man denies that he and others are dying, the terrible dissolu-
> tion [of his culture] is held up as a glorious ascent, and decline
> is viewed as an advance, the likes of which has never been
> experienced.[2]

The Plight of Christian Parents

Christian parents face an onslaught on their values and convic-
tions as intense and even demonic as at any time in history. Christian
parents will and do choose options and tactics for education that are
appropriate to their context and particular needs and abilities. Thank
God for Christian and faithful Lutheran teachers who render service
even in public schools! What bright shining lights! Thank God for the
parochial schools of the LCMS! Thank God for the growing number of
classical parochial schools of the LCMS! Yet there is another option.

I could not be more delighted with the book you, dear reader, have
before you. Cheryl Swope, her co-author Rachel Whiting, and a host
of contributors provide here the orthodox Lutheran manual for the
parent(s) considering classical homeschooling for children. The answer
to "the lie, which is the death of man, his temporal and eternal death,"
(Sasse) is the truth! It is the One Jesus, who remains "the way the
truth and the life!" The words of our Savior, "the truth shall make you
free," became the motto of many a great university in this land, but at
nearly all of the public schools where once hailed this truth even from

---

[1] Sasse, Hermann. "What is the State?" 1932.

[2] Sasse, Hermann. "Union and Confession," 1936.

the lips of the Son of God, His very words are engraved on capstones bearing witness to the fall of once-great institutes of learning. When neglected, those engraved words stand watch, instead, over a veritable slavery of the mind to untruth.[3]

To Liberate

Et veritas liberabit vos. And the truth will liberate you — make you free. Thus the goal of a genuine "liberal" education. The rebirth of classical Christian learning — learning which rejoiced in truth, in texts, in ideals, in faith in Christ, in source documents, in the views of those who spoke truth across the ages, in music, in mathematics, in Holy Scripture, in confessional documents, in the Small Catechism, in great books, in art, in great ideas and in genuine science — exploded during the Lutheran Reformation 500 years ago, beginning on October 31, 1517. Indeed, Luther's side-kick, Philip Melanchthon has forever since been known as "The Preceptor."[4] In this book, *Eternal Treasures: Teaching Your Child at Home*, Mrs. Swope provides you, dear parent or teacher, with the veritable powder and keg, including match and fuse, to bring a great education to your own children, today.

A "liberal" education was understood in the ancient world to be an education for "free" men, not slaves. Today so much education enslaves to half-truths, half-scholarship, anti-faith bias, and a rejection of the order and natural beauty of God's creation. The Christian "liberal" education, which awaits your children with the help of this book, shall free your children from sin, death, and devil, give your children biblical truths to live in, and share with them the words which shall bring your children joys unto eternal life! And this education shall provide the tools (the grammar!) of learning that they might come to know and understand truly (logic) and be able to take part in a robust dialogue and discussion with all the muses of the age (rhetoric).

I'm delighted by the revolution in liberal education.

Pastor Matthew Harrison

---

[3] See for instance the autobiography of the great LCMS classicist E. G. Sihler, in which he describes this very text (John 8:32) as the motto of Johns Hopkins University. Sihler was in the first graduating class of Ph.D. students at Johns Hopkins and taught there and for decades at New York University. Sihler was the son of Missouri Synod co-founder Wilhelm Sihler. See Sihler, E. G. *From the Maumee to the Thames and Tiber: The Life-Story of an American Classical Scholar*. New York: New York University Press, 1930, 249ff.

[4] See Chemnitz, Martin, and Jacob Andreae. *Church Order for Braunschweig-Wolfenbuettel: How Doctrine, Ceremonies, and Other Church-Related Matters Shall (By God's Grace) Be Conducted Henceforth*, 1569. Translated by Jacob Corzine, Matthew C. Harrison, and Andrew Smith. Edited by Jacob Corzine and Matthew Carver. St. Louis: Concordia Publishing House, 2015. This forthcoming volume contains a delightful "school order" with a host of specifics on how liberal education was to be implemented in orthodox Lutheran schools, written by the major author of the Formula of Concord.

The Pelican

The mother pelican spreads her wings around her young, as her babies raise their open mouths for food in time of famine. Drops of the pelican's own blood appear on her welcoming chest. Why does blood appear?

Born of a legend, this ancient church image depicts one who would pluck her own flesh to feed her offspring, even if this leads to her own death. Through the legend of the self-sacrificing pelican, we see Jesus Christ. From Christ's own pierced body, He feeds us mercifully with His own Body and Blood, shed for the forgiveness of our sins. He gives His life for us, so that we may have life in Him.

Parents: God's Mask

Created for the benefit of children, neighbors, and for all creation, fathers and mothers give of themselves, though never so perfectly as Christ Himself.[5] God works through parents. Dr. Gene Edward Veith and his daughter Mary Moerbe explain:

> Parents are in "God's stead." That is, parents are the face of God to the young child, doing what God does, giving life, nourishing, protecting, disciplining, forgiving, teaching, causing to grow. Actually, God is the one doing those things, using parents as his instrument, but God commands that they share his honor.[6]

Despite our failings as parents, we daily reflect the image of God in Christ through our love toward our children, our very closest neighbors.

Every Parent's Inner War

Admittedly, as fallen human beings we are naturally and grossly self-serving, turned inward, the very opposite of how we were created

---

[5] Fabrizius, Karl. *The Lutheran Catechesis Series*. Edited by Peter Bender. Bible Stories for Daily Prayer: Old Testament Stories, Year 1. Sussex, Wisconsin: Concordia Catechetical Academy, 2005. 4.

[6] Veith, Gene Edward, and Mary J. Moerbe. *Family Vocation: God's Calling in Marriage, Parenting, and Childhood*. Wheaton: Crossway, 2012. 180.

to be. There is no hope for improvement for our sinful nature. We hope instead for the mortification of the old man accomplished daily through God's Holy Word. The inner war between our selfish old man and our self-sacrificing new man, received at Baptism, is often magnified in our homes, and especially when we attempt to teach our children!

And so we see a paradox that is the normal Christian life. In the home, parents are "always being given over to death for Jesus' sake, so that the life of Jesus also may be manifested in our mortal flesh" (2 Corinthians 4:11). We die to ourselves again and again.

In His infinite mercy, God redeems us through the incarnation, life, death, and resurrection of Christ. In Christ, the image of God is restored in us. He has made us a new creation in Him. We will realize the fullness of this salvation at Christ's return, and "when He appears we shall be like Him" (1 John 3:2). In the meantime, despite our own failings, God cares for our children through us in manifold, merciful ways.

Our Children's Physical Wellbeing

As parents, we care for our children's bodies every day. In the early years, we find ourselves abruptly awakened to feed a baby, change a diaper, or welcome a sick child to sleep on our chest. We resist urges for rest, as we wash our children's faces, bodies, and clothing. Even the task of figuring out which clothes they have outgrown and what size they will need next is ongoing! Buying, preparing, and serving nourishing meals consumes our time. Transporting children to activities for physical exercise, shopping for new shoes to support growing feet, and attending doctors' appointments fill our calendars. All of this demands time and energy.

Indeed, at times the list of our children's daily physical needs seems inexhaustible. Additionally, the physical care and shelter for our children often requires difficult and exhausting work to obtain the financial means to provide. Yes, much is required to care for our children's bodies.

This Is Not All

Yet once our children's bodies have been washed, fed, and clothed, is our parental responsibility fulfilled? In his treatment of the Fourth Commandment, Martin Luther expressed grave concerns about the conditions of faith instruction in the home. He urged parents to "seriously and faithfully fulfill their office, not only to support and provide for the bodily necessities of their children ... but, most of all, they should train them to honor and praise God ... . Therefore, let everyone know that it is his duty, on peril of losing the divine favor, to bring up his children in the fear and knowledge of God above all things."[7] Our children are not just physical bodies but also eternal souls! In a sermon, Luther exhorts parents with these words:

> False natural love blinds parents so that they have more regard for the bodies of their children than they have for their souls …. It is of the greatest importance for every married man to **pay closer, more thorough, and continuous attention to the health of his child's soul than to the body** which he has begotten, and to **regard his child as nothing else but an eternal treasure God has commanded him to protect**, and so prevent the world, the flesh, and the devil from stealing the child away and bringing him to destruction. For at his death and on the Day of Judgment he will be asked about his child and will have to give a most solemn account.[8]

Our children are eternal treasures. They will outlast this world. They are not only bodies made for earth and time, but bodies and souls made for heaven and eternity.

Nurturing Souls

Just as we give sacrificially to care for our children's bodies, so we sacrifice to nurture our children's souls. We teach our children as human beings united in body and soul. We teach the Holy Scriptures, Christian doctrine, hymnody, and liturgy for their faith. We teach strong academics for their minds. Beginning in the home, we can give our children an excellent Christian education, "a beautiful preparation for this life and for the life that is to come."[9]

Who Is Equipped for Such a Task?

God Himself creates and sustains faith in us and in our children. God is at work, as He has been from the beginning, speaking through His Son and by His Holy Spirit. As our children increase in bodily strength through nourishing meals and physical exercise, so they increase in knowledge, understanding, and love through His Word and Sacraments. When we as parents place importance on these gifts and

---

[7] Luther, Martin. *Large Catechism.* In *Concordia: The Lutheran Confessions: A Reader's Edition of the Book of Concord.* 2nd ed. St. Louis: Concordia Publishing House, 2006. 378.

[8] Luther, Martin. In *Martin Luther's Basic Theological Writings.* Minneapolis: Fortress Press, 1989. 636. (Emphasis added.)

[9] Swope, Cheryl. *Simply Classical: A Beautiful Education for Any Child.* Louisville: Memoria Press, 2013. 108.

God's promises, we are reminded that we parent our children in the nurture and admonition of the Lord. Our children must be spiritually washed and spiritually fed. We find the Source of life and help in the Lord of the Church. The waters of Holy Baptism wash our children clean; the Words of Holy Scripture create, nurture, and sustain faith; and through the Body and Blood of our Lord Jesus Christ, we are granted remission of all our sin.

Fighting Our Enemies: Living in Two Kingdoms

We live in both temporal and eternal kingdoms. Enemies seek to confound our efforts to care for our children in body and soul. The world, the flesh, and the devil conspire to destroy the lives and faith of our children. The nourished soul needs to feast on truth, beauty, and goodness, because our enemies seek our children's demise. Just as poor food choices will malnourish our children, allowing them to consume what is false, ugly, and evil will fail to nourish our children's souls. We teach our children the faith to protect and to fortify them.

A child's mind will face starvation unless it is fed noble ideas. His ability to serve others will falter without strong skills. Through education in the home or day school, we can provide our children with needed skills in reading, writing, and arithmetic. We can strengthen their minds through memorizing, reciting, and imagining. We can cultivate wonder and delight. We can help them observe, analyze, and discern. We can teach them to defend, proclaim, and persuade with eloquence. We can incline our children toward wisdom and excellence through the Holy Scriptures and with the great literature, music, art, and ideas of Western civilization.[10]

We sacrifice ourselves to promote within our children the essential endeavor of learning and growing in every way. We devote ourselves to this task so that our children might live with dedicated service, noble character, and civil righteousness. We also sacrifice ourselves to nurture faith in Christ with renewed fervor, that by the working of the Holy Spirit, our children's lives may be preserved in His perfect righteousness for all eternity.

---

[10] For more on the topic of a Lutheran liberal arts education, see the following resources: Hein, Steven A. et al. *A Handbook for Classical Lutheran Education: The Best of the Consortium for Classical and Lutheran Education's Journals.* Fort Wayne, Indiana: CCLE Press, 2013. Korcok, Thomas. *Lutheran Education: From Wittenberg to the Future.* St. Louis: Concordia Publishing House, 2011. The Consortium for Classical Lutheran Education, *ccle.org.*

What Do We Teach?

To equip for both kingdoms, we teach strong academics and an active physical education alongside steadfast Christian catechesis. The intricacies of the language arts and the reliabilities of the mathematical arts equip and organize the mind, just as beautiful art, music, and literature form the tastes. Young bodies receive exercise through training in strength and coordination, while young minds receive exercise through academic discipline. Poetry and music speak directly to informed senses. The ability to see nature, appreciate a work of art, and hear an exquisite piece of music opens the created world to the child, as embers of appreciation are stoked into flame. Through studies in science and history, the world is revealed to our children. They learn what has happened and what has been discovered from the beginning until the present day. Imaginations awaken, as our children vicariously live through the stories they are told. They learn more than facts; they learn of heroes and evildoers throughout time, and they see historical implications as clear lessons to be heeded. "The discipline of such studies has worth in itself for the formation of mind and character."[11]

Home Education: Day by Day

Our children daily ingest small portions of nutritious food and regular periods of purposeful exercise for their bodies. Likewise, they can engage in a strong academic education for mind and character. We persevere in spite of our own inconsistencies and feelings of being underqualified. As we press onward, our children receive nourishment for their souls through the reading of Holy Scriptures, the singing of hymns, and prayer in the home.

"Day by day" eventually turns to years. As we plod along, sometimes our children reap immediate, tangible benefits from what they have learned; other times decades may pass till fruit comes forth. Regardless of the visible results, we pray that death would be at work in us, so that, by His grace and mercy, life will be at work in our eternal treasures (2 Corinthians 4:12).

Serving Others

Just as God loves and serves our children through us, our children likewise love and serve others. We show them what this looks like, often without a thought, in our vocation as parents. The ways in which God has gifted each child will help mold him to be the mask of God to others in his various vocations. This occurs even in our youngest children:

---

[11] Swope, *Simply Classical: A Beautiful Education for Any Child*, 93.

From an early age, the children learned that these Scriptures were meant not only to be learned, but to be shared. When an elderly neighbor struggled for breath just days before she died, the children and I visited her at the nursing home, quietly gathering at her bedside. We sang her favorite psalm, Psalm 23. Michelle held her hand. God was already working through these children, and through their education, to love and serve others in their lives.[12]

Our children grow, their knowledge increases, and their faith is sustained in Christ. Their unique interests, skills, and talents emerge. As God graciously permits, we are privileged to witness small moments of His work in our children.

Eternal Treasures

Much is required in loving service to our children, our eternal treasures in body and soul. When we look at or to ourselves, we know we cannot teach our children all they will need! Instead of attempting to be all our children will ever need, we come alongside our children on the trodden paths of humility. May our hearts "be comforted, being knit together in love, and unto all riches of the full assurance of understanding, to the acknowledgment of the mystery of God, and of the Father, and of Christ; in whom are hid all the treasures of wisdom and knowledge" (Colossians 2:2-3 KJV). As we discipline our children, we learn with them, and we grow with them. We forgive them, and we ask them to forgive us. We find strong teachers for them when we cannot teach them ourselves. We give thanks for faithful preaching and teaching from our pastors and for the unity in the body of Christ, His Church. As God graciously works in and through us, we persevere.

Like the pelican in the legend, as mothers and fathers of our children we give our own "heart's blood to nourish their souls."[13] In this task, as in all of life, we are never alone. Our merciful, risen Savior lives and serves us faithfully with His own Life, now and for eternity. Throughout our lives, our Savior's lifeblood flows sacrificially not only for our dear, beloved children, but also for their weak, faltering parents. Thanks be to God!

Rachel Whiting

---

[12] Ibid., 68.

[13] Ryle, J.C. "The Duties of Parents." Accessed October 27, 2014. *www.wholesomewords.org/etexts/ryle/ryleduties.pdf.*

As a homeschooling mother, I appreciate conferences for home-schoolers. Even so, intimidation initially kept me from attending one gathering: the annual summer conference held by the Consortium for Classical Lutheran Education (CCLE). I wish I would have attended sooner! Years later, I now appreciate the wisdom, edification, and companionship available in this unique setting. At CCLE conferences, Lutheran homeschoolers gather side by side with Lutheran pastors, headmasters, and school teachers. Synodical and district leaders attend, as do university professors. Joined in the common cause of historic Christian education, we all listen to inspiring plenary speakers. We learn together in practical workshops. With different but unified vocations, we sing, pray, and receive in daily chapel services. In each conference every year, we share the desire of recovering, preserving, and providing a strong Christian education for the children of the church.

One year I was asked to lead a session for homeschoolers. Afterward a regular attendee, the LCMS Director of Schools William Cochran, approached me with this simple declaration: "I want the LCMS to do something for Lutheran homeschoolers." We began by meeting in St. Louis.

Shortly after the Rev. Dr. Matthew Harrison arrived as president of the synod, I met at the International Center with Bill Cochran and the Rev. Bart Day. In a separate meeting, Bill Cochran and I met later with Concordia Publishing House (CPH). Bill's assistant director at the time, Terry Schmidt, attended this meeting. As a result of our early efforts, along with invaluable contributions from CCLE homeschoolers, CPH now has a Homeschool Resource Guide. This was a start.

Each time our paths crossed, Bill Cochran reiterated his intent. He wanted to do more. He sent me the names of Lutheran homeschoolers who contacted him. About this same time, I wrote *Simply Classical: A Beautiful Education for Any Child* (Memoria Press, 2013). Dr. Gene Edward Veith penned the book's insightful foreword. *Simply Classical* offers an examination of historic Christian education contrasted with "progressive education." Moreover, *Simply Classical* tells the story of my own adopted special-needs twins whom we homeschooled from their infancy through high school with a broad, Christian liberal arts education. The Rev. Day endorsed *Simply Classical* with one of the book's earliest reviews. He gave his proof copy to Bill Cochran, who then recommended it to Terry Schmidt who expressed enthusiastic appreciation for the book.

When Bill Cochran retired, Terry became his successor. The vision to help homeschoolers did not wither; instead, it grew with renewed urgency. With characteristic energy, Terry Schmidt contacted me with an idea late in the summer. He asked whether we could create a *handbook* specifically for Lutheran homeschoolers. The book would be published by the LCMS. The one-year deadline would be tight, but I would be allowed a co-writer.

I knew how gratefully our homeschooling families would welcome formal synodical support. I agreed. Suddenly I needed someone to write with me.

Rachel, A Young Mother

After the publication of *Simply Classical*, several Lutheran home-schoolers wrote heartwarming notes of thanks. I could have chosen any of them to be co-author of the upcoming Lutheran handbook. However, one young mother contacted me several times. When she did, I noticed how well she wrote, even in emails. Rachel secured my attention most powerfully with a heartfelt, online article written about her own children. I read this article, just as I was contemplating my need for a co-writer. From my home in Missouri, I contacted Rachel Whiting in North Carolina.

She said, "Yes, I have often wondered why there are no books on Lutheran homeschooling!" Although she did not consider herself a writer at the time, but rather just a homeschooling mother with tender reflections about her children, I knew she could write. We set to work. With little more than a preliminary outline, some words of encourage-ment from her husband, and welcome help from Rachel's mother who came to stay with the couple's four children, Rachel immediately dedi-cated large blocks of time to writing. As Rachel wrote and sent drafts, I edited them. We communicated often. Rachel submitted more and more narratives, and I continued editing. We added to our outline, but even as I compiled her beautiful pieces of writing, I knew we would remain far short of the goal for a comprehensive handbook.

Those early fall days passed quickly. The task loomed large. Our deadline drew nearer.

More Help

In a message to the 200 Lutheran homeschooling families in CCLE's online discussion forum, I shared the upcoming project and our need for contributions. The group includes pastors and published authors, so I was hopeful. I suggested topics such as vocation, academics, faith instruction, homeschooling large families, and more, with a requested deadline of Reformation Day.

Responses flowed! Opening my email became an exciting daily event. I received and sifted through everyone's thoughtfully crafted words, careful tips, and personal stories to weave them into our handbook. We culled descriptions, quotes, and insights, along with full-length narratives.

As we worked, all of the contributors' thoughts became so integrated throughout this book, we decided to attach names to the voices within the pages, rather than placing them in the Table of Contents as originally planned. Some are brief quotations, while others are full essays. Over time, we received even more submissions than we could include, so many became excerpted and rearranged. Throughout *Eternal Treasures*, homeschooling families added immeasurably to this handbook, just as they do throughout the sessions, meals, and discussions at our CCLE summer conferences every year.

The Lutheran Liberal Arts

In *Eternal Treasures: Teaching Your Child at Home*, you will notice the undeniable influence of the Lutheran liberal arts tradition, because so many of our contributors have come to appreciate the richness of this historic Lutheran heritage. At the time of the Reformation, Lutherans led a pedagogical reformation as well as a theological one. From Melanchthon and Luther to present-day leaders such as Dr. Gene Edward Veith, the Rev. William Heine, and Dr. Thomas Korcok, Lutherans across the centuries have embraced the joyous rediscovery and effective implementation of a Christian liberal arts education.

As I have learned, this confessional, "classical" education need not be intimidating. Rather, this is simply our heritage as Lutherans. Because it is rooted in the Holy Scriptures and proven by the test of centuries, it is the legacy our children need. Furthermore, teachable resources now abound! In *Eternal Treasures*, this new handbook unique to the world of homeschooling, we provide the recommended reading, curriculum suggestions, and doctrinal underpinnings to help families who seek strong academics alongside steadfast instruction in the Christian faith. We believe that all Lutherans benefit when we restore our focus on Christian catechesis within the humane, elevating, and beautiful liberal arts heritage. Toward this end, the varied voices of our contributors blend together, whether from the pulpit, the university, the school headmaster's desk, the classroom, or the home.

New Friendships

As we gathered contributions throughout the fall and winter, Rachel and I continued to collaborate. We met to read, to write, and to discuss. We worked to strengthen words and thoughts, and often even Rachel's own writings began to meld into our one voice.

I shared the early draft with our talented copy editor, Jennifer, who had helped me so faithfully with *Simply Classical*. At the same time, I shared the rough, unedited copy with a dozen proofreaders, including seven homeschoolers. Many hands provided the craftsmanship to weave the multitude of contributions into one book.

Rachel and I became grateful for a book characterized by community. As often happens with like-minded mothers, we shared personal conversations amidst the work. Rachel and I grew to be friends, and we hope you will find many friends among the pages here. We now refer to *Eternal Treasures* as the quilt we pieced together into a whole.

Schools Too

Even as we wrote for Lutheran homeschoolers, we requested contributions from Lutheran schools. We gratefully received them. In the section entitled "A Common Cause," *Eternal Treasures* emphasizes the unity we can share as Christian educators when we are unified by the clear vision to preserve our beautiful pedagogical and theological heritage for the sake of our children.

In this book, we provide a sampling of Lutheran schools with programs, classes, and activities for homeschoolers. We offer ways for more schools to invite homeschoolers. We hope that, in the freedom of the Gospel, this book will become an edifying work for the sake of all Christian education.

Why Specifically "Lutheran" Education?

With all Christians, we find our life in Jesus Christ. We affirm the Christian faith as given to us in the Holy Scriptures. We address Lutheran homeschoolers, because no other book exists to support home education specifically for Lutheran families. Every home-schooler, pastor, headmaster, and parent who shared contributions for this book is Lutheran.

In the Lutheran Confessions, we find the affirming articulation of that which we believe, and we find the clear condemnation of that which we reject. As Christian parents and educators, we appreciate the doctrine, hymns, and liturgy, which help us uphold and express biblical truth. Hermann Sasse explains:

> We are faithful to this church, not because it is the church of our Fathers, but because it is the church of the Gospel; not because it is the church of Luther, but because it is the church of Jesus Christ. If it became something else, if its teaching were something other than a correct exposition of the plain Word of God, it would no longer be our church. If it should ever be demonstrated that they contain essential errors, we would be the first ones to cast them into the fire.[14]

For You

Begun many years ago as a simple conversation at a summer conference, this book was initiated by the vision of one but is now a gift for many. On behalf of Rachel, our many contributors, and all who supported this work to its completion, we hope that *Eternal Treasures: Teaching Your Child at Home* will strengthen your own efforts in your own home no matter the trials and challenges you face. May God bless and keep you in Christ Jesus, even as you love, serve, and teach your children so that your children may love, serve, and teach others in Him.

Cheryl Swope

---

[14] Sasse, Hermann. *Here We Stand: The Nature and Character of Lutheran Faith.* Translated with Revisions and Additions from the Second German Edition by Theodore G. Tappert. Lutheran Publishing House, 1979.

PART ONE:

THE FOUNDATIONS
OF HOME EDUCATION

Where Do I Begin?
The Basics of Home Education

Advantages to Home Education

With an estimated two million children homeschooled just in the United States, and more across the world, reasons for homeschooling vary across families and over time. From dozens of homeschoolers, we received reasons which fell into eight general categories: teaching the faith, strong academics, family togetherness, unique interests, special needs, geographical flexibility, vocation, and (perhaps the most surprising) improved socialization!

Teaching the Faith

Let my teaching drop as the rain,
My speech distill as the dew,
As raindrops on the tender herb,
And as showers on the grass.
— Deuteronomy 32:2 NKJV

Whether beginning when children are babies or bringing children home from a traditional school setting, Lutheran families cite the unique possibilities for teaching the faith through homeschooling. Among the benefits, families who homeschool appreciate having more time for these activities:

- cultivating biblical literacy through teaching Bible stories as a family,

- conducting daily devotional readings and catechesis, whether morning, noon, or evening (or, for some families, all three!),
- consistent catechesis from year to year, including ample time to prepare for confirmation years and beyond,
- memorization of the catechism and hymns through recitations and songs played in the home,
- greater participation in the Divine Service by singing the liturgy and hymns or daily reading the upcoming lectionary readings for the week.

From California, homeschoolers Richard and Nicole note:

Over the years, as our two children have matured, we have realized the importance of grounding them in their identity as Lutheran Christians. Catechesis, therefore, is integral to our homeschool. It has been a delightful opportunity for our own spiritual growth, as we have rediscovered the ancient Christian faith alongside them. Delving into God's Word and the history of Christianity has also led to many hours of research into the history of classical education, especially as realized in the Lutheran tradition.

From New York, Susan echoes:

Homeschooling can allow faith-integrated conversations throughout the day as a part of family life, as well as allow flexibility in creating daily family devotional time together.

From Illinois, Heather reflects on her own homeschooling journey with four children over the past 15 years:

Did I achieve my initial goals? ... I confess, the answer is no ... . The path we walk as a family is not at all how I dreamt it would be. It is neither picture-perfect nor smooth sailing. I have a messy home and its inhabitants show themselves deficient and sinful in many ways. But we have been washed clean in the blood of the Lamb, and we give thanks for this above all else. My heart sings each Sunday my teenagers sit happily in the pew next to me. If our children remember only this — God and their parents love and cherish each of them — then I am a successful homeschooling mom, and this long journey has been well worth it.

Academics and a Love of Learning

[F]or though a child have all the gifts of nature at wish, and perfection of memory at will, yet if he have not a special love to learning, he shall never attain to much learning. — Roger Ascham[15]

Some traditional schools have abandoned the pursuit of strong academics, or they offer little to inspire a love of academic learning. Each of these factors contribute to the decline of true education:

- lack of pedagogical vision with a failure to embrace truth, goodness, and beauty,
- experimental teaching techniques,
- dull presentation of material,
- over-reliance on literary snippets or bland textbooks rather than "living" books (whole books, original sources, and true literature),
- the infiltration of progressivism,
- an emphasis on pragmatism,
- a misunderstanding of fallen human nature,
- relativism,
- catering to mandated testing.

[See Appendix F for readings on these topics.]

Families explore alternatives, so their children might receive a stronger academic education than they would receive in other settings.

Second-generation homeschooler Becky writes this from Missouri:

I was homeschooled through 9th grade, so I was inclined to homeschool our own children, ages 2, 4, and 6. My husband heard about excellent academics in classical Lutheran education from friends and professors while attending Concordia Seminary in St. Louis. We began with The Well-Trained Mind, *and our oldest son is already a strong reader.*

An excellent home education is not just for younger children. Children of all ages can be homeschooled either exclusively by their parents or with the assistance of online academies, flexible day school programs, co-ops, and community colleges. Many students homeschooled through high school enter college directly from their studies at home.

---

[15] Ascham, Roger (1515-1568). Quoted in *The Great Tradition: classic readings on what it means to be an educated human being.* Edited by Richard Gamble. Wilmington, Delaware: Intercollegiate Studies Institute, 2007. 453.

From Eastern Washington, Kimberly writes:

I homeschooled both of our boys. The 21-year-old is now in college, and the 17-year-old is still being homeschooled. I became interested in strong academics through the very first Veritas Press catalog about 14 years ago … . We have been heavily involved with NCFCA Speech and Debate. I coach our debate team, teach writing and humanities in our co-op.

Homeschooling for both younger and older students can offer these academic benefits:

- a tutorial approach, with the lessened likelihood of "slipping through the cracks,"
- flexibility to challenge the student in his areas of interest and aptitude,
- individualization for students who struggle with learning in one or more areas,
- parent-determined curriculum selection, so the best possible academic education can be pursued,
- efficient instruction — no time lost to assemblies, lining up for the cafeteria, or riding the bus!,
- integration across content areas, with learning across subjects as part of daily life.

From California, Nicole Manners reflects on her own education and adds:

In the "scientific" education to which I had been subjected … I encountered arbitrary instructions, disjointed facts, and a general lack of coherence. I began to ask myself in true Lutheran fashion, "What does this mean?" This led to a turning point in our homeschool, both in form and in substance.

As so many homeschoolers come to realize for the first time, learning is integrated! Nicole Manners tells this story:

I recall one day in particular, during a read-aloud from V. M. Hillyer's A Child's History of the World. *Suddenly I realized the import of Johannes Gutenberg's printing press. Not only had he built an invention which allowed for the dissemination of information at a hitherto unimaginable rate, but I considered (as I had never before realized) his placement in time, in such close proximity to Martin Luther and the fifteenth-century beginnings of the Reformation Church … . I realized with a sense of astonished indignation that I had never been taught to view history as an unbroken line of human beings stretching back to Creation, with the hand of a Divine*

Provider guiding its progression. I began to arrive at a sense of what true education might be ... . Although some might view homeschooling as an opportunity for laziness or idleness, the reality is often quite the opposite. Children who live in an environment which prizes learning for its own sake seem much more likely to value it themselves.

Brennick, homeschooled K-12, a graduate of Concordia University — Chicago, and now a teacher at a classical Lutheran school, reflects:

Within the family context, anything and everything can consist of a learning opportunity — whether family vacations, trips to the art museum, or visits to the grocery store. Of course, the path to a well-developed mind requires an organized course of study ... . In homeschooling, an organized curriculum of academic study with time for play and work on hobbies will mature and tone a child's mind.

Since a child is already on familiar terms with his home and parents, receiving instruction from his parents only seems natural. With no "going to school" shock factor or, "It's summer; I don't want to think," the home-schooler understands he is free to learn anytime, anywhere. His parents may even hear, "May I work ahead in my math after lunch?" or "Could I have a few more minutes to practice piano?"

Family Togetherness

But I will establish my covenant with you, and you shall come into the ark, you, and your sons, your wife, and your sons' wives with you. — Genesis 6:18

Some families choose homeschooling primarily to enjoy, strengthen, and extend time spent together as a family. In homeschooling, discipline issues cannot be deferred with "just three more weeks of summer until the kids go back to school!" Instead, bonds become forged with so much time spent together. When children begin to realize the sacrificial love given to provide them with a unique home education, homeschooling can create uniquely strong relationships characterized by affection and mutual devotion.

In home education, parents know what their children are learning, and they can reinforce this in ways that create favorite memories for their children. Whether creating a Lego model of Egyptian pyramids, reading *Detectives in Togas* while studying ancient Rome, or cooking a meal from the Middle Ages, family life is changed by homeschooling. For older students, dinnertime discussions may center around the latest selection from the Great Books or the text preached in the pastor's sermon on Sunday. When seminary students visit for dinner, the Latin or Greek verb charts can spark conversations to engage every member of the family!

Veteran homeschooler of two grown boys, Kay in Maryland shares this on an online classical Lutheran discussion group:

For some of us, homeschooling is not simply an academic choice. It is not just school at home; it is a different way of life altogether. [School] may contain elements parents do not want for their families: peer pressure, too much time not used for academics (time changing classes and getting the family out of the house every morning), rushing to the school's extracurricular activities that may interfere with family mealtimes. A family may choose a different lifestyle.

A homeschooling mom and pastor's wife in New York, Susan agrees:

The lifestyle developed in homeschooling can uniquely support and reinforce family relationships.

Mary Moerbe, author, deaconess, pastor's wife, and homeschooling mother of six adds this from Oklahoma:

All that time together keeps us honest, as everyone witnesses ups and downs. Time together lets us step in at a moment's notice, reminds us that some pains cannot be avoided, and instructs us that some things must heal with patience rather than become fixed in an instant. Time together, despite Satan's lies to the contrary, will not make you more likely to mess up your children! Indeed, time together lets us know our neighbor, that we might better serve him … . We continued homeschooling, as we saw our second child flourish when spending time with our oldest. The two girls grew so close and interested in life. I especially love how children of different ages can foster and nurture each other!"

Interests and Talents

Our life comes to us moment by moment. One moment disappears before the next comes along; and there is room for very little in each.[16]
— C. S. Lewis

Active homeschooling families dispel the lingering fear that home-schooled children will become recluses. Research also dispels the

---

[16] Lewis, C. S. *The Complete C. S. Lewis Signature Classics*. San Francisco: Harper, 2002. 91.

myth of the homeschool hermit! (See the National Home Education Research Institute.) Most homeschoolers are neither deprived of competition nor devoid of involvement. In fact, homeschooled children may find so many extracurricular opportunities available, parents need to establish boundaries and protect sufficient time for academics!

With a reasonable combination of systematic academics and ample leisure, one benefit of homeschooling is the flexibility that allows a child time for reflection, exploration, and delving deeply into his own gifts and interests. These interests may emerge in academic areas, the fine arts, or physical fitness. They may be honed through self-study at home. Assisted by co-ops, homeschool competitions, or community groups, homeschooled students participate in scholarly pursuits such as geography or spelling bees, science fairs, chess clubs, and speech or writing contests. They may enjoy church groups, 4-H, youth orchestra, swim team, or group sports.

A tip to the homeschooling parent: When discussing home-schooling with neighbors or grandparents, be sure to mention the child's personal interests and outside activities. Social involvement reassures concerned individuals that the child will indeed be "well-rounded" and is enjoying his young life in many ways!

From Wyoming, homeschoolers Randy and Michele write:

Our boys are 12 and 14. In addition to academic learners, both are piano players. Our older son is also becoming quite accomplished at the organ. With the help of God and a good pastor, both boys are confirmed, communicant LCMS members. Located in Casper, Wyoming, we spend much of our free time hunting, fishing, and camping.

From California, Nicole Manners contributes these thoughts about her children's freedom to explore interests through home education:

After a full morning of academics, my children might read books on various topics or build a birdhouse together out of scrapwood. Charlotte Mason dubbed the concept "Masterful Inactivity," and it is a beautiful consequence to diligent, thoughtful studies during the morning hours, with the remainder of the day left for pursuing interests in which the child delights. For example, my daughter is self-taught in arts such as crocheting, sewing, watercolor, acrylic painting, and scrapbooking. She also enjoys history, writing, voice, and piano. These affinities developed over years of having free afternoons; they are merely the result of her God-given talents coupled with the free time and encouragement to explore them."

Individual Needs

The possibility for individualized instruction may mean that a struggling child is given more time to master a subject at his own slower pace, or a child who excels may work a level or two ahead in his areas of strength.
— Susan Knowles, homeschooling mother

Whether special conditions require tailored therapies, frequent doctor visits or a slower (or accelerated) tempo with schooling, home education provides many families much-needed time to address an individual child's unique abilities and frailties.

Holly, wife of the Rev. Joshua Scheer and homeschooling mother of four children ages 2-10, explains:

Two of our children are girls and two are boys. When our oldest finished a year of 3-year-old preschool, we realized that although the school was nice, it was not the right fit for our daughter or for us. We started Lutheran homeschooling. We have seen many benefits. My husband's schedule is full of odd hours and time away. Homeschooling has allowed us to design the children's schedules so they receive as much time with both parents as possible.

It also allows us to encourage and engage our very different types of learners. One of our children has always been fast to grasp concepts. Another has special needs. We can select suitable curriculum by choosing and combining materials from many companies to provide the exact school experience needed by each child. Together, we can also focus on catechesis and religious scholarship. Homeschooling as Lutherans has been incredibly rewarding. Our time with our children is so short. Watching each of them devour learning and grow in their faith is such a wonderful part of every day.

Charles and Elizabeth, parents of two boys ages 8 and 16, share their experience:

For kindergarten, our first son attended an LCMS school that was wonderfully supportive and nurturing. However, his asthma worsened to a point that I just wanted to be with him, because the illness scared him and us. It was emotionally draining. So I quit my job teaching foreign language at the local public high school to be home with him.

While homeschooling, I became pregnant. We just continued homeschooling, while I was home with the baby anyway. When our baby became kindergarten age, we enrolled him in an LCMS school where he had the best teachers and education anyone could hope for. However, even though I feel that LCMS schools are the best schools, I learned with my older son that homeschooling is also a good medium of education for children. We recently decided to keep both boys home, and now I enjoy being with them all day.

Heather writes of the ways homeschooling helped in her oldest daughter's early struggles with reading:

My eldest daughter seemed to demonstrate signs of reading readiness, yet she did not learn to read until age 8. With homeschooling, I could not only give her extra help with reading, I could also make sure she never fell behind in anything else. I read out loud her history, science, and literature books. All that verbal language input resulted in a vocabulary that soared. I even read her math word problems out loud, and then she wrote the numerical answers. I found a piano teacher who did not insist that the child read English prior to learning to play the piano. (After all, music is a language in itself.) Home education allowed us to accommodate our daughter's needs during those early years.

Fast-forward a few years, and our daughter not only became a reader, but she was also able to articulate her troubles. Auditory processing disorder and borderline dyslexia might explain why she hears "The 'Grunch' who 'Took Away' Christmas." Yet by seventh grade, home-schooled the entire time, her standardized testing showed total reading abilities at the level a ninth grader would score, spelling as an eighth grader, and every other area at ninth grade through post-secondary. She entered the local college's enrichment program! Home education gave us the flexibility to understand, address, and meet our daughter's unique learning needs.

(See more information on homeschooling with special needs later in this book.)

Geographic Flexibility: The Military, Relocated, or Mission Family

We ask You not to forsake Your children but always to rule our hearts and minds by Your Holy Spirit that we may be enabled constantly to serve You. — Lutheran Service Book, Divine Service, Setting Three, 201

When families relocate frequently, homeschooling can offer a consistent education as the alternative to changing schools. Without creating gaps in education or an undesirable shift in scope and sequence, as often happens with changes in schools, education continues as usual. Teachers remain the same, rules remain the same, and educational materials remain the same, all to the benefit of the student.

From South Korea, Lisa reflects on homeschooling her four children (ages 11, 13, 15, 18) through many relocations:

We are a military family (Air Force) with four children. We started homeschooling because of our oldest child's learning disabilities and because of our nomadic lifestyle. We have continued because of the great quality of education and the opportunity to build deep relationships with our children. Before moving to South Korea this year, we have lived in six U.S. states and England. Our oldest graduated from our homeschooling high school, and he is doing very well.

Similarly, Kirsten writes from Virginia about homeschooling her five children (ages 6, 8, 10, 12, 13):

Courtesy of the Army, we have moved seven times since our oldest was born. We began homeschooling when our children were very young. We are now in our seventh year of homeschooling. Homeschooling has given us stability over the years.

International missionaries, Arthur and Eva share their experiences with home education in these extended thoughts:

Prior to our children reaching school age, we had considered homeschooling but were not firmly committed to it, until it became a necessity. With a rigorous travel schedule, we knew it was our only option if our family did not want to be separated for weeks or even months at a time. We now have three children, two girls and a boy, and our homeschooling journey actually began in the car! We traveled together several thousand miles around the country speaking at churches to raise funds for our service as missionaries.

The road has often become our children's museum, as we point out historical sites along the way. Sometimes geography links to literature in their young minds. We read Laura Ingalls' books. In Kansas, our children learned what a prairie looks like, and in Minnesota we saw Plum Creek and the dugout site near Walnut Grove, just a day after we finished reading On the Banks of Plum Creek. *Travel has allowed our children to experience the plant, animal life, terrain, and weather associated with forests and mountains, coasts and deserts. At the same time, they become* familiar with geography, maps, and directions. Just the other day, my six-year-old told me her "west" knee was hurting! ... .

Anyone can enjoy homeschooling lessons while traveling, even within the historic sites of one's own hometown. Our experiences are not unique, especially for missionary families. Homeschooling allows for learning to continue in both book form and in experience. As a family, we have traveled to the Dominican Republic several times, to Panama, and elsewhere without worrying whether our children were "missing" school. International travel has allowed them to enjoy different cultures, languages, foods, and climates, as well as to interact with people of various economic and social classes. Experiencing mission work first-hand has helped to give them the desire to tell everyone they encounter about Jesus ... . They see new experiences as a chance to learn something new. They also now have friends all over the world.

The Office of International Mission works with families to make sure they have the resources needed to school their children. Most families take these resources with them when they move to the mission field and "restock" every other year when they are back in the U.S. during furlough.

Vocation

God conceals his work of love to men in cross-marked vocation which is really of benefit to the neighbor. The cross of one's vocation comes without man's own doing, in the hour when God wills it ... . When God gives a vocation, he also gives his promise to be with him who endures vocation's cross and cries to God ... .[17] — Gustaf Wingren

In Maryland, Kay homeschooled her two boys all the way through high school. She explains:

To me the bottom line is vocation. As parents, it is our job to educate our children. We may do it ourselves, or we may employ a school to help us do it. But it is our job.

Deaconess Eva agrees:

Those who are parents have been given the awesome responsibility of raising the children God has entrusted to their care. Part of the vocation of parenthood includes providing for their child(ren)'s education. Some families decide to send their children to public or private school, while others are determined to homeschool, whether from the beginning or out of

---

[17] Wingren, Gustaf. *Luther on Vocation.* Translated by Carl C. Rasmussen. Eugene, Oregon: Wipf and Stock Publishers, 2004. 208, 228, 57-58.

necessity. Some parents decided the type of schooling they wanted for their children before they were ever conceived, while others may need to make that decision at the last minute depending on the specific circumstances of the family. Regardless, the education of children ultimately falls under the vocational realm of parenthood. Further, providing for spiritual instruction resounds in the calling as parents to share the Holy Scriptures with their children. "You shall teach them diligently to your children, and shall talk of them when you sit in your house, and when you walk by the way, and when you lie down, and when you rise" (Deuteronomy 6:7).

Nicole Manners adds:

Often as home educators we can be swept away by the myriad of options in curricula, style, and content, bogged down with the mechanics and minutiae of learning. Yet if we can step back far enough from the utilitarian aspects of education and approach it as Christians with a wider — even eternal — lens, we can see the ultimate end. We wish this for our children when they leave our homeschool: a full, caring life, lived in service to God and neighbor. Our identity in Christ calls us to anchor our homeschool to the one thing necessary.

Mary Moerbe admits:

It can be scary wondering whether you are making all the right choices for those you love so much. Regardless of the number of teachers in your child's life, God has given you the authority of parent. (That in itself is daunting!) God has placed you in the position of parent to educate your children in life and in the faith.

But God does not leave us alone, as if leaving our children distant from the help only He can give. God has given us Himself and so often neighbors who love and help sustain us through the compassionate gifts of God!

It is not a matter of being a theological expert … . Our God created a magnificent world, and there is so much to explore in beauty and science and to experience! And we get to do that together. Freed from the burdens of what we deserve, we can encourage one another to grow, to learn, and to appreciate what we have.

Improved Socialization (How Ironic!)

Through homeschooling, students can excel at interacting with people of all age levels and be less peer-dependent. School at home allows time for volunteer work in the church or community, which provides many opportunities for cultivating social skills. — Susan Knowles, homeschooling mother

Several myths exist regarding socialization and homeschooling. You may have heard some of these:

1. Myth: "Homeschooled children will experience only one teacher for ALL subjects K-12!"

Reality: Homeschooled children benefit from the wisdom and instruction of other adults, such as pastors, spouses, friends, additional teachers, tutors, or online instructors, mentors, coaches, and adults in the congregation.

Often homeschooling families become close with librarians, museum docents, piano teachers, or other education-minded adults who become lifelong mentors to their children with or without pay. Others appreciate instructors on DVD who teach with surprising passion and engagement, lesson by lesson. Extended family members often influence homeschooled children more than anyone, whether formally or informally, in person or via the Internet. Aunts and uncles, grandparents and others may impact children in ways they may not even realize, such as by reading stories to them, sharing family history, assisting with homework, and engaging homeschooled children in conversations throughout their lives.

2. Myth: "Homeschooled children never experience competition!"

Reality: Competition occurs within the homeschool and through outside activities.

Whether through flashcard contests, exercises on the white board, or science quizzes, homeschooled children may compete in academics within their own homes. Moreover, homeschoolers can enjoy healthy competition through spelling or geography bees, speech or writing contests, science fairs and talent shows, recitations and performances. Many homeschooled children will encounter competition in areas of their own interest, such as swim meets, team sports, auditions for vocal solos, or elections for group leadership positions.

3. Myth: "Homeschooled children always study alone in their own rooms."

Reality: Academic discussions happen for homeschooled children, and possibly more frequently than for a child in a classroom!

Peripatetic discussions occur daily with parents. Fathers can help children apply lessons in catechesis, logic, and civility to daily life. Mothers can align writing assignments and literature discussions to the family's shared experiences. Lutheran congregations provide Sunday School teachers or adult Bible classes where group discussions occur weekly. Many homeschoolers also appreciate book clubs, debate teams, and courses with other students, especially in the later years when analysis and expression become essential skills to practice and enjoy. Because social interactions can be more purposeful and less ubiquitous than in some educational settings, homeschooling may offer unique opportunities to teach common courtesies, mutual respect, and an appreciation for others.

Nicole Manners shares this:

I gratefully place socialization among the advantages to homeschooling! For all that is touted as a caution against homeschooling, the concept of socialization is one that actually works in our favor. Homeschooled children often receive compliments about their manners. Homeschooling parents hear this often: "Why, your children are so mature ...." "Your kids are so respectful and polite." "They are so well-behaved" — as though it has become a novelty for adolescents to respect their elders. Still the stigma persists, as even some of these admiring onlookers will finish up the compliments with their concerned caution about homeschooling: "Well, as long as they are receiving enough socialization ...."

I firmly believe that one of the greatest benefits to the homeschooling lifestyle is not that our children are hidden away from society, but that they receive appropriate socialization skills. Given the typical homeschooling family's penchant for socializing together as a family, home-schooled children become comfortable relating to various groups, which leads to respectful, mature conversations even with adults; firm and clear boundaries regarding peer relationships and suitable companions; and appropriate role modeling for younger ages. Indeed, in what other area of our modern lives are we segregated solely with respect to our chronological age? How ridiculous to suppose that one would demand to be seated next to other co-workers by age group at work, and yet this idea remains the basis for our modern schools. Homeschooling yields great social rewards by comparison."

In this first of several longer narratives provided throughout *Eternal Treasures*, we introduce you to Lutheran home education beyond mere snippets, quotes, and tips, as Nicole Manners, homeschooling mother in California, shares her journey with us.

Why We Homeschool

Nicole Manners

> *Two roads diverged in a yellow wood,*
> *And sorry I could not travel both*
> *And be one traveler, long I stood*
> *And looked down one as far as I could*
> *To where it bent in the undergrowth;[18] — Robert Frost*

"Oh, I already know that I'm going to homeschool my kids." I heard my new friend's statement ring with bald finality. I envied her almost arrogant assurance. Her statement hung in the air like a low-lying branch heavy with sun-ripened fruit. After my own admission that I anxiously anticipated sending my daughter, our older child, to kindergarten, my friend's assertion took me by surprise.

I quavered, "Homeschool? Really?" Mary and I had nurtured a strong rapport in the short months we'd known each other, but I didn't wish to pry. Gingerly, I asked a few more questions, but only until I could change the subject as unobtrusively as possible. Discomfited and rather dismayed by my own uncertainty in comparison to her unyielding and seemingly blithe dismissal of any other option for her children's education, I left our local moms' group play date in a state of cognitive irritation.

What was it about Mary's serenity that caused me such distress? Was it the fact that her oldest, and at that time *only*, child was merely two years old? Did I have a bit of a parenting seniority complex, since I had two children to her one, with my daughter nearing kindergarten age, a whopping three years older than hers, and with a baby boy nearly two? Could it be that I knew little of homeschooling, other than a caricature of pajama-clad lounging "students," much of which I based on mere speculation? This surely factored into my thoughts, but it was the sheer firmness of her conviction that boggled my mind.

Indeed, while I had secretly been worrying myself sick over what we would do with our daughter at the Magical Age of Five, this new friend of mine, with her husband's full support and blessing, had calmly and rationally made a life-altering decision before her child could even walk and talk! Certainly, I assured myself, this is mere

---

[18] Frost, Robert. "The Road Not Taken." In *A Treasury of Poetry for Young People: Emily Dickinson, Robert Frost, Henry Wadsworth Longfellow, Edgar Allan Poe, Carl Sandberg, Walt Whitman*. New York: Sterling Publishers, 2008. (All excerpts in this section are from this poem.)

hubris. No one can be so confident of the future!

Yet she was. That conversation, the first of many, was a pivotal moment in the future of my children's education, perhaps even the pivotal moment in my own education. College graduate though I was, it was only after that conversation that I was able to dip a toe in the waters of boundless possibilities available to us. I believe that the Lord brought this dear friend into my life, at the time and under the circumstances that He did, to open my mind and heart to the reality of an education outside the treadmill of modern schooling. Today I can look back to that shocking and uncomfortable statement and see with clarity the path toward the good, the true, and the beautiful, upon which we currently travel.

> *Then took the other, as just as fair,*
> *And having perhaps the better claim,*
> *Because it was grassy and wanted wear;*
> *Though as for that the passing there*
> *Had worn them really about the same,*

Of course, my earnestness to learn more about this hitherto unrecognized path led to countless hours of research. I knew that my dear children deserved nothing less than my best efforts at seeking answers. When a move across the state took me far away from my friend, not only did I begin to scour the overwhelming plethora of homeschooling methods and philosophies on the Internet and in the library, but I began to research our local school district. This included the highly touted test scores, which somehow proved our district to be of good reputation, always brought up in conversations regarding school choice.

I had no aim other than the nebulous idea to gather as much information as possible. I was on a deadline! My daughter, Madisen, was soon to be enrolled for the following fall! The decision weighed heavily on me, until I found this one small golden nugget of information, which blessed me with an immediate sense of peace: In California where we live, kindergarten is not compulsory. Before October of the year in which the child turns six years old, state law did not require that she be enrolled in a school. What did this mean for us? We now had the luxury of a whole year in which to make a firm decision regarding our children's educational future. Albeit, there was still a part of me that waxed nostalgic, Norman Rockwell-style, imagining the exciting first day of the school adventure for Madisen, little backpack bumping against her scrawny body, princess lunchbox clutched in her eager hand, as she walked toward her future—smiling, eager, ready to learn. Yet in the back of my mind lurked a niggling voice of disillusionment, reminding me of the unhappiness that had plagued my own school years: the bullying, the tears, the boredom. Did I really wish to send her off hoping for the former, yet knowing the latter was probably closer to the reality?

Armed only with the morass of confusing information gathered thus far, I presented the most comprehensive case I could muster to my husband, Richard. After all, I reasoned, since law did not prohibit us from keeping her home the following year, what would be the harm? In his usual patient fashion, he listened to my reasons, asked a few pointed questions, and pronounced with a resounding tone of finality, "Whatever you think, dear. You have obviously given this a lot of thought. I trust your judgment."

The wind gushed sickeningly from my sails. This is awful, I thought. Expecting him to be completely sold on the whole homeschooling idea by the depth of my fervor and the firmness of my arguments, I did not know how to proceed with such an apparently lackluster response. Didn't he understand that our children's future, and our own, lay in the balance?! This couldn't be all my decision. What if I made the wrong choice?

Since that day, I have come to realize that this was his wise way of tempering my enthusiastic, all-or-nothing mentality with a healthy dose of prudence. Why rush into such a huge decision with the weight of Forever looming over it? Instead, just as a baby does not learn to walk all at once, at these beginning stages my husband wisely insisted that we take this whole business one step, or year, at a time. I will be ever grateful for his discernment, because it enabled me to realize that homeschooling, like life, requires nothing if not practicality, persistence, and, patience.

> *And both that morning equally lay*
> *In leaves no step had trodden black.*
> *Oh, I kept the first for another day!*
> *Yet knowing how way leads on to way,*
> *I doubted if I should ever come back.*

We were on an adventure, that first year of homeschooling. The Lord blessed our family abundantly, although often in ways that seemed the opposite of blessed. When it came time to share our decision, friends and family often became uncomfortable. In some cases, conversations became downright awful. While some were simply bemused but supportive, no doubt thinking this a passing whim, others seemed to take our family's choice to homeschool as a personalized criticism of their own choice *not* to. Similarly, when my husband and I had made the firm decision that I would remain out of the work force to raise our children, well-meaning onlookers seemed confused that I wouldn't be "using" my college education, especially for the elusive Something Worthwhile Out There. Friends seemed to delight in sharing homeschooling horror stories about "friends of friends," whom no one seemed to know personally. As when a woman is expecting her first child and birth stories come out of the woodwork by well-meaning veteran moms, we felt bombarded by people's unsolicited opinions about our educational choice.

Over time, my greatest challenge would come not from outside my home, but from within it. That first year, I realized that our daughter would not be able to learn to read as I had envisioned and expected, in kindergarten.

Books in our household were plentiful, and both children, young as they were, enjoyed listening to story upon story, as we had been reading to them consistently from birth. My daughter was extremely creative and articulate, with an exceptional vocabulary for a five-year-old; so by extension I assumed that she would be an early reader. After all, my mother claimed, I read by age four! Could my progeny be any less than miraculous? With the pressure of feeling that I was performing a circus act, as the onlookers waited for me to careen headlong from my tightrope, attempts to teach her phonics proved disastrous. Her young mind was not ready, and we ended the year, I believed, as failures.

Reflecting back, I now know that I needed to understand some-thing: my success as a homeschooler was linked not to the academic performance of my children, but only to the faithfulness of the good and gracious God who upheld me. Moreover, my children's successes would never determine their worthiness in the eyes of their Creator and Redeemer, but rested completely on His grace.

The following year, with a rambunctious three-year-old boy and a non-reading first-grade girl who was beginning to dislike "school" time because it meant frustration and tears for both of us, we determined to try homeschooling for another year. Despite what I viewed as our failure, I feared that Madisen might be labeled as deficient because of her inability to read, if we were to take a different route and put her in school. Inwardly I quailed at the knowledge that among her little group of church friends, all girls of the same age, she was the only one not able to read more than a few three-letter words. Indeed, their mothers cheerily shared that their children were reading scads of sight words and being assigned homework most days of the week from school. Knowing that an admission of failure would result in raised eyebrows and conversations about reconsidering our decision, I could do no more than listen and congratulate them. I felt alone, scared, and exceptionally powerless, praying every day for God to give me the strength to continue, when it seemed that I might have chosen unwisely. I struggled mightily against doubt in my own ability to teach my children and in my own judgment.

In an attempt to fill some of our schooltime with meaningful and tearless activity, I enrolled the three of us in a unique parent participation program run by the local adult school. We gathered once a week for an opening, a play time, and the requisite discussion of various parenting topics — all with snacks included. And there, by God's grace, I met a real-life homeschooler! Not yet having found a homeschool community in my small locality, I had to staunchly resist following her around like a lost puppy dog. Throughout the duration of the program, I was able to discuss homeschooling with her. Albeit, her oldest child was only four, but she was unwaveringly convinced that homeschooling was her future, probably because she was married to a grown-up homeschooler. Eventually, when I met her husband, I found out that we had been in the same degree program at university and had been in several upper-division classes together. God certainly used this family to open my eyes to a deeper understanding of education, as this man shared stories from his childhood. Both he and his brother were homeschooled through high school in an extremely relaxed manner, which he jokingly dubbed benign neglect. Yet, though his brother had not learned to read until age eleven, they were both successful at their upper education endeavors and further pursuits. Now ankle-deep in homeschooling waters, I found the water refreshing, rather than icy. My heart sang to hear that we were not alone. I found hope for our darling girl and for our future as homeschoolers.

I shall be telling this with a sigh
Somewhere ages and ages hence:
Two roads diverged in a wood, and I —
I took the one less traveled by,
And that has made all the difference.

At that point, I determined to make the best use of our days, while I waited for God to open up Madisen's mind to the written word. We read scads of books together, took nature walks, participated in church life, memorized Scripture, and went to the library for story time. In our tiny yard we planted a tinier garden, learned together how many shoes a puppy could devour in one week, and found out that the jays liked one particular tree in our backyard because it was full of figs. We drew, we counted, we picked berries. Tidepools became science experiments. (How close *does* your stick have to be before the anemone closes up?) Hikes along the coast became fodder for an increasing rock and shell collection. In other words, we lived. Together. Abundantly. Yes, daily phonics instruction remained a small part of our school day, but it was no longer the focus. Some of our very sweetest memories were made during that year when I gave up my imagined control of the *when*, and just concentrated on the *how*. My own education flourished, as I continued my search for knowledge of man, of God, and of the universe. In many ways, I learned more of significance during these short years of homeschooling than I ever did during my own public school and college education.

Our family has since moved upstate from where we began our homeschooling journey, but when we all remember back to those years, it is flavored with honeyed memories of those carefree days. It took our daughter until she was almost nine before words became real and living for her, and when they did, there was no holding her back! Presently, at fourteen, she is in the midst of writing a fantasy novel and can explain the most obscure intricacies of Tolkien's *Lord of the Rings* series, which she has now read multiple times. Madisen can be found at her piano or with her art supplies when not hidden in a corner with a book. Our son maintains a vast Lego experimentation laboratory, otherwise known as His Bedroom. He boasts an affinity for Frodo and Gandalf's adventures, which is exceeded only by his love for Star Wars trivia. His favorite homeschool day is the one in which he can take something, preferably complicated, apart.

My friend Mary, whose adamant decision to homeschool influenced my own so long ago, now lives close enough to visit. Our homeschooled children appear poised to become lifelong friends. That road less traveled, once hidden by clusters of seemingly impassable brambles, twigs, and thorns, we have traveled together.

God has proven extremely gracious in His provision for our life together as a homeschool family. Our homeschooling community has broadened to include many families who have made the same choice, to keep (or bring) their children home and provide the best possible education they can. While this looks different in every family, we no longer feel unsure about our decision. Today, when we receive the occasional raised eyebrow at the grocery store while most children are tucked away in a school building, we no longer feel defensive or pressured. Instead, we are thankful to share the joy we have found in learning and living together.

Getting Started

As examined in the previous narrative perhaps the most challenging part of homeschooling is simply the decision to begin! For those families exploring home education and for any homeschooler seeking reminders of home education "basics," we share the following suggestions:

Learn the laws of your state or province.

Search online for the latest homeschooling regulations in your area. You can search by state to find groups to help.

You can also visit *HSLDA.org* in the U.S. or *HSLDA.ca* for Canada. Consider joining HSLDA for legal protection and counsel throughout your homeschooling years. Your HSLDA membership card gains discounts at various bookstores and office supply stores. After you learn the laws, follow these suggestions:

- Plan to follow every requirement for your state or province. Understand that the legal criteria may be far more minimal than your own, so feel free to exceed these standards! You need only document the required coursework, testing, and hours.

- Keep good records for each child. Set up a file cabinet or accordion file for each child. Have necessary documents ready to produce at a moment's notice. [See Chapter Two for more information on record-keeping.]

- Find out when compulsory education begins and ends in your state or province. Maintain good records for these ages. HSLDA recommends that you do not offer to the state any information that is not required.

Select a curriculum that will assist your teaching goals:

- Consider excellent, proven, and easy-to-teach curriculum programs to provide strong academics, integrate the great languages and literature of Western civilization, and uphold historic Christian teachings. One favorite is *MemoriaPress.com*. At Memoria Press, all curriculum is developed, taught, and tested at the acclaimed Highlands Latin School. These teaching resources are made available for homeschoolers, co-ops or cottage schools, and day schools to provide academics within a historical, creedal, and classical Christian context.

- If you prefer to plan your own curriculum, you can select individual resources from one publisher or from a combination of publishers. Some favorite publishers among Lutheran homeschoolers include Concordia Catechetical Academy (Lutheran), Concordia Publishing House (Lutheran), Peace Hill Press, Veritas Press, Rod and Staff, the Institute for Excellence in Writing, Classical Academic Press, the CiRCE Institute, and Memoria Press. See Appendices C and D for specific resources.

Be true to your faith.

Feel free to research options, but do not overwhelm yourself with too many choices. You can quickly rule out many publishers whose curricula will consistently undermine Lutheran catechesis. For options most consistent with Lutheran teaching, turn to the new Homeschool Resource Guide (Concordia Publishing House), the *Curriculum Resource Guide for Classical Lutheran Education* (CCLE Press), or ask fellow Lutheran homeschoolers for assistance.

Keep it easy.

Combine children where possible. For example, teach two children in a particular curriculum, if the children's skills and motivation lend themselves to combined teaching. After all, far wider disparities exist in any single classroom. While individual tutoring is recommended when teaching a child to read, combined instruction can occur effectively with such subjects as history, science, and literature. To reduce time needed for homemaking tasks, plan to assign household chores just as you assign schoolwork, so everyone assists. This may include cleaning, folding laundry, and helping with younger children.

Ask questions.

Ask the families at conferences for Lutheran homeschoolers or in online discussion groups for Lutheran homeschoolers on Yahoo, Facebook, and elsewhere. To learn about the Lutheran liberal arts, join *ClassicalLutheranHomeschoolers* via *www.ccle.org*, and post questions. Attend CCLE's summer conferences to meet other Lutheran homeschoolers, hear Lutheran speakers, and gather with families. If you enjoy researching independently, see Appendix F on Family and Education.

Outsource tough subjects.

When you need help with difficult subjects or would like to provide discussions for your teen with someone other than Mom, consider classical Lutheran online courses through Wittenberg Academy or Faith Lutheran School in Plano, Texas. You can find other reputable online academies or instructional DVDs through Memoria Press, The Well-Trained Mind, Veritas Press, and others.

Special needs?

Yes, you can homeschool a child with special needs! Research the laws, or visit HSLDA's Struggling Learner website for state-specific information. For therapies, assemble a good team of professionals to help you. Ask your pediatrician for referrals. Options include evaluations for pediatric occupational therapy to assist fine-motor skills and sensory processing; speech and language therapy for speech articulation and language abilities; physical therapy for gross-motor skills and coordination; a neurologist, psychoeducational examiner, or neuropsychologist for more comprehensive assessments. Consider reading *Simply Classical: A Beautiful Education for Any Child*. See also the *Simply Classical Curriculum* (Memoria Press) for children with special needs.

Find in-person support.

Start a Lutheran homeschooling group in your congregation or among neighboring Lutheran churches. Find a host church or meet in a public park. Even two or three families can be sufficient to create enjoyable park days, field trips, and book clubs. Create special outings or classes based on the talents of the participating adults. Consider asking a Lutheran pastor to provide regular Matins services for these Lutheran homeschool families, so your children can share in the Holy Scriptures, Lutheran hymnody, and liturgy together.

Take your time.

Be patient with yourself and with your children. One mother reflects on how demanding she was with her two grown girls during homeschooling. She realizes now that she tried too hard to duplicate the least humane aspects of "school," the very things she had sought to avoid by homeschooling! Now she states it this way quite honestly: "If I had to do it all over, I would yell less and take more breaks!"

Many successful homeschoolers look back now and realize that the best times were those spent delving deeply into subjects, enjoying "down time" together with excellent read-alouds, and sharing the most precious elements of the faith — listening to and singing hymns, reading and memorizing the catechism together, confessing and forgiving sins, and discussing Bible stories with the comfort of mercy, forgiveness, and hope in Christ Jesus. We explore these elements more fully in Part Two of *Eternal Treasures*.

Choosing Curriculum

Before selecting curriculum, determine your ending goals. Consider what you hope your child will achieve in high school:

- wisdom and eloquence,
- strong academic preparation,
- being well-rounded in the language arts and mathematical arts,
- disciplined habits of study,
- in-depth reading of the essential literature from Western civilization,
- a love of learning,
- strong character,
- biblical literacy,
- an appreciation for the Holy Scriptures and Lutheran doctrine.

Ask these questions or create your own:
- What will be the daily routine?
- How will we manage housekeeping and meal-planning?
- Do I wish to devise my own plan or teach from a full-year curriculum?
- How will I best engage my child in discussions through the materials?
- How will we divide instruction between Mom and Dad based on interests and strengths?
- How will we teach hymns, prayer, and God's Word within our home?

For recommendations in teaching math, reading and spelling, writing, history and science, Christian catechesis and more, you might appreciate *The Curriculum Resource Guide for Classical Lutheran Education* (CCLE Press, 2015), *www.ccle.org*, for recommendations from early childhood through high school. In the guide, you will find resources reviewed from a Lutheran perspective. Many "veteran homeschoolers" recommend purchasing curriculum only one year at a time and re-evaluating options annually. You may select all-in-one curriculum options or design your own homeschool curriculum with individual resources selected by area of study.

All-In-One Curriculum: Everything You Need for One Year

Many new homeschoolers and "veterans" appreciate the trend toward all-in-one curriculum packages. With these sequential programs and daily checklists, parents may be less likely to allow gaps in learning. All has been researched and integrated into one intentional, cohesive whole. Parents retain flexibility to modify for scheduling, interests, and depth of study. Programs offer daily lesson plans to be followed or modified as desired.

Recommended all-in-one curriculum programs are listed here:

- Memoria Press, *www.memoriapress.com*, gives your child strong foundations in early academics in a context of beautiful literature and the Christian faith. While you will want to supplement with Lutheran teachings, hymns, and prayers, your older child will receive an excellent education, with preparation and engagement in the Great Books and the classical languages in a Christian context. These award-winning curriculum packages provide daily lesson plans with adaptations for accelerated, moderated, and special needs. Large families may combine closely skilled children into one level for ease of teaching. Whether teaching from this curriculum or not, homeschoolers may appreciate the free catalog from Memoria Press, *The Classical Teacher*, for articles with an emphasis on truth, goodness, and beauty.

- Peace Hill Press, *www.welltrainedmind.com*, offers some all-in-one curriculum packages. The companion book, *The Well-Trained Mind: A Guide to Classical Education at Home*, assists homeschoolers with providing a strong academic education.

- Veritas Press, *www.veritaspress.com*, offers grade-by-grade curriculum suggestions with total packages. The catalog provides good read-aloud recommendations and resources for teaching art.

- Online options: As previously mentioned, Lutheran homeschoolers who seek online classes will find exclusively Lutheran teachers in Wittenberg Academy and Faith Lutheran School in Plano, Texas (live, online). Other online options include: Memoria Press Online Academy, Wilson Hill Online Academy, Veritas Press Scholars Academy, the Well-Trained Mind Academy, and HSLDA Online Academy (formerly Patrick Henry Preparatory Academy).

Design Your Own Curriculum

If you would prefer to assemble your own curriculum, you have thousands of choices. Each of the above publishers provides teaching resources for any age and any subject. You can assist the process with any of these resources written by Lutherans:

- *Concordia Catechetical Academy* Sussex, Wisconsin
- *The Curriculum Resource Guide for Classical Lutheran Education*, by Cheryl Swope and Melinda Heine, CCLE Press
- *Homeschool Resource Guide*, CPH
- *Simply Classical: A Beautiful Education for Any Child*, by Cheryl Swope
- Appendix C and Appendix D within this this handbook

Other helpful resources for selecting curriculum:

- *All Through the Ages: A Literature Guide to History*, by Christine Miller (a collection of resources)
- *Designing Your Own Classical Education*, by Laura Berquist (Roman Catholic)
- *The Latin-Centered Curriculum*, by Andrew Campbell (helpful for learning how to streamline your homeschool)
- *The Well-Trained Mind: A Guide to Classical Education at Home*, by Susan Wise Bauer (a collection of resources)
- *Follow the recommended sequence by one of the reputable publishers listed on page 243.*

Above All: Teach the Faith

Reading Bible stories and reading from God's Word at increasing levels of detail and understanding can improve wisdom and knowledge while strengthening faith at each level. For a sample course of study in the Christian faith, see pages 240-242.

From Early Childhood to Teaching High School

For Eunice and for Lois
  We sing our thanks and praise.
Young Timothy they nurtured
  And led him in Your ways.
Raise up in ev'ry household
  True teachers of Your Word
Whose lives will bear clear witness
  To Christ, our risen Lord.[19]
– Herman G. Stuempfle, Jr.

For some families, homeschooling young children becomes a logical, natural extension of parenting young children. We read to our children, explore the outdoors together, learn God's Word, forgive one another, and love one another. We walk side-by-side together as Christians united with family bonds. As our children grow older, we become more structured and purposeful, as academic instruction and formal catechesis shape the hours and content of our mutual study. Other families decide to "bring their children home" after the children have experienced traditional classrooms. We explore these various experiences through the voices of Lutheran homeschoolers.

Beginning Early
These homeschoolers began homeschooling early in their children's lives.

Megan in California:
  When my husband entered seminary, our oldest was just six months. We met homeschooling families. When we received a call to a small town, we decided to homeschool. We now have four homeschooled children (3, 4, 6, 8).

Charmaine in Indiana:
  I started looking into homeschooling when my oldest was preschool-aged. Our four homeschooled children are now 4, 11, 13, and 15. As a pastor's daughter, I began to realize what a great education my dad had received. I knew he would not be here forever for me and for my children to teach us all things historical, theological, literary, and classical. I began exploring classical Lutheran homeschooling.

---

[19] *Lutheran Service Book.* St. Louis: Concordia Publishing House, 2006. 855:13.   **49**

Dan and Sallie in Iowa:
We have two children, ages 18 and 14, whom we have homeschooled from the beginning. Currently, our teens attend classes online.

Jared and Rebecca in Colorado:
We have six children (4, 5, 6, 8, 9, 12). After some research while attending the seminary at Fort Wayne, and after hearing a lecture by the Rev. Joel Brondos, who was headmaster of Zion at the time, my wife and I have been homeschooling since our oldest started school. As a pastor in Denver with a somewhat flexible schedule, I teach the children three mornings a week.

Yvonne in California:
My husband and I have three children, twin 16-year-old sons and a 14-year-old daughter. We have homeschooled our children from the beginning.

Jenny in Minnesota:
A few weeks after my husband received his first call, our first child was born. We have homeschooled our children, ages 7 and 9, from the beginning.

Ken and Sarah in Arizona:
My husband and I have two girls, ages 5 and 7. We are Lutheran, so we knew teaching the faith would be part of their education. Our first "official" years of homeschooling have been great. My oldest loves to learn and is a great reader. I am amazed at how much our 5-year-old learns, even while I'm going over things with her sister!

Michael and Claudia in Ontario, Canada:
My husband and I began investigating schooling options for our children when our oldest was an infant. We now have four children, one girl (age 9) and three boys (3, 6, and 7) whom we have homeschooled. My favorite thing about homeschooling has been teaching my children to read! This is the most rewarding thing ever, and something I would never delegate to anyone else.

Bringing Your Children Home from School

Jesus, all Thy children cherish
And keep them that they never perish
Whom Thou hast purchased with Thy blood .... [20]
— Wilhelm E. Arends

These families offer encouragement to those who desire to bring their children home for their schooling:

Rachel Pollock in Michigan:
Both graduates of Hillsdale College, my husband and I majored in education. We sent our oldest son to a charter kindergarten, but that lasted only about five months. We now homeschool our four children—three boys (ages 6, 8, 9) and one girl, age 5. Homeschooling has been one of the best decisions we've made as a family.

Jim and Emily, parents of five children (ages 2, 7, 9, 12, 13):
After our oldest survived a year in an all-day Catholic school kindergarten, we began homeschooling. I appreciate the freedom to teach the Lutheran Confessions as part of my children's education.

Michelle and her husband, homeschoolers of two boys (ages 2 and 9):
Frustrated with what our son was learning (or not learning) in school, we decided to embark on a classical approach through homeschooling.

From Ohio, Mark and Sue speak to the unexpected benefits of bringing their young son home:
For preschool through mid-second grade, our son attended a Lutheran school, but the day school experience left our family with very limited family time, given my husband's many evening commitments and seasonal obligations. Countless times the association day school programming conflicted with the congregation's schedule, leaving us all frazzled trying to juggle everything. We started homeschooling when my husband accepted a call to a congregation with no Lutheran school within an hour drive. Having now lived both ways, I can readily say that homeschooling is the best thing that ever happened to our family.

---

[20] *The Lutheran Hymnal*. St. Louis: Concordia Publishing House, 1941. 444:4.

Tips for Bringing Your Children Home

- **Go slowly at first.** Give yourself time to establish a new rhythm and routine for the family. Changes will occur. Family life, once seen as the "break" from school, will become the primary place where learning occurs. Perhaps classroom teachers were once deemed the "experts" and parents viewed as mere bystanders; but now mom and dad become the educational authority. Siblings, once separated by age and grade restrictions, suddenly become both classmates and playmates. True leisure, once swallowed by school calendars, now becomes untapped opportunity for wonder, curiosity, and exploration.

- **Enjoy the changes.** Children who may have dreaded reading books due to the reports attached to them may begin embracing reading as a shared pleasure. But this may take time. To change drudgery to enjoyment, one homeschooling family began a paper chain onto which any of their four girls would add a "link" upon completing another book. The chain eventually zigzagged across the finished basement family room with a sense of cheery accomplishment.

- **Establish a sense of order.** Routine and structure will assist learning. Remember to allow frequent physical breaks. One homeschooling family walks three times a day. Others interperse academic lessons with household tasks, such as carrying loads of laundry or taking trash to the curb. Other families play games or sports, jump rope, or ride bicycles. A gentle but predictable routine need not stifle the child. Rather, this may serve to promote harmony and well-being within the family.

- **Determine the most important areas of study.** Begin with these. Teach the most important areas in the first part of the day. Allow adequate time to teach, assess, and remain organized. Then add other subjects, perhaps one at a time, as you feel comfortable.

- **Rest!** Be sure to plan a few enjoyable outings or activities each week. Consider posting these on the calendar or white board, so both children and adults can look forward to these activities as they work.

Teaching High School

Home-educated students have been accepted into post-secondary programs with a parent-generated diploma for the last 25 years ... . In fact, the high school years can be the most exciting.[21] — FPEA

Many families homeschool through high school, with their children entering college directly from their home-education programs. Often by the time homeschoolers are high-school age, they can study far more independently than their public-school peers. In Wisconsin, Lutheran homeschoolers Alex and Jenni witnessed their older daughter complete Advanced Placement courses at home without much instruction from her parents! Cacia received scholarships to enter college directly from homeschool, and she graduated from Concordia University in Mequon. Thanks to their parents' dedicated homeschooling K-12, she and her sister Sara (who shares thoughts later in *Eternal Treasures*), along with their brother Andrew, found themselves well prepared for the academic challenges of college.

Transcript templates, diplomas, and even caps and gowns can be obtained through *HSLDA.org* and many state homeschool groups. If homeschooling through high school seems daunting, whether or not you have not homeschooled from the early years, you can easily find support for those upper-level subjects. Consider any of these options:

- DVD instructors with outlines, lessons, and readings for the student to accomplish independently (Memoria Press for Latin, Literature, Logic, Rhetoric; Classical Academic Press for The Art of Poetry, The Art of Argument, and more),

- private tutoring,

- dual enrollment through the local community college or university often at a greatly reduced rate,

- independent learning with occasional assistance from a family member, congregation member, or local teacher,

- online classes (See page 246 for options.)

For a uniquely affordable approach, consider the book written by Missouri homeschoolers, *College Without Compromise*, which explains ways to rely on placement testing for college credit.

---

[21] "Starting Point." Orlando: Florida Parent Educator Association, 2014. 18-19.

Hear from these families who homeschooled through high school. Eric and Kay in Maryland:

We have two grown sons whom we homeschooled through high school graduation. Our older son is now an Aeronautical Engineering graduate from Rensselaer Polytechnic Institute, and our younger son is in the Marine Corps.

Scott and Tressa in South Carolina:

We have three children. After our oldest was homeschooled all the way through high school, he entered Bethany Lutheran College. Our middle child, a daughter, is finishing high school now. Our youngest is a freshman. Homeschooling high school has been challenging and wonderful at the same time.

Lisa in Wisconsin:

We have been homeschooling over fourteen years. Our oldest is now in college. The others are in 11th grade, 9th grade, 7th grade, and 5th grade.

Mark and Laura in Texas:

We have six children (6, 8, 11, 14, 16, 18). We are actively involved in our LCMS congregation. I taught in a Lutheran classroom for five years before coming home to begin kindergarten with my now high-school-aged child. My husband is an architect and is currently handling the geometry and advanced algebra at home.

Glenda in Minnesota:

Our five children are 11, 12, 13, 16, 18. My husband David and I attended a CCLE conference in the summer of 2001 before we began our first official year of homeschooling. That conference shaped much of what we chose for curriculum. My husband serves as pastor of the church next door, so this provides us with the ability to attend daily Matins, have all meals together, and for him to teach Latin and upper-level math. We also appreciate the Wittenberg Online Academy, where I serve on the Board.

Special Needs

Lord Jesus Christ, the children's friend,
To each of them Your presence send.
— *LSB, 866:1*

You can teach your special-needs child at home! In this section, we offer several tips. We follow these suggestions with some helpful thoughts from a Lutheran pastor who is also the homeschooling father of a son with special needs.

Know the laws.

Search *HSLDA.org* to learn the legal requirements in your area. Consider joining for legal protection. Search *WrightsLaw.com* for additional legal information on special needs.

Assemble a good team to help you.

Request referrals from your child's pediatrician, if needed, and obtain thorough evaluations in each of these areas as soon as possible:

- vision and hearing to include auditory processing,
- neurological functioning (neurologist),
- educational achievement and intellectual capacity (educational psychologist or psychoeducational evaluation),
- cognitive and processing function (neuropsychologist),
- speech and language (speech and language pathologist),
- sensory, fine-motor, and self-help skills (occupational therapist),
- coordination and large-motor skills (physical therapist),
- state or regional centers for the developmentally delayed (various services, funding).

The earlier you can obtain ample, specific information with coordinated recommendations, the better prepared you will be to provide an excellent education for your child. For information on navigating this process, see the chapters on Assessment and Modifications in *Simply Classical: A Beautiful Education for Any Child*.

Read. Listen. Attend conferences.

Read books and attend conferences on your child's specific

disabilities or challenges. Read any of these handbooks on educating the special-needs child at home:

- *Homeschooling Your Struggling Learner,* by Kathy Kuhl
- *Homeschooling Children With Special Needs,* by Sharon Hensley, M.A.
- *Different Learners,* by Jane M. Healy, Ph.D.
- *Simply Classical: A Beautiful Education for Any Child,* by Cheryl Swope, M.Ed.

Obtain modified or targeted curriculum.

Use the creative strategies recommended by your child's evaluators and therapists. As mentioned previously, if your child is significantly challenged or delayed, consider the new all-in-one *Simply Classical Curriculum* packages (Memoria Press) designed just for children with special needs.

Ask questions.

Join *SimplyClassical.com,* the free online Memoria Press forum for special-needs and struggling students. Search *ClassicalSpecialNeeds.com* for information and various resources.

New homeschooler Michelle V. writes:

My young son, born three months early at just 2.5 lbs., amazes me. When we began homeschooling him this past fall, he spoke only ten words. Now he speaks so many, I cannot count. I truly believe the Simply Classical Curriculum *from Memoria Press has helped his oral skills more than anything else. The lessons gave me exactly what I was looking for, something concrete to do with him to work on oral language skills and more.*

Mother of three, Elaine teaches with the same curriculum:

Our youngest son is fourteen. He has low-functioning autism, is non-verbal, has auditory processing disorder, has involuntary muscle spasms due to a Chiari I malformation, has sensory integration disorder, and sleep disorder. I was very excited last year to find the book Simply Classical: A Beautiful Education for Any Child. *I have been using Level A of the* Simply Classical Curriculum *with my son since last September. To help him understand, I take pictures of things, especially food, which is highly motivational for him. I create albums from which he can make* choices. *We use pictures to explain the activities of school. Although some days end in tears (mine), God comforts me, as I teach my son. I love Psalm 139.**

Find support.

Receive information to address the topic of your own child's diagnosis (e.g., autism, intellectual disability, learning disabilities, mental illness). Join (or form) local or online support groups based on your child's diagnosis.

Remember that your baptized child is God's child.

You can rest assured that the Holy Spirit works through His Word, even when our children fail to comprehend fully. John the Baptist's leaping in the womb has comforted me many times. Keep speaking God's Word, teaching the stories from the Bible, and singing hymns. And of course keep bringing your child to the Divine Service. Our special-needs children remind us that we are safe in His loving care, through no effort or ability of our own.

*Psalm 139:4-10

Before a word is on my tongue
    you, LORD, know it completely.
[5] You hem me in behind and before,
    and you lay your hand upon me.
[6] Such knowledge is too wonderful for me,
    too lofty for me to attain.
[7] Where can I go from your Spirit?
    Where can I flee from your presence?
[8] If I go up to the heavens, you are there;
    if I make my bed in the depths, you are there.
[9] If I rise on the wings of the dawn,
    if I settle on the far side of the sea,
[10] even there your hand will guide me,
    your right hand will hold me fast....

Continue reading Psalm 139, and consider memorizing verses 11-18 with your children day by day:

If I say, "Surely the darkness shall cover me, and the light about me be night," even the darkness is not dark to you; the night is bright as the day, for darkness is as light with you.

For you formed my inward parts; you knitted me together in my mother's womb. I praise you, for I am fearfully and wonderfully made. Wonderful are your works; my soul knows it very well. My frame was not hidden from you, when I was being made in secret, intricately woven in the depths of the earth.

Your eyes saw my unformed substance; in your book were written every one of them, the days that were formed for me, when as yet there was none of them. How precious to me are your thoughts, O God! How vast is the sum of them! If I would count them, they are more than the sand. I awake, and I am still with you." – Psalm 139: 11-18

Take comfort.

For our edification, a homeschooling father of three explores this area of Christian education more fully. In this essay dedicated to his son with autism, the Rev. Erik Rottmann shares thoughts generously written for *Eternal Treasures: Teaching Your Child at Home*.

The Christian Faith for Children With Special Needs
Erik Rottmann

For my son Adam, who daily homeschools me in subjects that truly matter.

Perhaps our special-needs children are not always at the disadvantage. Perhaps their mental, neurological, and even physical limitations place them at some advantage over their peers, at least when it comes to the matters of the Christian faith. Jesus turns weakness into strength.

In this essay, I will offer concrete suggestions for teaching the faith to your special-needs child. First I will prepare you for these suggestions by briefly explaining my statement that our special-needs sons and daughters might have an advantage over their peers in matters of the faith. I take into account 1) the subject matter of the faith and 2) the perspective of a special-needs child. To close, I will point to some divine Words that will speak hope and consolation into the battle-scarred precincts of your special-needs home.

Children with special needs face no disadvantage in spiritual matters.

The subject matter of the Christian faith "regardest not the person of men" (Matthew 22:16), as the King James Version so beautifully worded it. The subject matter of our faith is Jesus Christ, the living Word of God in a human body (John 1:1, Philippians 2:6-7). "He took our illnesses and bore our diseases" (Matthew 8:17). Jesus does not need us to overcome our limitations in order to believe. Jesus overcomes our limitations so that we may believe. No disability of any sort — blindness (John 9:1-7), deafness (Mark 7:31-34), paralysis (Luke 5:17-28), or any other affliction (Matthew 4:24) — places anyone at any disadvantage when it comes to being Christian. God gives understanding (Psalm 119:169). God gives faith (Romans 10:17).

In science and math, our special-needs children may indeed struggle more than their peers in order to understand. They do not struggle more to understand the faith. It is a divine miracle for anyone to understand the faith. Reading and writing might take longer for children with special needs, but they became Christian instantly, in the moment of their baptism and in the speaking of a Word. In this faith, we all have special needs because we were all dead in trespasses and sins (Ephesians 2:1, Colossians 2:13). But "God made us alive together with Christ" (Ephesians 2:5).

Special-needs children possibly view the faith from an easier perspective.

The same health conditions that place our special-needs sons and daughters at a disadvantage in almost every area of life might prove advantageous for their faith. They daily feel in their bodies and their minds the effects of living in a fallen, sinful world. They viscerally understand weakness. They routinely experience the thoughts and emotions that weakness creates: jealousy, rage, sorrow, despair, grief, denial, desperation. This is more than the "normal" tantrums or fears experienced by their peers. Stated in the familiar terms of the Lutheran confession of faith, everyday life is an unavoidable and graphic preaching of the Law for our special-needs children. Because of this, they might be in a position to appreciate the Gospel more quickly (more deeply?) than their peers.

Here are some things you can do to teach the faith to your special-needs child:

1. Because God alone creates faith and understanding, the basic nuts and bolts of teaching the faith remain the same for every child. Sunday worship remains a priority because that is where God acts for all His saints, including those with special needs. Brief but regular chapel services during the week, simple and repeated forms of prayer, illustrated Bible stories, and manageable memory assignments can all be integrated into a homeschool schedule. Your child's special needs might dictate the amount of material you cover, the time of day for chapel, etc., but these disciplines build a firm foundation for every Christian.

2. Adopt the language of the liturgy for your everyday speech. Every Christian home has space available for such phrases as "Lord, have mercy!" and "Thanks be to God!" and "I forgive you." Sometimes children with special needs struggle to express themselves. Your patterned speech, spoken in "sincerity and truth" (1 Corinthians 5:8), will help to orient their thoughts and guide their tongue.

3. As part of your child's regular spiritual diet, you could highlight passages of Scripture that show how God uses weakness, limitation, and need to create blessings for many people. The blind man in John 9 is a particularly beneficial example for children with special needs. "'It was not that this man sinned, or his parents,' says the Lord, 'but that the works of God might be displayed in him'" (John 9:3). Paul likewise carried a daily burden that he desperately asked God to remove. God preferred to make good use of Paul's burden: "My grace is sufficient for you, for my power is made perfect in weakness" (2 Corinthians 12:9). As you continue your own reading of the Scriptures, ask God to open your eyes, so that you may see wondrous things in His Word (Psalm 119:18). Likewise pray that God would give you "an instructed tongue, that [you] may know how to sustain with a Word [your child] who is weary" (Isaiah 50:4). Who knows the wondrous ways God will lead you to use Joseph's imprisonment (Genesis 39-41) and David's courage (1 Samuel 17) and Job's endurance (Job 19) for teaching the faith to your special-needs child!

Anecdotally, my son is aware of his health. He knows it by name — Autism — and he considers it his enemy. He often asks, when the dust finally starts to settle, "Why do I have this?" I hope my various answers do not sound too pat: "Because our God is gracious. Because He intends for you to bless many people in unimaginable ways, as you already have. Because Jesus gives every Christian a cross and this one is yours. Because Jesus wants you to live on His strength instead of your own."

4. Teach your child to pray, but not in the standard American way of praying. Find a copy of Martin Luther's *A Simple Way to Pray*. Concordia Publishing House has one available. Read it and teach it in a simple way to your child. Luther stated in another place that spiritual growth consists of the interplay between hardship, prayer, and meditation upon the Scriptures. Hardship creates the need for prayer; prayer, in turn, draws our eyes and ears to the Scriptures. Why should we speak to God without expecting to hear Him respond? In the Scriptures, God responds. Children with special needs already have the hardship. (Their families have the hardship, too.) In *A Simple Way to Pray*, Luther will teach you and your child how to pray with your eyes on the Scriptures. Therein the miracle of the Christian faith begins, continues, and remains.

5. Working with your pastor, diligently prepare your child to receive the Holy Communion of our Lord's Body and Blood. Make the *Small Catechism* part of your homeschool curriculum and ask your pastor to examine your child as soon as the child is ready. (*The Pastoral Care Companion to Lutheran Service Book* contains help for examination.) Perhaps your pastor and congregation will graciously allow you to dispense with the traditional age for confirmation, or even admit your child to the Holy Communion prior to confirmation. (*Lutheran Service Book* has a rite for that too.) The life-giving Body and Blood of our Lord will serve for your child's daily strength as surely as these things will serve for yours.

To him who has no might, the Lord increases strength (Isaiah 40:29).

Children with special needs often feel isolated. So do their parents. You are not alone. My wife and I live in exile with you. We do not know what to do either. Certain Bible verses breathe life into me. They have the power to fill your lungs too:

"We had boldness in our God to declare to you the gospel of God in the midst of much conflict" (1 Thessalonians 2:2). Earlier I made reference to "the battle-scarred precincts of your special-needs home." Perhaps I should have included the phrase "war-weary." In our family, the struggle is always mental, usually emotional, and frequently physical. But our Lord Jesus Christ voluntarily chose to enter a world of chaos. The good news of forgiveness and life in Christ creates the very best form of peace, and it does so in places where there is no peace.

"The Light shines in the darkness, and the darkness has not overcome it" (John 1:5). Mental, neurological, and physical disabilities carry a dark side. In this darkness, the light of Christ often seems to shine like a tiny candle on a distant hill. But it still shines, and it will not go out.

"Thy will be done on earth as it is in heaven" (Matthew 6:10). In order for God's good and gracious will to be done, my will must be broken. I owe thanks to my son. He has humbly allowed the heavenly Father to use him as a hammer and anvil to forge a more patient father, a more attentive husband, and a more understanding pastor. The student is the teacher.

Nuts and Bolts: The Logistics of Home Education

For everything there is a season, and a time for every matter under heaven. — *Ecclesiastes 3:1*

When speaking with prospective homeschoolers, one hears a common statement, "I just do not know whether I could do this." In this chapter we offer suggested priorities, tips for homeschooling large families, recommendations for organization and record-keeping, and caveats to help you avoid common pitfalls of home education. We then provide a longer narrative with a thorough description of one family's homeschooling day. We conclude with applications for celebrating the Church Year, because opportunities within home education reach far beyond academics.

Priorities for Making it Work

With a vision or "mission statement" of devoting your family's priorities to the child's growing years, saying "no" to unnecessary commitments and distractions may become easier. After all, whether you begin early or later, Lutheran homeschooling is only for a season.

Suggested priorities:

- Sunday morning Divine Service, along with family devotional reading, prayer, and singing together in the home,

- the husband-wife relationship: guarding time to rest, refresh, and have good conversations with friends and with each other,
- physical exercise, fresh air, and good nutrition for all family members,
- strong academic teaching with steadfast faith instruction,
- service to one another in the home, among neighbors and extended family, in the congregation, and beyond.

Homeschooling a Large Family

When interviewed, many families cite "flexibility" as the key element to successfully homeschooling a large family. After teaching for the first year or so, the family develops a rhythm. For enjoyment and efficiency, many large families appreciate reading aloud together and exploring subjects such as history, science, and nature study together. With little ones in laps, large families can gather around the table or living room for daily prayer, reading, and hymn singing.

From Wyoming, Holly Scheer shares her thoughts on managing a full household while homeschooling.

Juggling Big Kids, Toddlers, and Babies
Holly Scheer

I am the mother of four children, ages 10, 7, 4, and 2. A common question when someone sees my children and then hears that I am homeschooling them is to ask how I do it all. People want to know if you can nurture a baby and still teach all of the subjects that are planned.

It is possible to have your whole family thrive with homeschooling, from the littlest to the biggest. It can be helpful to shift the academic focus for a few weeks after the addition of a new baby to baby care and helping to get the household running again. Time with a very small new baby can be well spent reading to the children, baby included, focusing on practical "home ec" type skills, and working on helping the older children find ways to help their nearest neighbors — their parents and new sibling. Homeschooling can allow your family to draw closer during these times, as parents and children work on serving one another in changing ways.

As soon as the baby begins to have a rhythm to his days, you can begin to work the home and school schedule back to normal. Breakfast works well to start the day with devotions together. While the baby is awake, reading aloud for history or science works well, as does music practice. It is also a good time to take everyone outside, weather permitting. When the baby goes down for his nap, you can then do more hands-on subjects or things that need more direction, such as math, science experiments, and language arts.

Lunch can be combined with more reading, conversation, or listening to music or audio material for lessons. Many foreign language and Latin curricula, for example, have an audio component that works well with table time for reinforcing vocabulary. There are also wonderful audio options for listening to hymns or parts of the liturgy to aid memorization.

After lunch, small children will often nap again, and this provides more time either to have lessons with full parental attention or to have quiet time for all of the children. Quiet time provides a wonderful opportunity for children to read books, work on puzzles or Legos, write in a journal, or finish work not completed earlier in the day. It also provides time for supper preparations and to put the house somewhat back in order.

A daily rhythm is a framework that can and will change as the ages and needs of the family change. It can be easy to become so focused on the schedule that you lose the very flexibility that makes home-schooling shine. If there needs to be more down time to just hold and feed a baby or toddler without something else happening at the same time, then take it. Move academic activities to the evening or in the morning, when the littlest family members are asleep.

The very most important thing I have learned about a schedule is that the schedule should serve the family. If trying to get everything done or following the schedule exactly causes upset and stress, then it is time to shift things around. The pattern and flow of each family will look different. Homeschooling affords flexibility for individual needs and for the family as a whole. Homeschooling allows you to craft the schedule that works best for various aspects of your life.

Rachel Pollock, homeschooler of three school-age boys (6, 8, 10), adds this suggestion:

Take educational opportunities for memorization with you when away from home! All ages benefit. Older children receive review, while younger children absorb more than we realize. If I know we are going to be in the car traveling to activities or have a long time to wait some place, I can take our playlist, loaded with many educational songs. Before we had our iPad, I took a small book of CDs in the car. These are our favorites:

- poetry: *Linguistic Development through Poetry Memorization, www.iew.com,*

- grammar: jingles from *www.shurley.com,*

- history: *Wee Sing America* (patriotic), *www.weesing.com; The Presidents Song, www.suedickson.com,*

- classical music: Companion CDs for Opal Wheeler's books, *www.zeezok.com,*

- geography: *www.audiomemory.com,*

- science: *www.lyricallearning.com, www.ellenjmchenry.com,*

- arithmetic: *www.mathusee.com and www.audiomemory.com,*

- Lutheran liturgy and hymnody with catechesis: *Sing the Faith* CD, *Treasury of Daily Prayer, For All Seasons,* Kantorei CDs, and *Evening and Morning: Music of Lutheran Daily Prayer, www.cph.org.*

Organization and Record-Keeping

Kelly Rottmann, M.A., homeschooling mother of three boys, provides recommendations for order and efficiency.

Organization and Record-Keeping in the Homeschool
Kelly Rottmann

A few essentials may assist in structuring your homeschool. For the purposes of developing and maintaining a well-organized education, consider each of the following needs:

- day-to-day plans,

- week-to-week schedule and overview,

- record-keeping of hours logged and courses taught to comply with state requirements,

- a master schedule for all children of compulsory school age.

Day-to-Day Plans

For day-to-day and week-to-week organization in the homeschool, a standard teacher's planner can be useful. Options for teacher's planners vary in price, and they come in several styles. Interactive teacher's planners, like the *Homeschool Tracker* or *Schoolhouse Planner*, are usually more expensive. Less expensive options include printed teacher's planners such as *The Homeschooler's Journal* or *The Homeschooler's High School Journal*. The most economical choice is to create a customized "do-it-yourself" planner that utilizes free organizational templates offered either through pre-purchased curricula or the Internet. Whichever planner style is chosen, consider functionality as well as affordability, because each classical homeschooling family is unique.[22]

Pocket or accordion folders make great day-to-day organizational tools for both teacher and students. Two-pocket folders with a different color for each day of the week can be a good method for the teacher to organize worksheets for daily lesson plans. Each student's daily bundle of worksheets for every subject can be paper-clipped together, as each daily bundle is put into its corresponding daily folder. Each student can be given his own two-pocket folder to store daily work. Differently colored two-pocket folders can help students stay better organized. One inside pocket is labeled "To Do," and the other inside pocket is labeled "Done." Every day, the teacher puts the appropriate bundle of paper-clipped worksheets for that day's lessons in the "To Do" side of each student's folder. When the student completes a worksheet, he puts it in the "Done" side of his work folder. Accordion folders can be utilized in a similar manner, with sections labeled to indicate a specific day of the week or individual student, and paper-clipped daily worksheet bundles are distributed accordingly.

Additional and differently colored two-pocket folders, one for each subject, are also good for storing each student's completed and graded papers, as some states require a portfolio of student work. Additionally, students could label each section of an accordion folder by subject, and place completed work in this folder. Both two-pocket and accordion folders can help teacher and students save time, minimize loss, and keep good records.

---

[22] Desmarais, Kathleen. "Scheduling a Classical Education." *Classical Home Education*, n.d. Accessed June 5, 2012. *http://classicalhomeeducation.com*.

Weekly Goals on Weekly Worksheets

Daily goals or lesson plans within the quarterly unit can often be best recorded on a weekly chart or worksheet inside the teacher's planner. For example, weekly worksheets on the *Tapestry of Grace* online page indicate days of the week in columns along the top, with enough rows to accommodate various "stage-appropriate" classical subjects of the trivium and quadrivium. When writing weekly and daily plans, remember to focus "on one problem, one author, or one epoch long enough to allow even the youngest student a chance to exercise his mind in a scholarly way: to make connections and trace developments, lines of reasoning, patterns of action, recurring symbolisms, plots, and motifs."[23] This focus is especially important when teaching multiple children at different learning stages, because good plans keep the teacher's time with each student running smoothly and efficiently.

State Requirements

Well-organized records are necessary, especially because many states require tangible evidence both for what is learned and for the amount of time spent on academics in the homeschool. Knowing and complying with state educational standards is in keeping with the Fourth Commandment, in which we are required to honor more than fathers and mothers; we are called upon to "serve ... other authorities by gladly providing what they need or require ... ."[24] There are several tools available to assist with record-keeping, such as standards lists, grading scales, and grade books.

Standards lists offer objective means for assessing students' academic progress. Consider the Core Knowledge Sequence,[25] the World Book standards found on the Donna Young website, or lists in classical curriculum packages. Standards can serve not only as academic skills checklists, but also as informal report cards for lower grammar students. Skills and content knowledge can be checked off as they are mastered.

For upper-grammar levels through rhetoric levels of learning, more systematized records will be needed. Consider the two separate

---

[23] Bauer, Susan Wise, and Jessie Wise. *The Well-Trained Mind: A Guide to Classical Education at Home.* Rev. ed. New York: W. W. Norton, 2004. 17.

[24] Luther, Martin. *Small Catechism.* St. Louis: Concordia Publishing House, 1991. 75.

[25] Holdren, John, and E. D. Hirsch, Jr., eds. *Books to Build On: A Grade-by-Grade Resource Guide for Parents and Teachers.* New York: Dell Publishing, 1996.

grading scales used by Memoria Press Academy, one for lower school (3rd-7th) and one for upper school (8th-12th). Record grades in a spiral-bound grade book from an office supply store, inside the teacher planner, or in an interactive grade book, like Edu-Track Homeschool (PC).

Annual Goals

With methods for day-to-day organization and record-keeping chosen, another helpful step is to schedule yearly goals based on an organized plan for home education. Some follow the patterns of their favorite homeschooling publisher or curriculum. Others prefer to spend more time on historical periods, especially classical periods and church history, and will devote an entire year to ancient Greece, another to ancient Rome, another to Augustine, and another to the Reformation. Others recommend dividing twelve years of education into "three repetitions of the same four-year pattern: the ancients, the medieval period through the early Renaissance, the late Renaissance through early modern times, and modern times."[26] Some publishers will determine this outline and reflect the decision in teaching resources.

When the overall pattern is determined, school years can then be chunked into quarters or trimesters. The divided annual goals determine quarterly or trimester lessons for each school year. These, together with each student's age and abilities, can then determine weekly and daily goals.

A Master Schedule

Creating and using a master daily schedule can be a good way for organizing time with each student. This provides each school day with a definite beginning and ending. Though some prefer more flexibility, a structured school day assures that every student has a guaranteed time slot with the teacher, and ensures that long-term projects move forward. The master daily schedule also gives an at-a-glance estimate of how much time each student works on each content area, and this is especially useful if a state or province requires a certain number of hours per subject.

---

[26] Bauer and Wise, *The Well-Trained Mind*, 15-16.

The Benefits of Organization

For all of the practical benefits, perhaps the most important benefit of an organized, efficient homeschool is that, through this means, well-educated students can be stimulated toward academic achievement, independent learning, and hard work. They can be encouraged through disciplined study to act in accordance with what they know to be right and work against "baser tendencies" like laziness.[27] Each day, students can be given periods of instruction with the teacher and periods of independent study or "homework." Whenever students cannot discover solutions to academic problems themselves, they can be taught where to look or which older student to ask for help.

For many, such structure — whether through a master daily schedule or independent study planner — assists in teaching children organizational *and* thinking skills over time. These skills support a main purpose of classical Lutheran education, which is the development of virtuous learners able to measure the worth of new knowledge, as they serve their neighbor daily in their God-given vocation.

In one of his many prefaces, Martin Luther points out the benefits of living under the rule of a prince educated in the liberal arts tradition, "who seeks, increases, and upholds the glory of God and the well-being of the commonwealth."[28] After hearing two young princes' impressive Latin orations, Martin Luther reflects on "what a good education is and how much it can achieve, particularly when brought to bear … on a teachable nature and an apt mind."[29] It is through the coherent and orderly teaching methods of a liberal arts education that teachable natures and apt minds have been and continue to be developed.

For Further Reading

- "How to Write a Lesson Plan: Five Secrets of Writing Great Lesson Plans." Busy Teacher. N.p., n.d. Web. 5 June 2012. (*busyteacher.org*)

- Lockman, Diane. "Homeschooling Plans." Accessed September 30, 2015. *ClassicalScholar.com/homeschooling-plan/#Records*.

- Phelan, Thomas W. *1-2-3 Magic: Effective Discipline for Children 2-12.* 2nd ed. Glen Ellyn, IL: ParentMagic, Inc., 2011. Print.

---

[27] Ibid., 17.

[28] *Luther's Works*, Prefaces II, Vol. 60:314. St. Louis: Concordia Publishing House, 2011.

[29] Ibid., 60:313.

- Young, Donna. Printables and Resources. Accessed September 30, 2015. *DonnaYoung.org/forms/planners/administrative.htm.*
- Wise, Jessie. "Encouraging Your Child to Work." Accessed September 29, 2015. *www.WellTrainedMind.com/encouraging-your-child-to-work.*

Avoid Common Pitfalls

Sometimes the most helpful advice comes from those who are no longer homeschooling! With the advantages of perspective and reflection, they offer wisdom for others. Melinda, wife of the Rev. William Heine and mother to their four grown children, provides this description of their experiences, followed by a list of seven caveats for those engaged in home education:

Due to various calls and school placements, we homeschooled intermittently as the need arose. We homeschooled our eldest child four different years. She now homeschools her own children. We taught our second daughter at home with a structured K-1 curriculum. We homeschooled our third child, a son, three different years. Our youngest daughter was taught at home in phonics and reading only.

If I could do it all again, I would homeschool them all K-12! Times were much different twenty years ago. Society is more open to the concept, and the availability of good homeschooling materials has exploded ... . Even so, over the years, I have noticed a few common errors to which new homeschoolers often fall prey.

Seven Common Traps to Avoid with Home Education
Melinda Heine

1. Putting the cart before the horse

In other words, do not pick your textbooks or publishers before creating a comprehensive vision with objectives and content you intend to teach at each level. This approach is hard to sidestep, especially for former teachers. Design your homeschool in the proper order:

Start with Grade 12, not the current year. What do you want your children to study and know by the time they leave for college, career, or employment? Work backwards until you have a framework for your homeschool. Read. Research. Take your time. Have conversations with knowledgeable Lutheran homeschoolers. Attend CCLE conferences. Find what best meets *your* objectives and approach to education. Then, and only then, should you start your curriculum research.

2. The bandwagon

I remember well when Bob Jones vs. A Beka Books was *the* conversation among homeschoolers. Then came the consumable craze (Alpha Omega Lifepacs, etc.). Then Spalding and Saxon seemed to have a corner on the market for years among classical educators. Today Susan Wise Bauer's histories are all over the place, and so on. My advice, after being swept up in those waves myself, is related to #1 above: Do your own research.

Take marketing gimmicks and the recommendations of others with a grain of salt … unless you *know* they share your theology, educational philosophy, and academic standards. Even Lutheran families will have very different ideas when it comes to curriculum! In my living room one evening, Cheryl Swope and I discussed how to make this process easier for Lutheran homeschoolers. We created a guide of strong academic and catechetical curriculum options reviewed by Lutherans. This eventually became the *Curriculum Resource Guide for Classical Lutheran Education* (CCLE Press, 2015.) Consider this guide for help with your selection process.

3. The false dichotomy of the spiritual vs. the academic

Anyone who has attended a mega-homeschool conference has probably heard such arguments, often in the context of dismissing classical education. After all, so it goes, "What good is stuffing your child's head full of facts about the pagan Romans and Greeks, teaching students the classical languages and literature, or even helping them learn to write? All they need is the Word of God!" Others argue, "My child just wants to be a mother. She does not need to worry about academics." Still others explain, "My son is not going to seminary. He does not need Latin or Greek!" This is not the view of the Reformation-era educators, such as Sturm, Luther, and Melanchthon, who promoted the strengths of a liberal arts education for all, including peasants, girls, and others who would not become pastors.

A strong academic education supports, not undermines, catechesis and sound theological training. It is not an either/or scenario. A solid biblical training is not antithetical to a sound academic foundation. Aspire to both. Too often I've heard the "spiritual angle" used as an excuse to soothe the consciences of parents who are failing to provide quality academic instruction for their children.

4. False expectations

While statistics show that homeschoolers, as a group, score better than public or private school students on academic tests such as the SAT, homeschooling is no guarantee that your child will be academically high-achieving or accepted to medical school. Motivating stories of homeschooled achievers abound — e.g., the homeschooled Eagle Scout, admitted to Harvard, who performed at Carnegie Hall, started his own business, qualified for Nationals in gymnastics, and still had time to tutor his eight homeschooled siblings while volunteering at the nursing home and leading the Youth Servant Event. Beware of this trap. God has distributed talents and abilities to each of us at levels of His choosing. This includes athletic, leadership, and academic abilities. Homeschooling, if done well, can provide a framework for our children to develop their God-given potential in any vocation to which God calls them. Do not expect the miraculous from the mere setting of homeschooling. Rather, trust God and expect hard work.

5. Thinking no one will criticize

Criticism is likely. Criticism is especially likely for pastors' families, parents in congregations with a Lutheran school, and for those residing in small towns where community pride is focused on the local school. You would do well to realize that no matter how well you teach your children, some people may *never* be won over to homeschooling. Bearing the disapproval of relatives, friends, and parishioners is a burden to be prepared for. Understand, too, that rightly or wrongly your children's public behavior (and academic prowess) will be more critically judged than those children who attend local public or Lutheran schools. Many of those who criticize are genuinely concerned, so reassuring comments often serve better than defensive ones.

6. Flighty curriculum chasers

Many of us love spending hours upon hours perusing textbooks, looking at catalogs, and evaluating resources! The danger is that curriculum selection can continually take precedence over actual teaching. One common sub-trap is to change curriculum each time something new comes out, because it looks better than what you have. Again, you are letting the book determine your goals, rather than the other way around. Make sure that so-called curriculum weaknesses are truly that, and not just your own instructional weaknesses! Many curriculum options, especially integrated packages, have been carefully crafted to avoid gaps in your child's learning. Research well ahead of time, select, and commit. When something new comes along, you will be less easily distracted and swayed.

7. Overcommitted mothers

When you "don't work," you will be asked to join assorted community activities, garden clubs, women's circles, altar guild, Sunday School staff, and the soprano section in the congregation's choir. Always remember that you are a full-time teacher. If you find yourself with extra time after your commitments with your husband and extended family, meal preparation, household management, and educating your children, only then consider involvement while homeschooling. However, if you find you are already struggling to provide a full daily education to your children among your other duties, you may wish to consider deferring acceptance of these invitations until a different season in your life.

A Sample Daily Routine

I trust in you, O Lord; I say, 'You are my God.' My times are in your hand. — Psalm 31:14-15a

What does a typical homeschooling day look like? Rachel Whiting, wife and mother of four, invites us into her home. Rachel and her husband homeschool an imaginative boy, a creative girl, and delightful young twin daughters in North Carolina.

A Day in the Life of One Homeschooling Family
Rachel Whiting

Preparing Our Children

One day a kind lady was trying to make conversation with my then three-year-old son. She asked, "What do you want to be when you grow up?" Perhaps she anticipated the response of "fireman" or "astronaut." After pausing, my little boy answered with exasperation, "I want to be a man!" (In his simplification of her question, he wondered how the lady did not know that boys become men.)

Our little boys and girls will grow up to become men and women. The foundation we lay in their education can equip them academically and spiritually, benefiting them both as children and as adults. Even though we do not know exactly in what manner of vocation they will love and serve others in their adulthood, we are preparing them for the future. We provide solid content, impart needed skills, and form character through the day-in-and-day-out habits and routine of homeschooling.

Our Daily Routine

A typical day will look different for every family. Moreover, not all days turn out the same when homeschooling within any given family. Some days our schedule changes around, so we can make time to stock up on books from the library or go grocery shopping. Sometimes we attend theater performances or cultural festivals. Other days we might get together with friends in the afternoon. When the children are signed up for extracurricular activities which only run for a number of weeks (soccer, fencing, swimming, theater class), the schedule of lessons at home gets moved around as well.

For our family, less is more. I have found that with a piano lesson one morning and each of the older children having an evening activity, we can usually add only one more afternoon activity in a week, but anything more than that makes us too busy. So occasionally we sign up for special classes which only run for a number of weeks. This provides variety without overtaxing the daily routine.

Some families schedule each day by the hour, but we do not follow the clock for our day. While caring for younger children, it does not always seem realistic to plan an allotted time for subjects. Our approach to homeschooling is task-oriented, as opposed to time-oriented. We follow a routine whereby we do most of our work in the

75

family room with a table in the middle, books organized by subject on shelves, and walls "decorated" with these items: a world map, a white board, a chalk board, and a bulletin board. We do move around to different parts of the house, and sometimes we take our lessons outside when the day is too beautiful to stay indoors.

My lesson planner not only records our subjects, but it also keeps my brief notes of covered content. I use my lesson plans to plan the year, monitor what is being studied, and keep track of the required number of homeschooling days for the year. My goal is to have steady progress in the subjects I am teaching my children, while taking planned breaks. We homeschool all year, so this allows us breaks for holidays, extended family visits, birthdays, and also time off just to enjoy a brief vacation from our regular routine.

Options in Homeschooling

We cover the essentials of reading, writing, and math to provide a firm, necessary foundation and fulfill state obligations. While these are non-negotiable, there is much freedom in what we include and how we structure our homeschooling day. On busiest days, audio recordings on car rides can even provide the opportunity to review certain subjects (e.g., geography, Latin, and the catechism). We also listen to familiar musical compositions, hymns, or audio story books while traveling. With two school-age children and twins younger than school age, this is the way our average week unfolds:

Daily Subjects

Individual Reading

While the house is dark and quiet, as some are still sleeping, the children wake up on their own and begin to do their "reading for fun" for the day. They choose their own book from the parameters of acceptable books. They read according to their ages and abilities.

When a book is completed, they write a narration about the story in their Book of Narrations. They often include an illustration. I enjoy reading these! When my oldest was eight years old, he summarized E. B. White's *Charlotte's Web* with his own drawing of a pig and a spider, with cobwebs dangling all over the page. He wrote, "Wilbur is a pig and his best friend is Charlotte, a spider, whose great love for him would not let him die, but live; as Jesus did on the cross." After we talked together about the nature of love, my son finished his narration on his own with this: "Love bears all things. Love is the most greatest thing in the world to have."

Bible and Catechism

Following breakfast, all four children and I have a time of morning prayer. We gather in the living room together and we say the Apostles' Creed and the Lord's Prayer. We have a Scripture reading and use a catechetical curriculum to support our discussions. My younger children enjoy using a Bible felt set to reenact stories. We go over key terms with flashcards that accompany the catechetical curriculum we are using. We focus on the meditation or summary at the end of the lesson, which helps us see what the text is teaching us about Jesus Christ.

We then review a section of the Small Catechism and work on memorizing another line in the catechism. We use the *Sing the Faith* CD, as the children enjoy memory work more when accompanied by a tune. Often I use a blackboard to write the selection we are working on. We pray together about what we are learning through the Scriptures and Small Catechism. This is my favorite time of the day.

Piano, Math, and Spelling

Next, the older two children take turns practicing on the piano. While one child is practicing the piano, I work with the other one individually. I teach each math lesson and assist with difficult problems. I correct the work, and I help as needed, while they work on correcting their missed problems. When my older children were younger, we frequently used math manipulatives. Playing store with pretend bills and real coins was always their favorite. Now that they are a little older, we use flashcards for drilling math facts. I also teach an individual spelling lesson at this time. Often my younger children repeat the word that I have an older child spell, so this gives them a vocabulary lesson.

The delightfully unique personalities of my children shine through in their studies. My passionate son approaches his piano playing with fervor, like a descendant of Beethoven. In early geometry lessons, when asked to "name the shape," he gives a personal name to a parallelogram with a twinkle in his eye. Meanwhile, my gentle daughter cautiously but gracefully plays the piano. She diligently reminds me to add words she does not know to her list of spelling words, so she can practice them. As homeschooling parents, we have the privilege of witnessing these differences emerge in their studies and in their daily lives.

Memory and Recitation

During our time of memory work together, we remember the Latin saying *Repetitio est mater studiorum* (Repetition is the mother of learning). I write their memory selection on a white board. The children try to add a line or two of the Scripture or poetry selection they are working on memorizing. We include copywork of the piece they are learning. Our memory selections are kept in three-ring binders.

The children recite some of their previously learned pieces. They recite as far as they can continue on their current selection. They hold themselves to high standards, as they attempt to execute a selection with precision. "A child with a rich repertoire of memorized poetry will inevitably demonstrate superior linguistic skills, both written and spoken, because of those patterns which are so deeply ingrained in the brain."[30] Occasionally throughout the day, I overhear my younger children repeat parts of what the older children are memorizing.

Latin

In Latin, as in many areas, I am a student along with my two older children. The children learn Latin grammar and vocabulary more quickly than I do, but they love to find out how Mom did on her test! We use a DVD for instruction and follow a lesson plan from our curriculum. Every day consists of reviewing previously learned material through an oral recitation and doing workbook activities to learn the week's new material.

We use charts, flashcards, games, CDs, early Latin readers, and even books from other Latin curricula, which encourage our learning of Latin together. We also occasionally study Greek and Latin roots during this time. The children are learning English grammar and vocabulary in the context of their Latin studies. As *The Latin-Centered Curriculum* suggests, this greatly streamlines their education.

Poetry and Character

While we are eating lunch together, I often read a poem, either from a book with a collection of poems by one poet or from an anthology, or I read a short story, such as a selection from the *Book of Virtues: A Treasury of Great Moral Stories,* by William J. Bennett. We talk about what I read while we are eating. We try to summarize the

---

[30] Pudewa, Andrew. "One Myth and Two Truths: Nurturing Competent Communicators." Institute for Excellence in Writing. Accessed October 27, 2014. *http://iew.com.*

poem and identify its rhyming structure. We also discuss the language used in the poem, noting literary devices. After reading a short story or poem, we discuss character-forming elements from the selection.

Writing

I teach composition with our two older children at the same time. I follow the lesson in the writing curriculum book and expect my older child to complete thoroughly the assignment as intended, but I modify the work for my younger child due to her age. In homeschooling, one is free to adapt a curriculum to suit particular teaching goals. My children are learning how to write through copywork, dictation, and narration exercises. They are continuing to practice these skills as they learn how to write by delving into fables and exploring the nature of descriptive narratives. They are learning grammar rules in this context as well.

The children do their writing in cursive. They learned how to write in cursive before print, as the movement of cursive letters was easier for them to form than the printing of letters. If their writing is sloppy, I have them rewrite their assignment.

The other day in our writing curriculum, we read the Greek myth of the goddess Athena, who disguised herself as an old woman while she spoke with the mortal Arachne. The assignment was to amplify the story with a description of the old lady. Evidencing the difference in their ages, my daughter wrote, "She had wrinkly skin and a cane in her hand. She had rags as clothes and big gloomy eyes." My son, the older student, wrote, "Her nose was like the crooked beak of a crow. It went so far out of her head that it was intolerable. She had wrinkly skin, like the skin on a vulture's head. Her head was bald except for three strands of long graying hair. Her hands were dry, like a piece of old cheese. Yes, she was an ugly sight to see." Homeschooling parents can combine their children, even when the students are at different stages, so they can work at their own level on the same assignments.

Science and History (Personal Study)

At this early stage of his education, my oldest child reads on his own every day, in either history or science. He takes notes on what he is reading and writes a narration of what he read, often adding scientific sketches as well. He has studied scientific discoveries and zoology. He has learned much about ancient and medieval times. He has read biographies and good books with an overview of history. Not only does he learn content, but he learns habits of personal study.

Thankfulness Journal

The older two children write an entry in their Thankfulness Journals.[31] They write in full sentences, describing one or two things they are thankful for and why. This has helped the children realize what they have to be thankful for, and this has improved their attitudes. Their journals draw their focus to the simple things in life otherwise taken for granted but that, when noticed, promote gratitude. One day my eight-year-old daughter wrote, "I am thankful for my bed because it is so cozy and warm." Sometimes her entries reflect a growing understanding of spiritual truths, as one day she wrote, "I am thankful for Jesus because He saved me from death and from the devil."

Literature Read-Aloud

Before our learning time together is done for the day, I read aloud to the children. With the desire to read the best literature, I read all sorts of books, from fables and fairy tales to abridged and unabridged classics. We sit together on the couch, or we take a blanket outside on the back porch or in the grass. I read aloud to them, and we talk about what was read. My husband also reads aloud to the children in the evenings before bed. We have a binder where we keep track of what the children have read individually and what we as parents have read aloud to them. We also use this binder to keep notes of what we would like to read aloud in the future.

Once-a-Week Subjects

Art Appreciation: Picture Study

My children enjoy looking at a piece of art as they try to take in all the details. We briefly study an artist's life and then spend a number of weeks learning about the artist's works. We study a variety of artists, from Pre-Renaissance Giotto to modern Picasso. This activity does not take long. We sit together looking at an artist's work. Then I take it away, and the children describe the picture in their mind's eye.

---

[31] I was inspired to have my children begin thankfulness journals after reading *Simply Classical* by Cheryl Swope. Parents can now find My Thankfulness Journals through Memoria Press. See *Simply Classical: A Beautiful Education for Any Child*. Louisville: Memoria Press, 2013. 171f.

The picture is then displayed on the wall so that we become better acquainted with it.

Composer/Music Study

We spend a little time every week learning about a composer and becoming familiar with a specific musical composition. When my children's piano playing is finished for the day, I often put on a musical piece that we are gradually becoming familiar with through repeated listening. We have learned about symphonic instruments and their families, as well as basic musical concepts. We try to identify instruments and musical themes in our listening.

Oral Reading

Although both of my older children are reading well, I still have them read aloud to me at a level past their current reading level. This helps them learn to enunciate and learn proper punctuation. This usually turns out to be a lesson in vocabulary, as often the children must sound out unfamiliar words and decipher their meaning from the context or consult a dictionary.

Science

I read aloud, or the children take turns reading aloud, from books with content related to science topics. We sometimes expand our readings with activities. For example, we have studied the human body by making life-size paper bodies onto which we glued various organs. With continued reading and some supplementary activities, we have learned about weather, animal and plant life, ecology, and astronomy. We use the Internet and reference books to try to identify flowers, trees, insects, and birds, and make sketches of what we have learned.

Geography

We review the names of countries around the world with the *Geography Songs* CD. The children identify each country on a blow-up globe, a laminated world map, or an atlas. They make their own maps of countries and acquaint themselves with the surrounding countries. We read cultural books, including facts about specific countries as well as mythological stories. They enjoy learning about how people live in other countries and how different their lives are from their own.

I teach them geographical terminology. We also assemble puzzles and play geography games.

Drawing

My older children wanted to capture more accurately the entries they were putting in their Nature Journals, so we decided to focus on some drawing basics. They have been learning about basic elements of shape and training their eyes to see as they practice making various lines. They have learned about proportion and how to break down figures into geometric units. My children enjoy the creative process, as their individual perspectives create unique renderings.

History

In the afternoon each Friday, my husband teaches history to the children. He follows a curriculum by reading aloud to them and discussing the questions in the guide. He enjoys linking history to current events, economics, and philosophical ideas. When teaching, he lists key individuals, events, and dates. The children use colored pencils with handouts and map work. They write a narration on what they learned. They record entries into a history timeline notebook.

Pausing Together

Time to Share

During homeschooling we have the freedom to temporarily stop structured activities to notice beauty. A Great Blue Heron lives at our pond. One day we all ran to the window when the heron killed a fish on our dock, just before he ate it. We stopped, watched, and then captured the heron with pencil on white paper. Another day we paused when we knew it was the approximate day for the Black Swallowtail Butterfly to hatch from its cocoon. My children grew quiet as the new butterfly slowly moved its new wings for the first time. We watched in awe, as the wings began to dry, and the butterfly prepared to fly.

The days are busy and full, but there is time. When all children's chores and lessons are finished, the children have free time in the afternoons. It is essential for them to have time to be reflective, to have time just to think and daydream. Having this restful time is neither boring nor unproductive. It is often after time alone that creative ideas blossom, such as an idea for a poem, a play, or book, or an idea of something to build or make.

Free time also gives all of us time to get outdoors, which is a much-needed part of each day, as appreciating God's world is good for the body and soul. Nature is refreshing and helps one's perspective. Spending time outside gives the children needed exercise and enjoyment as they ride bikes, kick soccer balls, and play in their tree fort.

Special memories are made in our afternoons. There is time to teach the dog a new trick, practice a new instrument one is trying to learn, or perform a puppet show. We recall afternoons spent creating the Colosseum out of cardboard and eating the Parthenon made from cookies. We take pictures of unique creations, as most of our constructions do not last for the long term! Sometimes afternoons find us planning or preparing a meal for a neighbor, writing letters, or creating friendly notes to keep in touch or offer encouragement. Sometimes the children just take time to play.

Time to Serve

Homeschooling family life is more than academics. We serve one another throughout the day. The older children take turns reading to the younger children. The older children and I work together to help keep the younger children cared for and busy while homeschool lessons are going on. My younger children, twin girls, are kept occupied as they cut and glue old magazines, making collages. They "cook" with play dough, or do art with watercolor paint, crayons, or markers. Most of the day, these younger twin girls are decked out in dress-up clothes as they care for their baby dolls.

Much learning occurs in our relationships with one another. There are continual opportunities to learn how to get along with one another in the course of our days together. We bear with one another's weaknesses and love one another as 1 Peter 4:8 instructs us: "Above all, keep loving one another earnestly, since love covers a multitude of sins."

Inspiration for Mom and Dad

"A mother's heart is a child's schoolroom."[32] I have learned that my own attitude can set the tone for our studies and for the whole day together. When I approach learning with enthusiasm, it is often contagious to my children. Some days are relatively easy and studies are

---

[32] Welcome to the Quote Garden. Accessed October 27, 2014. *http://www.quotegarden.com/mothers.html.*

tackled smoothly as kids work hard applying themselves and concentrating. Other days, almost every aspect of the day feels like an uphill battle with distressing academic and disciplinary issues.

When I become overwhelmed with the quantity of curriculum choices and the amount of content I could be teaching my children, I can remember, "Education is not the filling of a pail, but the lighting of a fire."[33] My own education in public school was largely an unending process of "learning" only to pass a test, and then forgetting the information once I turned the test in. I always received good grades, but I did not retain knowledge or gain wisdom. I am choosing a different route for my children, because I want them to love learning, to wrestle with what they hear, and to acquire critical thinking skills. My goal is not to just have them learn isolated bits, but rather to have tools to learn with the desire to learn deeply, while keeping curiosity and wonder intact. There is content that must be mastered, but through books and discussions, we can also foster ideas that ennoble the spirit and enliven the mind, as fires in their hearts are stoked into flame.

"Enjoy the little things, for one day you may look back and discover they were the big things."[34] Small moments all strung together make up our days. We can notice the moment-to-moment "little" things: conversations at breakfast, talking together while we are folding laundry, praying with a child over disciplinary issues, laughing together at the dinner table, and crying together over a touching story. These passing moments are building blocks that form and shape my children. They are truly the "big things" after all, as the effects are lasting. When I take time to reflect, I am grateful to be able to spend these often trying, yet always worthwhile, days with my children.

When Homeschooling Is Interrupted

"All things work together for good, for those who are called according to His purpose" (Romans 8:28b), and this is a truth we cherish more dearly when times of trial interrupt the regular routines in our home. The reality of the Fall upon our bodies — resulting in suffering, sickness, and death — is often heightened when these effects break upon us. We agonizingly try to go about our day while we await looming results from a diagnostic test performed on us or our children.

---

[33] Plutarch. Quote Investigator. Accessed October 27, 2014. *http://quoteinvestigator.com/2013/03/28/mind-fire/.*

[34] Brault, Robert. Accessed October 27, 2014. *Rbrault.blogspot.com/p/note-november-23-2013-today-to-my.html.*

At such times, academic goals are difficult to pursue. We may find ourselves looking upon a child who has an elevated fever, or upon cords connected to their small bodies as they lie in a hospital bed. Our regular schedules are placed on hold. When the phone rings and news of a loved one's critical sickness or death enters the home, the atmosphere of academic home education instantly changes.

Unexpectedly, we find ourselves in the "school of suffering" with our children as we ourselves or those we know go through difficult times. These interruptions do not need to be seen as a time when we are failing to homeschool our children. For a time, the focus may be off academic lessons; yet great lessons are being learned through physical and spiritual trials. We cling tightly to Christ who has defeated sin, the devil, and death. We hold on with a stronger firmness than on days of ease and in times of health.

We can take the time to stop the regular routine, to grieve together and pray. Together with our children, we can minister to others in pain, whether by spending time with those who are hurting, offering acts of kindness on their behalf, or praying together for others in our lives. Every day, we await with our children the Last Day, when the effects of the curse are completely wiped out, as our ears hear the last trumpet and Christ gathers us to Himself.

A Prayer for Our Children

The other night I tiptoed up to each of my children as they slept soundly in their beds. I made the sign of the cross upon them as I thought about how God's holy name was placed upon them in their baptism and that they are His children. I prayed that He would keep them in their baptismal grace. I found a prayer that gave me words to say for all that I felt and hoped:

> *O Lord, almighty God, Father of all grace and mercy! Behold among other gifts of Thy grace Thou hast also given me children, for which I praise and bless Thee with all my heart. But oh, my God, when I look upon my children as precious pledges which Thou hast placed in my keeping, which Jesus has redeemed with His holy blood and Thou hast received as Thy children in Holy Baptism, oh, I am filled with anxiety lest through my fault one of them should be lost … .*
>
> *Therefore, O Father of all grace, I come to Thee, and present before Thee my children. I shall do for them what I can, but the best part must be done by Thee … .*

Bestow upon my children Thy temporal blessing; provide for them, nourish them, give them food and clothing, and deal with them as a faithful Father. Give them a good heart, a good intellect, and a sound body, that they may live before Thee and honor and praise Thee … . [L]et them grow up under Thy blessing, that I may have comfort and joy in them.

O God, hear my prayer, and remember that they are Thy children as well as mine; therefore let my sighings on behalf of my children ascend to Thy throne of grace, and hear them … . Yes, my God, grant that none of my children may perish, but that they may enter into Thy glory with me and I with them … Amen.[35]

The Church Year

The Church Year brings the life, death, burial, and resurrection of Jesus into your life, into your space and time.[36] *— Arthur A. Just, Jr.*

Parents can bring readings, hymns, and visible elements of the Church Year into the space and time of the home. Rachel Whiting offers these thoughts, as she and her husband Todd seek to share liturgical traditions with their children.

The Church Year in Our Home
Rachel Whiting

The Passage of Time
The first time I held my firstborn son, I felt as if time stood still. I could barely see him through the myriad of my tears, as his fresh new eyes looked up at me and his entire hand wrapped itself around my finger. I felt as if I had all the time in the world just to hold him. And hold him I did, all the time. Yet he grew so quickly, he seemed to be in a hurry to grow up.

I rejoiced in his milestones, but sometimes deep inside I quietly mourned the little baby that disappeared into a toddler. He was on the go, and so was I. There seemed to be not enough hours in the day.

---

[35] Starck, Johann Friedrich, and W. H. T. Dau. *Starck's Motherhood Prayers for All Occasions from the German Edition of Dr. F. Pieper.* Kansas City, Kansas: Emmanuel Press, 2011. 64-65.

[36] Just, Jr., Arthur A. *Heaven on Earth: The Gifts of Christ in the Divine Service.* St. Louis: Concordia Publishing House, 2008. 129.

Soon another baby, his sister, was cradled in my arms. Both children grew. Then two more precious baby girls, twins, entered our family. With all my babies, as each birthday passed, the delusion that I had unlimited time faded.

The Church Year

As days fell into weeks and months, seasons came and went, and years unfolded. I felt an urgency to embrace the time our family had together. I wanted to create traditions to build the culture of our home. I learned that the Church Year already had a framework for using time in a meaningful way. The Rev. Dr. Arthur A. Just Jr., explains:

> Time is marked by Christians in a special way in their liturgical life because Christ entered time. By His presence in the creation to make all things new He changed our reckoning of time forever. From the beginning, early Christians lived with clarity about how, through Christ's resurrection, eternity now bore in upon our finite time. They lived in that tension between a life lived toward the endtime within time itself, that tension between the now and the not yet. By their accounting of days and weeks and years, Christians gave meaning to time.[37]

The calendar of the Church Year centers around the birth, life, death, and resurrection of Jesus Christ. What better way for us as Christians to live out and order our days?

My husband and I wondered how we could impress upon our children the value and significance of the Church Year in our home. As we brainstormed, we evaluated ways we already observed Advent, Christmas, Epiphany, Lent, and Easter. During Advent we would put up a tree with white lights, strings of red wooden berries, and Baby's Breath. After Christmas Day we would take it down. And ... well, that was it.

We desired for the readings from the Scriptures in the Divine Service of Word and Sacrament to saturate our home. We wanted the colors, meanings, stories, and moods of the Church Year to infuse our home and linger in our hearts. With the impressionable little faces of our children looking up at us, the desire was mounting to build a more intentional culture in our home.

---

[37] Ibid., 116.

Ideas

I am sharing with you what we developed in our home to celebrate the Church Year not because it is the "right" thing to do. Far from it. Many wonderful Church Year traditions will not even be mentioned here. For example, the Advent Wreath and Chrismons are beautiful and helpful traditions, yet our family has not yet adopted these.

Perhaps our ideas will spark some of your own. With four children (10, 8, 4, and 4), we share our journey here, because our home has been enriched as our lives have become more synchronized with the rhythm and richness of the Church Year.

The Tree: Traditions with a Theme

We decided to stay with a "tree theme" for Advent and carry that imagery all the way through the seasons of the Church Year. It seems fitting. Our fall into sin came through the eating of forbidden fruit from the Tree of the Knowledge of Good and Evil. Our redemption came through Christ's bearing our curse, as He hung on the cross made of wood from a tree. Our partaking of the Body and Blood of Christ, our Tree of Life, gives us eternal life in Him. Of course there is nothing salvific about the trees in our home, but they are visual reminders of the details of our spiritual lives in Christ.

For all the Church Year seasons, we have binders coordinating with the Church Year colors. We keep the binder out on the living-room coffee table during the corresponding time of the Church Year. It is a homemade resource with information we developed on commemorating each season of the Church Year.

Advent

Advent is a time of waiting for the coming of Christ, as He will come again at the end of time. While we await His second coming, we also prepare our hearts for Christmas. We reflect on His first coming as a baby, born of the Virgin Mary. In our home, we set up our Advent tree on Thanksgiving weekend, decorating it with white lights and red porcelain hearts symbolizing God's love for the world in sending His Son as a baby. We are ready for the beginning of Advent by December 1st. In this four-week period of anticipation, our home is filled with the air of expectation. The days are normally greeted by the question of "Who goes up on the tree tonight?"

The children take turns decorating the tree with characters in the Matthew and Luke narratives. On the first day of Advent, King Herod is hung from our tree as the story begins with "In the days of King Herod ..." (Luke 1:5). All these figures, King Herod, Zechariah, Elizabeth, baby John, Gabriel, Mary, Joseph, baby Jesus, angels, Caesar Augustus, shepherds, animals, Simeon, Anna, wise men, Roman soldiers, prophets, and more, have been sewn by hand with felt. As we place the various ornaments, we read the correlating Scripture passage and review previous narratives.[38] The story builds. Each day the tree is decorated more, as the branches grow heavy with ornaments.

We also remember St. Nicholas during Advent as the children awake to stockings stuffed with little treats, hung from the fireplace mantle, on December 6th. They giggle as they put their feet on the "snowy" (white flour) bootprints throughout the house. We cuddle together as we read aloud the children's books we own about the true story of St. Nicholas of Myra.

During this time, we also set up a nativity set, which consists of a gray cave made out of baked dough, which we use to set up small figures (Playmobil) in a nativity scene. The cave was made with a hole in the ceiling, so a round book light can sit on top, hidden under moss, enabling rays of light to shine directly on Jesus, the Light of the World. One year as we set up the cave, I talked with my children about how it was probably very dirty, damp, and dark. My three-year-old daughter assured me, "Momma, it was beautiful, because of the angels and the Baby."

Christmas

On December 24th all the characters are up on our tree and we are ready to celebrate the incarnation of Christ. We review the Matthew and Luke narratives, trying to locate all the characters on the tree. We open gifts from each other, and we attend the Christmas Eve Candlelight Service of Readings and Hymns at our church.

The next morning is Christmas. We attend the Divine Service of Word and Sacrament, the Feast of the Nativity of Our Lord, as

---

[38] Along with Scripture readings for seasons of the Church Year, we use a Harmony of the Gospels and these resources from the Concordia Catechetical Academy: *The Lutheran Catechesis* series with *Bible Stories for Daily Prayer, Catechism Stories*, and *Miracles and Parables of Jesus* Study Cards. We pray from the *Lutheran Book of Prayer*, St. Louis: Concordia Publishing House, 2005. We also teach from Maier, Paul. *In the Fullness of Time: A Historian Looks at Christmas, Easter, and the Early Church*. Grand Rapids: Kregel Publications, 1991.

with joy we rejoice in our Savior who has come and who sustains us with His Word and Sacraments. We light twelve white candles, as we anticipate the twelve days of Christmas, celebrating that the Light of the World has come. Through special readings we remember the commemorative days in this celebration. Our Emmanuel, the Babe humbled and lying in a lowly manger, has come. Our hearts and minds are filled with reverential wonder. Hidden amid a hectic contemporary culture, we enjoy the freedom of truly appreciating these twelve days.

Epiphany

The Light of the World has come for the entire world, and He manifested Himself among us. On January 6th, we remove our nativity scene and replace it with a biblical house scene with Playmobil wise men visiting Joseph, Mary, and the child Jesus.

We focus this time on the life of Christ, His Baptism, parables, miracles, and Transfiguration. We use a metal tree, as the branches can hold paper in their wire tips. The kids place small cardstock cards of colored-pencil drawings of the stories and teachings of Christ's life. We save these cards from year to year and choose a few from years past to decorate the tree at the beginning of Epiphany. When our older daughter was three, she drew Jesus and John the Baptist. Each year we also include the card of Jesus calling His disciples. Our son drew this image when he was six years old. We also use miniature paintings of Christ's life as well as church symbols for Christ. All of these decorate our Epiphany tree. As Epiphany comes to a close, our little metal tree is full of the teachings and events of Christ's earthly life. Our home is touched with a visible reminder of the One who is the Way, the Truth, and the Life.

Lent

With ashes placed on our foreheads in the shape of a small cross, we enter into a 40-day period of somber reflection and repentance. We place in our home a black tree with bare branches. We add minia-ture ornaments symbolizing key events mentioned in the Gospels. The children hunt for the miniature branches, as my husband reads about the Triumphal Entry of Christ riding into Jerusalem. They find the temple (made from foam) when he reads about Jesus cleansing the temple. They look for the sheep and the goat when they listen to the Olivet discourse, in which Jesus teaches about the final judgment.

They find coins to symbolize those Judas received in his betrayal of the Lord. They look for the Passover lamb, the bread and cup from the Last Supper, the swords and clubs that were carried to arrest Jesus, the chains that bound our Lord, the rooster that crowed after Peter's betrayal, the scourge used to beat our Lord's body, the crown of thorns, the purple robe, a reed, the sign above the cross, hammer and nails, and more. While we needed much initial preparation, these lasting emblems bring the events into our home during the readings.

As our eyes look upon the small emblems on the Lenten tree, our hearts ponder the sufferings of our Lord. Beside the dark tree sits a trial scene with a porcelain Roman ruin and small characters (Playmobil), such as Roman soldiers and Pilate beside Jesus, who is bound. The gravity of Lent permeates our home in this visible way.

Holy Week

The Lenten tree helps to prepare our hearts for Holy Week. On Palm Sunday, the beginning of the week, we cry "Hosanna!" On Maundy Thursday our faith is fed with the Lord's Supper and Individual Absolution. Then we watch with somber reflections the Stripping of the Altar.

The next day, on Good Friday, we hear the Ringing of the Somber Bells, 39 times, symbolizing the lashes of the whip upon our Lord Jesus Christ. The eerie chanting of Psalm 22 sinks into our ears. We watch as seven candles are extinguished after each of the seven last sayings of Christ are spoken. We sit humbly in blackness during the sermon. We hear the reading of Isaiah 52:13 - 53:12, followed by a very loud noise, representing the cosmic chaos of the death of Christ and the shutting of the tomb. While the startling noise still reverberates between our ears, the Christ candle is extinguished. On Good Friday, our mouths are silenced. We leave the church in the darkness of the Tenebrae Service, and we enter the solemnity of Holy Saturday.

We return to church on Saturday evening for the Vigil of Easter. This Service of Light offers hope. After all the darkness, we watch with joy as the Paschal candle is ignited. Death did not conquer our Lord. We hear the history of our redemption, and we remember our baptism into Christ. We receive the Word and Sacrament of the Altar. Our souls glimpse the eternal joy of Easter.

Easter

With "Alleluia!" on our lips, we rejoice in the celebration of Easter. As the children awaken in the morning, they find that the black tree has been replaced. A lightly colored, almost white tree with small green leaves greets the children with colorful dangling eggs. A basket full of red and purple wooden eggs sits on the coffee table as we remember Jesus' blood and Passion. Candles are lit, because our Light of the World has risen from the dead!

In the place of the Roman trial scene, a booklight sits on top of an empty tomb to shine down and show that it is empty. Made from baked dough with small white flowers adorning it, the open tomb reminds us of the angel's words: "He is not here, for He has risen, as He said. Come, see the place where He lay" (Matthew 28:6).

With an air of celebration, we hold brightly colored dyed eggs in our hands. One person says, "The Lord is risen!" then another responds with, "The Lord is risen, indeed. Alleluia!" as eggs are joined together with a crack! With joy and comfort, we attend the Divine Service of Word and Sacrament, the Feast of the Resurrection of our Lord. The afternoon is full of festivities as the children hunt for eggs and Easter baskets. But there is more.

On our Easter tree, 25 drooping eggs await opening. Every other day for the 50-day celebration that Christ has conquered death, defeated Satan, and atoned for our sin, we open one egg. Inside the eggs, objects help us remember Christ's resurrection and post-resurrection appearances. For example, in one egg a child finds miniature objects of three nails, a sword, and a fish, as we read in the Scriptures how Christ appeared to His disciples, showing them His wounds and eating fish with them. Other eggs contain these items: spices the women brought to anoint Jesus' body; gardening tools (because Jesus was initially mistaken for a gardener); a linen wrapping found in the tomb; a loaf of bread, as Jesus revealed Himself to the Emmaus travelers; a fishing net and fish (because Jesus cooked breakfast for the disciples); a wispy cotton ball representing Jesus' Ascension; and so on. The children take turns choosing which egg to open. We are all blessed through the Easter readings of Holy Scripture. During Eastertide, hope and promise pervade our home in a special way.

The Season after Pentecost, The Season of Holy Trinity, The Time of the Church

Now the question for us is what to do with the season of Holy Trinity. Because this is a time of spiritual growth, I am thinking about using some sort of green tree decorated with historic symbols of the Holy Trinity. Our development of family Church Year traditions is still a work in progress. Nonetheless, observing the Church Year in our home has enabled our family to better focus on Christ in the seasons of the year.

As the Rev. Dr. Arthur A. Just teaches:

> Liturgical time allows the Church to proclaim time's sacred character as Christ-centered. Through Sunday as the day of worship and rhythms of the Church Year, the Church teaches how our days and weeks and years are shaped and formed by the reality that Jesus entered our time and space. This rhythm shows us how we are to truly live in God's gift of time as temporal beings baptized into Christ's eternal life.[39]

Summary

We are grateful for the Church Year, because "the Church Year tells the Church its story, which is Christ's story ... . [It] serves as a reminder and teacher that Jesus entered into the suffering and shame of our sinful flesh to deliver and sanctify us, and that it is His life that defines our life."[40] Truly, Jesus' life defines ours, for we are the baptized children of God! We have been placed into Christ and united with His life, death, burial, and resurrection.

Eight years have passed since my husband and I began the initial discussion on how to have the Church Year infiltrate our home. There was much work at the beginning, with sewing, painting, whittling wood, raiding the children's miniature toys, digging through dollhouse sections of craft stores, making ornaments, figuring out how to hang objects, studying, planning, and putting it all together. As a result, the traditions of our home are now in full swing year to year.

The years still pass by too quickly for me, as I watch all of the shoes by the front door increase in size. When my son and I put our hands palm to palm together, our hands are nearly the same size now. Yet we embrace our time together as a family, as the seasons and stories of the Church Year enliven and strengthen our home.

---

[39] Just, *Heaven on Earth*, 116-117.

[40] Ibid., 128, 133.

VOCATION: SERVING OUR CHILDREN THROUGH HOME EDUCATION

The human being is self-willed, desiring that whatever happens shall be to his own advantage. When husband and wife, in marriage, serve one another and their children, this is not due to the heart's spontaneous and undisturbed expression of love, every day and hour. Rather, in marriage as an institution, something compels the husband's selfish desires to yield and likewise inhibits the ego-centricity of the wife's heart. At work in marriage is a power which compels self-giving to spouse and children. So it is the 'station' itself which is the ethical agent, for it is God who is active.[41] — Gustaf Wingren

Mother to a Homeschooled Child
Erik Rottmann

She is a rock, a willow, a metronome.
She chisels clay, she pummels dough
And hammers house into a home.

She is aloe, curtain, and crowded room.
She pulls weeds when seedlings show
And finds a jar for every bloom.

Mother to a homeschooled child.

---

[41] Wingren and Rasmussen, *Luther on Vocation*, 6.

She is a rose, a sparrow, a ray of light.
She keeps anchor in the blow
And walks with dawn into the night.

Mother to my homeschooled child.

Thanks will not do. Every gift, each crafted line
Will fall too short, sing too low,
And not repay her selfless time.

She is a cloud, a gate, a twist of lace.
She holds hands to let them go
And gives to love its frame and face.

Mother to a homeschooled child.

Parents, Teachers, and Vocation

Deaconess Mary Moerbe is a published writer and homeschooling mother of six. Mary graciously shares these thoughts for *Eternal Treasures* from her family's home in Oklahoma.

Parents, Teachers, and Vocation
Mary Moerbe

Vocation

Vocations start in one clear, unmistakable place: words. Specifically, these are the powerful words of God spoken in Scripture, echoing in creation. He says, "Be fruitful and multiply," and the vocation of parent is established as a foundational orientation of human society. He says, "Be baptized," and our gracious Lord takes us as children into His own family, united to His only-begotten Child, and brings our tasks into, in a loose sense, His family business of caregiving.

Vocation, of course, also gets associated with things we do. Vocational schools teach toward particular paths within the economy. Vocational discussions often include questions like "What are your strengths? How do you excel?"

Some people think that, in order to be a part of any vocation, they must be really good at something — even competitively so — in order to participate. They think of vocation as a goal to be obtained, as something loftier than a job that hard work and serious effort can achieve. But, notice, a lot of people mentally leave God out of the picture, or, perhaps, see Him as the distant one who sets into order your bits of talent and discipline though now you proceed on your own.

How differently Scripture speaks of it! One does not apply for or earn vocation, nor are we ever alone in our vocations. As baptized children of God, our talents and disciplines are not qualifications but blessings to ourselves and for others. In faith to God, we trust Him to provide, and in love to others we share what He gives us.

God calls us all to love and serve our neighbors. Different vocations speak about different neighbors. Parents serve children, and children serve parents. Teachers serve students, and students serve teachers.

Vocation of Teacher

Education falls within the loving service we give to one another. Although truth is the jurisdiction of God, He lets us share and spread the truth in our little ways, even as He reveals it through His Word and His Son.

Vocations participate in what is rightfully God's. Vocations love, although, strictly speaking, God is love. Vocations give, though every good gift comes from above. Vocations speak in word and deed, though God's Word and Deeds triumph through all.

Teachers teach what God has revealed, either in His Word or His Work of creation. A teacher serves his or her neighbor, the student, and tailors his or her service for a particular goal: the individual student's education.

When instituting this vocation, God's word is simply "instruct." We may think in terms of Galatians 4:1-2, in which Paul refers to guardians and managers, or we can consider the repeated admonition that believers should teach their children.

After Moses climbed to the top of Pisgah and looked into the Promised Land he could not enter, the Israelites remained in the valley (Deuteronomy 3:23-29). Moses instructed the people once more with the Law.

> Only take care, and keep your soul diligently, lest you forget the things that your eyes have seen, and lest they depart from your heart all the days of your life. **Make them known to your children and your children's children** — how on the day that you stood before the LORD your God at Horeb, the LORD said to me, 'Gather the people to me, that I may let them hear my words, **so that they may learn to fear me all the days that they live on the earth, and that they may teach their children so'** (Deuteronomy 4:9-10).

God has given the Law not to one generation, but to all generations. Likewise, God's *promises* are not to one generation. God's Word
rings out, echoing its power and truth, throughout the ages. Simply
put, education is a primary place for Word and truth to meet the ear,
and Scripture seems to be entirely in favor of such ongoing catechesis
for life! Consider this description for the Israelite kings:

> And when he sits on the throne of his kingdom, he shall write
> for himself in a book a copy of this law, approved by the
> Levitical priests. And it shall be with him, and he shall read in
> it all the days of his life, that he may learn to fear the LORD his
> God by keeping all the words of this law and these statutes,
> and doing them, that his heart may not be lifted up above his
> brothers, and that he may not turn aside from the command-
> ment, either to the right hand or to the left, so that he may
> continue long in his kingdom, he and his children, in Israel
> (Deuteronomy 17:18-20).

Children must be educated. "But shouldn't teachers be experts?! I
have never done this before!" Not to worry. God offers a big beautiful
world that can be explored together on various levels. He often prods
parents with questions from their children. He creates opportunities,
often through a combination of both curiosity and need. He works in
ways we cannot always see. Resources abound, and He will sustain us,
as we teach our children.

Education is strongly advocated throughout Scripture. There are
certainly classes of teachers and educators in the history of Scripture,
but repeatedly the task is assigned to parents. Family is given as the
setting, and parents are the primary teachers. Additional teachers
supplement, as the community gathers around God and one another
to meet each others' needs and complete the economy.

Vocation of Parent

Economy, let us note, originally referred to household management. Economy involved bringing in food, paying for services, raising
the children, tending the property, etc. In tribal communities, such as
Abraham's and his lineage, a household could be huge, gathered under
a primary father figure, incorporating siblings, cousins, grandchildren,
servants, etc. We find the excellent wife who looks "well to the ways
of her household" (Proverbs 31:27), including real estate, handling

merchants, producing merchandise, caring for her family, and opening her mouth with wisdom, while the teaching of kindness is on her tongue.

The household is a central unit and a formative place for life. The parents, father and mother, are to be honored and obeyed. They are tasked with the wellbeing of their children (Ephesians 6:2) and their upbringing in the family, the world, and the people of God. Martin Luther spoke of three realms of vocation: family (including all forms of bread-winning), state/society, and church. Parents are uniquely positioned to raise up and support the family and its additional, growing families which spread forth; to affect how individuals respond and interact with peers and levels of authority; and to prepare children for the life to come, both in this world and the next.

Encouragement

Parents can be full of doubt regarding themselves. How can one know what is best without knowing a child's future? How can one avoid misunderstandings when a child's needs and abilities can shift every day? How can we be all that our children need us to be? But parents are not called to be perfect for their children.

God does not depend upon parental competency in order to raise a child. While parents may feel overwhelmed with a full schedule and providing for the physical needs of their family, God is still present, providing daily bread and *everything* that is needed for both parent and child.

Parents do not have to be confident, consistent, or perfectly prepared. Rather, Christian parents are blessed to be children of God. As His beloved children, we love our children. We share what our own Father has given us. We do what we can and grow as we may. Ultimately, we go to sleep at night and rest in the care of Him who is far greater than we are.

We might *feel* like we need to be confident. We might *feel* like we need to be in control, but a beautiful, gracious thing is already at work, helping us and raising our children: God's Word. Within creation, the young rise up to grow in wisdom and stature, in favor with God and with man. Within the church, sins are being forgiven and faith is given into the ears of even the youngest listener.

God speaks and things happen. In the vocation of parent — particularly the vocation of *Christian* parent, as unbelievers are not yet "called" by Baptism — God is active. He is present through His Word in creation and through His Word in Scripture made flesh as our Christ.

A parent sins, and God teaches that all fall short. A parent forgives, and God teaches that mercy comes from above. When a parent instructs in the Word, God teaches right and wrong, and He provides the way, the truth, and the life in Christ. And when parents instruct in the world, God is shaping relationships and interactions, enlarging neighborhoods and future families.

Chapters and Phases

Children start with very few neighbors and with the simple command to honor and obey their parents. As their neighbors increase, they have a lot to learn. Loving our neighbors can require intricate and varied services. As children grow, they can begin to see each believer as a fellow child of God, and each person as one for whom Christ died.

Or, put another way, children begin under the authority of God and their parents. Then they learn to interact with those who are not in authority over them, like brothers, sisters, cousins, and other peers. Gradually they usurp authority or actually gain it over others through employment (camp counselors, for instance, or babysitters).

Parents go through the stages of childhood differently. First, they provide everything, including the clean diapers. Gradually things go from sitting to chasing, and parents marvel at their children's development. In a sense, parents go from an active/passive relationship to an active/active one.

Throughout it all, parents are to teach their children the things of God. Most importantly, they teach about sin and salvation, about Jesus Christ, the power of the Word, and the means of grace. But of course God's work on our behalf also includes creation and giving us relationships with one another. Parents are to raise children up with the two great commands: "'Hear … you shall love the Lord your God with all your heart and with all your soul and with all your mind and with all your strength.' The second is this: 'You shall love your neighbor as yourself (Mark 12:29-31).'" Then parents assure their children that all their righteousness is found in Christ alone, as only He perfectly obeyed the will of His parents. This righteousness is given in Him and bestowed freely to us.

Mutual Gifts

God gives children to parents. As Proverbs 27:17 says, "Iron sharpens iron, and one man sharpens another." Heart tends to heart, soul to soul, mind to mind, and strength to weakness — even strength against strength — as God works through us to impact our children. Though the instigators may vary, patience grows and challenges are met by the grace of God.

You will not always steady their newly found toddler gait. You will not always potty-train or clean up their messes. You will not always speak in small words with simple messages. But as a parent you will teach your children all the time, whether you intend to or not. You cannot help being an example and a powerful source of words and love.

Too often the stereotype is that *eventually* parents need to become more intentional with development and training. We wait in tension hoping something will finally click and make our parenting choices seem right. Confidence is not what makes the vocation, and right answers are not what makes a parent; rather, the promise of God accompanies His Word. The gift of life He has given in your children is a blessed opportunity and a mercy in itself, as your children serve you and God works through all.

One may be tempted to think that parenting is a matter of control, but it is not. The authority God gives is neither for power or external submission, as though that merits anything. Instead, "the Son of Man came not to be served, but to serve, and to give His life as a ransom for many" (Matthew 20:27-28). The greatest authority is *to forgive sins*, and even the Perfect Father seems to have a great many black sheep.

While all we do in this life is indeed tainted by sin, there is still very good news. We are washed clean in the blood of the Lamb, forgiven, and restored both to our Father in heaven and to new attempts to love and serve our neighbors. He who makes Himself Father of the fatherless has mercy on us and our children.

Services End

There is only one vocation which lasts forever: being a baptized child of God. All other vocations belong to this world and end in death, as we ourselves and our neighbors bend to the frailty of our flesh.

But God is so kind that He, time and again, turns our eyes to look on Jesus, the author and perfecter of our faith. He defines us by our relationship with Him, united in Baptism and judged not guilty before God because of His life, death, and resurrection on our behalf.

We may define ourselves as one thing or another, focusing on our tasks or talents, but even those we serve do not define us. We may parent

24 hours a day or focus twelve hours a day on a specialty of some sort, but even this is too narrow to encompass us as human beings.

When God called us into being with those same words, "Be fruitful and multiply," He made us children. We became siblings, either within our nuclear family or with the brothers and sisters of God. Many enter the vocation of marriage, but there are the vocations of aunt and uncle, cousin, grandparent, godparent, and more. There are expanding vocations entirely outside our control, and there are times when vocations abruptly shift, like when a child moves away from home.

As our vocations change, one thing remains the same: God's Word. God provides us with our daily bread, and God gifts us with neighbors. He gives us opportunities to serve, and even if the day were to come where we can serve no longer, He offers us opportunity for prayer and thankfulness.

If you are a homeschooler, you are also much, much more. And, if you are a parent scared of becoming a homeschooler, you are still already a home educator!

God grants children, and God grants neighbors. He commands us with explicit words to serve our neighbors and then allows us to serve them under different circumstances with the gifts and talents He has given us — and which He sustains every moment.

A parent's service will look different yesterday, today, and tomorrow, but God remains constant as Father and Brother to us. Thanks be to God!

> *For this reason I bow my knees before the Father, from whom every family in heaven and on earth is named, that according to the riches of his glory he may grant you to be strengthened with power through his Spirit in your inner being, so that Christ may dwell in your hearts through faith — that you, being rooted and grounded in love, may have strength to comprehend with all the saints what is the breadth and length and height and depth, and to know the love of Christ that surpasses knowledge, that you may be filled with all the fullness of God. Now to him who is able to do far more abundantly than all that we ask or think, according to the power at work within us, to him be glory in the church and in Christ Jesus throughout all generations, forever and ever. Amen.*
> *— Ephesians 3:14-21*

Am I Doing the Right Thing?

I would advise no one to send his child where the Holy Scriptures are not supreme. Every institution that does not unceasingly pursue the study of God's word becomes corrupt.[42] *— Martin Luther*

Am I Doing the Right Thing? Lord, Free Us From Fear
Cheryl Swope

We begin to understand our vocation as parents. We bring our children to the waters of Holy Baptism. We teach our children the Holy Scriptures. We attend the Divine Service with our children. We tend to our children's souls.

Yet when we determine to begin (or continue) homeschooling, doubts about home education can assail us. Such doubts may arise from friends and extended family members, or they may creep into our thoughts because of our own fears. Doubts may even bubble up unexpectedly when speaking with other homeschooling parents, when such conversations are intended for refreshment!

The decision to homeschool — or to continue homeschooling — is not always easy. We may hear our own questions behind the ones commonly spoken by homeschoolers:

- "Which curriculum do you teach for math?" *(Would this be better than the math program I selected?)*

- "Which lesson is your daughter learning from the curriculum right now?" *(Is my child behind? Or am I moving too quickly?)*

- "When does the public school cover our state's history?" *(Should I follow the public school for this? For anything? How do I know?)*

- "How many hours do you spend 'doing school' each day?" *(Am I overloading my children? Am I doing enough?)*

Christian parents cannot escape doubts and fears, especially because we know the duty is ours for parenting, training, and educating our children in every way. Whether we enroll them in a private or parochial school, a public school, a co-op or cottage school, or even when we homeschool full-time, we fear that we will not give our children everything we desire for them. We compare our own inconsistent day-to-day routine to our good intentions. We find our "programs" lacking, given our desires which may include these:

---

[42] Luther, Martin. Treatise of 1520, "To the Christian Nobility." Vol. 44 of *Luther's Works*. American Edition "(AE). Philadelphia: Fortress Press, 1966. 207.

- sound teaching and nuturing in the faith through the Holy Scriptures and Sacraments, the Lutheran Confessions, and Lutheran hymnody and liturgy,

- a well-designed curriculum and literature list to incline the student to truth, goodness, and beauty without undue influence from contemporary culture,

- lessons in civility to raise well-mannered children;

- strong academics at every level,

- exemplary physical fitness programs for the development of strong bodies and healthy minds,

- the liberal arts carefully blended with Christian catechesis to teach the language arts, the mathematical arts, and the liberal sciences in a Christian context,

- a broad education in the Great Books, the great music, art, and ideas of Western civilization,

- our own wisdom, love, patience, discernment, and kindness as we teach each day.

No matter our educational choices, no earthly setting will ever give our children everything we desire for them. In fact, we do fail our children! We fail them every day. Yet we teach them, even when we admit this to ourselves, to our children, and to our God. In Christ, we ask for forgiveness, and we receive forgiveness.

We turn to the God who gave us these children, and we know that He alone can allay our fears. Our children, in spite of our own inadequacies, are safe in His loving care. He strengthens us, so we can take heart.

> While it is good, right, and healthy for us as parents to try our best and be as prepared as possible for the sake of our children, we can give thanks every day that our children are in the hands of our gracious God. The same God who knit our children together in their mother's womb now remains active in their lives for all their days.[43]

As parents, we research, we make informed decisions regarding our children's education, we teach our children, and we love them. We can do this free from fear. We guide our children, secure in the knowledge that our gracious God is at work in our children through His Word and

---

[43] Veith and Moerbe, *Family Vocation*, 147.

through us as His chosen instruments. We even have the freedom to change direction with our educational decisions, whenever this seems necessary for our children or for the family. At the start of the day, and at its end, we rest in our Father's merciful care.

Luther writes of parental devotion, born of God. Truly the "love toward their mother is not so great in children as the love of their mother toward them. As the proverb has it: *Amor descendit, non ascendit*" (Love descends; not ascends).[44] Freely forgiven in Christ Jesus who descended to earth for us, who died for us, who rose again for us, and who lives to make intercession even now on our behalf, we can be freed from fear. As we press on, we rest in Him. Our children are forever kept in His strong and loving care. And so are we.

> *Fear not, for I am with you;*
> *Be not dismayed, for I am your God;*
> *I will strengthen you, I will help you,*
> *I will uphold you with my righteous right hand. — Isaiah 41:10*

> *The Lord will keep your going out and your coming in from this time*
forth and forevermore. — *Psalm 121:8*

Homeschooling mother of two, Nicole Manners adds these thoughts:
While a legitimate fear for our child's safety and well-being are gracious gifts of our God-given vocation as parents, moving past what is healthy and into a detrimental state of mind can negatively influence our decisions. We begin to believe that throwing money at weak areas, changing curriculum yet again, or arbitrarily "redesigning" our homeschool will fix all our problems. We constantly compare ourselves to others, and we breed our own discontent. It is difficult at times to see past the trials of the moment, be it a crying toddler, an unhappy math lesson, an argumentative child, or a struggling reader. Yet, in the midst of these, we are called to pursue our vocation as homeschoolers, indeed as parents, in humility and grace. We can only love because God in Christ first loved us. We remember with gratitude that there is "no fear in love, but that perfect love casts out fear. — 1 John 4:18a, 19

---

[44] Luther, Martin. *Luther's Works*, Vol. 52. Philadelphia: Fortress Press, 1974. 811.

Sample Families With Younger Children

The Rev. Benjamin Pollock, Idaho

During my years in seminary, my wife taught at Zion Lutheran Academy in Fort Wayne, Indiana. She also attended several classical education conferences. With my first call to small churches in rural Minnesota, we had no LCMS day school nearby.

We decided then it would be best to attempt to teach our children at home. Homeschooling allowed us to adjust our routine to a pastor's busy schedule. If I was called to visit a member in the "big city" hospital three hours away, we would all go along and make a day of it. Homeschooling also worked well, because we had three young children close in age. It was much easier to teach them at home, instead of having one on a school-oriented schedule with two younger children on a home-based schedule. My wife Rachel joined the Martin Loopers email list at that time, and she gained much wisdom from Lutheran homeschoolers while making many like-minded friends.

Several years later, I received a call to be pastor of one church in Meridian, Idaho. Some friends were surprised that we wanted to continue homeschooling despite our move to a larger city. However, homeschooling made it much easier to transition in the middle of the school year. Homeschooling also helped us transition to life in a large city after living in our rural small town. Even though we have access to more homeschooling resources here, we have not utilized these, because we enjoy being on our own schedule and teaching from our own curriculum. We count the greatest blessing of home education to be the freedom to teach LCMS doctrine and hymns to our children every day.

Homeschooling has also assisted our eight-year-old son with his mild learning disabilities. Last year we spent four hours a week at different kinds of therapies. We could focus on these therapies and exercises, and we could slow down the academic pace for a time. The other boys went along while their brother had therapy, and we continued school lessons in the break room of the doctor's office. I believe our son achieved so well academically, both before and after this period of therapy, because he was homeschooled. With one-on-one instruction, he can progress ahead of grade level in some subjects and work on strengthening his skills in other subjects. He just keeps learning.

Our entire family loves to read. Homeschooling has fostered this love in our children. Together, we shop library book sales to add to the estimated 9,000 books in our home collection. Rachel has placed all of these in Dewey Decimal order. Our ten-year-old read every *Boxcar Children* book that he could find through the library system when he first learned to read. All of our boys (6, 8, 10) enjoy being read to daily. Favorite family read-alouds have included books by A. A. Milne and E. B. White, books about musical composers by Opal Wheeler, *The Adventures of Tom Sawyer, The Borrowers, The Cricket in Times Square,* and nonfiction selections about animals and other topics. The love of learning spills over into other areas. Recently, the boys have enjoyed studying Usborne's *Famous Paintings* art cards and memorizing a few facts about each painting. We appreciate the many blessings to our family God has given us through homeschooling.

Sarah Koehneke, Florida

I always imagined that my children would attend a Lutheran school. Having been a Lutheran school teacher, this seemed reasonable. However, when the geographic obstacles of living in Florida made this impractical, we had to get creative. Surrounded by failing public schools, we looked resignedly to homeschooling as a last resort. As it turns out, it was not until we began homeschooling that I really began to truly understand what Lutheran education could be.

Forgiveness and vocation are the core of our school day. Each subject is viewed as an ongoing lesson to better love our neighbor. The classical Christian model inclines the little mind to truth, beauty, and goodness within God's good order, and salvation is found in Christ alone.

Of course, with three children (18 months, 3, and 6), our school runs a little differently than most Lutheran schools. We drill memory work while marching around the block. We practice skip-counting and Latin vocabulary with sidewalk chalk. We do "early bird" math before Daddy leaves for work, so he can keep an eye on the little boys. We impulsively belt out hymns, and we observe God's creation while keeping a Nature Notebook. We can readily accept an invitation to meet Papa or head across to the neighbor's for a lunch break. A trip to Grandma's house includes sewing lessons. Best of all, we can cuddle up to read! Unrestricted by bells and car lines, we have the luxury of time. In humility and love, we can begin and end each day in the Word which artfully weaves our studies and conversations together into a unified whole-colored with the unending ribbon of forgiveness held together in Christ alone.

Families With Teens

Susan Knowles, New York

We are in our fourteenth year of homeschooling. We initially began homeschooling during our time at seminary, because we anticipated multiple moves. Homeschooling seemed to make sense to provide academic stability for our children (4, 11, 16, 19).

Later we found that the flexibility of our schedule also allowed us the opportunity for the children to see their father at times which fit around his work schedule. As a pastor, he would be busy in the evenings, and as a military chaplain through both stateside and overseas separations (e.g., Iraq and Afghanistan), we could continue to communicate with him despite the odd hours and time differences.

We soon discovered many privileges of becoming our children's primary teachers. As parents and children, we grew as learners together — both in academic subjects and in faith. Our family established school routines and approaches similar to those in Lutheran schools, where there can be both intentional study of God's Word and the infusion of our faith throughout every subject.

Over time we became familiar with classical Lutheran education. As our lives settled down into a routine, we chose to continue homeschooling primarily because of a desire to provide consistency in a classical Lutheran education since there was no classical school nearby.

As an expression of our faith within our parenting, we have intentionally studied the interaction of Law and Gospel with our children each year. We wanted our understanding of God and His work to grow along with our children without focusing simply on external behavior. From the time they could communicate, we spoke with our children about the ways we can be loving and unloving toward our neighbors (even those in our home!). We helped them interact with the Law in the most direct terms, so even the smallest of children could see their thoughts, words, and actions more clearly, and thus see their need to run to their Savior. We run to Him together, as we recognize the role of confession and forgiveness in restoring relationships.

Much of our time homeschooling has been spent supporting outreach activities in our community through our church, with a special emphasis on homeschoolers through our church's Educational Resource Center. The classes and activities offered have been a true blessing to our own family as well as to families throughout our church and community.

The Rev. Christian Tiews, Oklahoma

Our three children (8, 11, 14) have never experienced a traditional school setting; yet they are not only thriving, but they are also best friends. Reading, writing, math, and history are priorities for us, but we appreciate the freedom we have to study subjects in seemingly unorthodox ways together as a family. These include regular walks and talks with Dad in the morning (Deuteronomy 6:7 and "As the head of the family should teach it in a simple way to his household," Small Catechism), breakfast devotions (from the Small Catechism and the *Treasury of Daily Prayer*), heated lunch conversations, field trips on days nobody else seems to be on the road, visits to sick and shut-in congregation members, family trips to Germany, and just reading great books. Homeschooling gives the children time to pursue their own individual interests: photography, blogging, ballet, Boy Scouts, piano, gymnastics, cooking, baking, or just playing with neighborhood friends. The flexibility of homeschooling is a great gift.

The continuity of homeschooling is also a gift. When we moved to St. Louis in order for Christian to pursue his seminary education, the transition was so much easier for the children, since a school transfer was not needed. When his first call was to Grace Lutheran Church, Tulsa, Oklahoma, we had many new things to discover, but our schooling remained the same.

During high school years we have found supports for our children's education. We supplement with online classes from Veritas Press, Patrick Henry Preparatory Academy, community college (dual credit!), and Latin/Biblical Greek classes taught by Christian at our church. We have found resources online and in the local library for individual study, AP/CLEP preparation, and more. We appreciate *EdEx.org, Ted.com*, Khan Academy, Coursera, and YouTube educational channels. Private tutors, jobs and internships with local companies, starting a photography business, writing a book, volunteering, mission trips, keeping backyard chickens, and even helping the family to move and renovate a house have all given our students real-world experiences within the homeschool setting. In academic study, we can skip school "busy work" and turn directly to assignments that matter.

Most importantly, we feel blessed that we are able to center our life on Christ and His Church. We have time to go often to receive His gifts in Word and Sacrament. We can strengthen each other in our faith. We can learn how to apply His word in everyday situations. We can take the time to daily forgive and be forgiven.

Graduated and Grateful

Homeschooled K-12 by Lutheran parents Alex and Jenni in Wisconsin, Cheryl Swope's godchild Sara shares these thoughts composed for *Eternal Treasures*.

Graduated and Grateful

Sara Scheler

My years of homeschooling taught me many things, but if you ask me to condense those twelve years into one common theme, it would be this: Lutheran homeschooling strengthened my faith by teaching me to know truth and question error. Homeschooling taught me to be skeptical of the world in a healthy way, as a critical thinker, a curious learner, and a practical problem-solver. In the end, Lutheran homeschooling taught me how to become a capable adult with strong, family relationships. I see this all the more clearly, now that I am away from home.

Leaving the Nest

You need at least three things to be successful in college: skills for communication, the desire to stand out favorably, and the ability to think. Through Lutheran homeschooling, my parents gave me all three. I reflect often on such things, because I see the contrasts in some of my peers who were not so fortunate.

College students need to be able to communicate with adults. A common misconception is that "socialization" is synonymous with having a lot of friends, because the most common response to finding out someone is (or was) homeschooled is something along the lines of, "Do you have any friends?!" One problem with this response is the assumption that the key point of school is to obtain friends. This, unfortunately, is more than an assumption. For many people, it is a reality. Conventional schools offer so much time and extended contact with one's peers, few opportunities exist in school for prolonged, meaningful exchanges with adults. When some students come from such a peer-centered environment, teachers are easily disrespected, criticized, or shunned as being severely "un-cool."

Such peer-focused students may bring these attitudes with them outside of the classroom. Several college friends from traditional school settings have told me they are afraid to talk to adults. One asks a friend to make her doctor's appointments, because she does not want to speak to the receptionist on the phone. Another asks me to flag down the waiter when we go out to eat, because she feels too uncomfortable to ask for a napkin or spoon. How did this happen?

Homeschooling *encourages* conversations with adults, and especially engaged discussions with one's parents. While such engagement can happen in any family, many homeschooled students feel equally comfortable chatting with adults as with peers. I notice myself doing this naturally. Just as my mother or father might, I frequently strike up conversations with complete strangers in the checkout line at the grocery store. One college friend usually laughs nervously and tells me how awkward it was that I spoke to someone I don't even know. Such social tunnel vision can be debilitating in higher education.

I have come to believe that peer dependence, fostered in some school environments, cripples *true* socialization. Instead of raising a hand to ask or answer a question, students remain silent for fear of being ridiculed by fellow students. I have seen peers afraid to talk to their professors after class, afraid to call them on the phone, even afraid to send them a simple email. My history professor illustrates this for our benefit. He shows us a complex paragraph and asks if there are any words we do not know. Of the twenty-three students present, despite five minutes of silence, not a single student volunteers a lack of knowledge. He then calls on students, none of whom can define the words. He has done this several times with the same result. Poorly "socialized" students are so resistant to communicate with adults, they would rather not learn than risk embarrassment before peers. None of these observations makes me better than my peers, but the realizations make me grateful for the engaged homeschooling education I received.

The second thing college students need to be successful is the desire to stand out in a favorable way. Many public schools operate like factories. They become efficient at squelching individuality and turning out a steady, homogenous product: the student who knows exactly how he should behave in order to fit in. Students learn which clothes, cell phone, and car they need to obtain the status of conformity, and exactly what minimal academic information needs to be "learned" and forgotten. By the time they enter college, many conventional students have spent twelve years of their lives learning standardized, watered-down material, being moved along from one grade to the next regardless of their grasp of this material. They are not seen as individuals. They are not expected to be special.

In college, students who truly value individuality are not afraid to put away their cell phones and engage with the material presented in class. The more adventuresome students raise their hand and ask questions, they stay after class to speak with their professors, and they value their education as their first priority, far ahead of late-night bar crawls. Confident that they have the tools necessary to succeed, they do not let the negative pressures of those around them impair their education.

College students must be able to think. This last point sounds absurdly obvious, but I have witnessed too many students in my classes who struggle with this. It seems as if they are so accustomed to merely assimilating information on the lowest levels of understanding, only to return these facts onto test papers, it is as if education bypasses their minds. When the previously mentioned history professor asked a simple, straightforward question in class one day, a student immediately turned to the textbook and started looking furiously, as if expecting to stumble upon the answer. She later realized she knew the answer to the question, but she got so caught up in trying to find it, she could not think. It does not help that our textbooks are laid out in an overly simplistic manner. Each chapter has a summary of the main points, which is certainly helpful but it makes it far too easy to skim the summary and never delve into the material. This process of skimming gets rid of all the context students need to understand the big picture and think critically about real issues.

Teachers in traditional settings can make this worse. Our college professors often say, "You don't need to know this for the test, but … ," as if unaware that immediately after they say those words, many of the students shut off their brains. Learning is an engaging process. True education, whether in the home or classroom, requires students to absorb, process, and think (read, mark, learn, and inwardly digest), not simply binge on information only to purge it out on exam day. The discussions and interactive, engaging daily learning within our Lutheran homeschool taught me to be a critical thinker, analyzing and evaluating everything I read, no matter the source. Our homeschooling science textbooks offered secular explanations for how the world began, and my parents were not afraid to expose me to these topics; in fact, they encouraged us to explore controversial ideas, but they always brought us back to biblical truths and helped us value God's word as the standard by which to evaluate secular viewpoints. I now see the value in this form of education more than ever.

The Dangers of Self-Discovery

Many people will tell you college is a time to discover who you really are and who you want to be. Such inward focus is dangerous at any age, but especially so during a teen's first prolonged absence from home. I witnessed many of my friends experience harsh transitions at the beginning of college, as they realized their freedoms to "be themselves" and rebelled against many things their parents had taught them. One of my friends said she had "an awakening" that showed her homosexuality is not a sin, despite being taught the contrary by her Roman Catholic parents. She and others encouraged me to be similarly enlightened, and when I explained that I would stand by my biblical viewpoints, they treated me like a child who had not yet learned how the world really works. Rather than being thrust into college with a weak sense of self, a confused identity, and a precarious faith like many of my peers, my strong and consistent Lutheran homeschooled background taught me to be certain of absolute truth, to discern right from wrong, and to hold fast to my faith.

Being a conservative Lutheran homeschooler puts you in the smallest of minorities on most campuses across the nation. If you attend a liberal or secular school, you will be teased, ridiculed, looked down on, and opposed on almost every issue that comes up in the classroom. The protective, nurturing, and intentional Lutheran homeschooling background never could have instructed me in the pain of having classmates team up against me, having professors single me out in class for public humiliation, or having close friends criticize the very foundations of my faith. However, it did prepare me with the tools I needed to survive the harrowing journey of "self-discovery." All the things I had learned in years of sermons, Bible studies, and confirmation classes brought me hope and comfort, as my faith was continually challenged. Verses like Matthew 5:10, "Blessed are those who are persecuted because of righteousness, for theirs is the kingdom of heaven," reminded me that pain and suffering in Jesus' name is neither futile nor unexpected. I looked forward to attending church every week, because it was the one pure, quiet, refreshing hour. The Divine Service was consistent and comforting, rich in forgiveness; something I admit I never truly appreciated until I went away to college.

Some Things Homeschooling Does Not Teach You

My transition to college was, as transitions usually are, a bit rough. Everything I had heard from adults, peers, and especially from the administrators at my school made me think the first few weeks would be one giant, non-stop party full of adventures, new friends, and independent bliss. It was not. I spent much of the first month in my dorm reading my textbooks word-for-word while trying to live with a struggling roommate who suffered from a drug addiction and accompanying emotional difficulties. Unfamiliar with such things prior to college, this brings me to my second point: There are some things homeschooling may not teach you.

There are certainly things I was not prepared for when I embarked on my college journey. I was unprepared to choose the more apathetic seat in a lecture hall, so I just sat front and center. I brought a hundred pages of college-ruled lined paper and three ballpoint pens to class, but everyone around me whipped out their MacBooks. Though this might have seemed intimidating, I soon realized this was the way many college students pretend they are taking notes when they are really on Facebook. I was not aware that skipping class was an option, and I did not know what house parties were, but I soon learned they had little to do with anything my homeschooled brother, sister, and I would call real fun. I did not know that when your Resident Assistant calls a mandatory floor meeting, you can choose not to attend. I did not know where to obtain a fake ID or how to imbibe with an absurd level of illegal abandon. Yes, there was much homeschooling had not taught me. And while I feel for my classmates, I am grateful for the more beneficial education my dedicated parents provided.

One semester my sociology professor instructed us in a section on marriage and family. She spent most of the first hour criticizing the nuclear family. She belittled all conservatives. She explained the concept of "the second shift," which she describes as the oppressive and brutally unfair time when mothers come home from their day jobs to cook, clean, and spend time with their children. While coming home to a dirty house after a long day of work is certainly not a mother's idea of a good time, my professor treated any time spent doing domestic activities as akin to torture.

In contrast, my eighteen years of Lutheran homeschooling taught me that my parents' favorite part of the day was coming home. As soon as we heard the garage door open, my brother and sister and I would rush downstairs to give Dad a big hug. With family dinner on the table, we all sat down to talk, laugh, and enjoy one another's company. The nuclear family is terribly scorned and undervalued today, but I now know that it is invaluable. I have gained a deep and permanent appreciation for my family. My siblings and I were blessed to grow up in a loving, functional home.

People think I am odd when I say my siblings are my best friends, especially when I add that I actually enjoy spending time with my parents. In a staff meeting at school, we were divvying up holiday duty days. As a Resident Assistant, I worried I might be assigned holiday duty in some brutal competition for vacation. To my surprise, several students volunteered to work the Thanksgiving and Christmas holidays. "I hate my family," one laughed. I remember feeling a deep sense of distress for her after she said that. When I first left for college, I counted the days until I could go home and visit my family. I naively assumed everyone else felt the same way. I quickly learned many students deemed their families broken and dysfunctional, and they viewed college as a place to escape. This is fostered and perpetuated by intentional teachings against the honor of parents, against the duty of children, and against the strength of the family.

Dedicated Lutheran homeschooling can surround children with countless examples of healthy, successful relationships. Growing up, I saw numerous examples of biblical, forgiving marriages, with loving parents and respectful children. I never had the desire to date casually. Instead, when I entered college, my plan was to meet a Lutheran man, marry him, and homeschool my children. My friends thought I was "completely insane." They looked down on me for not having more self-focused priorities. They even criticized me for selling myself short. Several of them encouraged me to follow their lead and have a string of casual flings.

My friends still speak critically of an acquaintance who got married immediately after graduation and had a baby the following year. Ironically, they have no problem with the two freshman girls in my class who found themselves pregnant. "Don't judge," they say over and over, yet they are consistently critical of conservative viewpoints. While Lutheran homeschooling could never have prepared me for this baffling double standard, it did teach me what is biblical and true. This is what I revert to when I encounter the puzzling liberal notions so common in higher education. With gratitude, I realize that so many years with the teachings, relationships, and consistency of Lutheran homeschooling made me strong.

Do Not Be Afraid

When the time comes, do not be afraid to send your children out into the world. Know that, as recipients of your efforts, they possess the ability to think, question, evaluate, and learn in almost any environment. Know that, in many cases, parents are their most trusted confidants. Keep this relationship strong, and they will come to you when they are struggling to reconcile their solid upbringing with our tumultuous modern-day society. While there are no guarantees, and while your children will change and grow in many ways, trust that the God of their faith will see them through it all. Know that your children will be a witness to many and a light in a world of darkness. You can be proud of their accomplishments and gracious with their failures, because you know that, armed with a strong faith and God's Word, they will never be alone.

Take the helmet of salvation and the sword of the Spirit, which is the word of God. — Ephesians 6:17

What, then, shall we say in response to these things? If God is for us, who can be against us? — Romans 8:31

"And surely I am with you always, to the very end of the age." — Matthew 28:20b

My Life as a Homeschooler

Homeschooled from infancy through high school graduation, Cheryl's daughter Michelle shares these thoughts.

My Life as a Homeschooler
Michelle Swope

My name is Michelle Lynn Swope, for I have been adopted. Delivered by emergency C-section in fetal distress, at three pounds, I suffered with oxygen loss in the womb. Born in a St. Louis hospital, I am a true Missourian by blood. I was raised by foster parents till age one. With my twin brother and lifelong chum, I then gained my "forever family."

Raised and homeschooled by loving parents, they taught us the best of everything they knew: kindness, love, and self-control. Yes, we fell into our spats, and we were disciplined. One time when we were still young, not quite six, I had a favored baby doll named "Michelle" after me. Michael took her from me, sat on her atop a small white rocker, and broke her head clean off. He was, of course, chastised for his crime. When he apologized, I forgave him. We learned very early to forgive, for "we daily sin much," and we are daily forgiven much.

Mom taught me to read my ABCs and to know my 123s. From there, the graceful writing that soon flowed from my pen. We sang the music of the church. We learned the liturgy of the Divine Service when we were still in diapers. Later we learned Latin, arithmetic, grammar, science, history, literature, geography, logic, and more. We celebrated many years of education with a large gathering for our graduation. Never had we seen so many people in our house!

Today I sing French and German folk songs with Les Petits Chanteurs. I have been honored by them more than once. I am surrounded by family and friends. I work with disabled adults as both a client and helper at a day program, and I volunteer at a nursing home. I help set the table, sweep after meals, and play card games with the clients. I tuck them in for rest time and clean the rabbit's cage when needed. Sometimes the staff asks me to sing songs. Other days I arrange flowers, help with Bingo, or read poetry. In the center for disabled adults, they once gave me my own corner where I could retreat to write poems, as the words came to me.

At home I take long walks with my brother, who remains my best friend. I read the many books in our home yet unread. I listen to music. Being taught at home has given me more than any gift I could share.

Every good and perfect gift is from above. — James 1:17

DELVING DEEPLY: LEARNING TOGETHER

OUR CHRISTIAN FAITH: THE WORD FOR US

The doctrine or teaching drawn from the prophetic and apostolic Scriptures is confessed in the Small Catechism of Dr. Martin Luther and expressed in the Divine Service. The Small Catechism serves as a road map to the very heart and core of the Bible, saving us from making wrong turns in our reading of God's Word.[45] *— John T. Pless*

Teaching the Catechism

In the first of several longer narratives within Part Two of *Eternal Treasures*, Rachel Whiting shares her thoughts with an examination of the language of our faith, a glimpse into the catechism's Six Chief Parts through the eyes of a family, a discussion of the Table of Duties, and more.

Teaching the Catechism
Rachel Whiting

The Language of Our Faith
When my baby boy was only a few months old, I began putting him in a bouncy seat so I could complete tasks around the house. I would move the bouncy seat all over the house, as I folded laundry,

---

[45] Pless, John T. *Didache*. Fort Wayne, Indiana: Emmanuel Press, 2013.

cleaned, and made dinner. During all of my activities, I would talk to my son. Of course, it was a long monologue, but his big eyes sparkled as he looked up at me. Occasionally his chubby legs would kick whenever I spoke with enthusiasm. I would tell him what I was doing and what I was thinking. I didn't expect him to understand all my words, but I knew he would learn the meaning of words over time as he was exposed to them. Slowly he began making grunts and tones to copy sounds in the words he heard. How exciting this was for my husband and me. We said a word, and his sweet little voice mimicked it. It was only natural for him to try to repeat what he heard.

When this same son was much older, I read aloud to him a Greek myth about a nature goddess who was full of incessant chatter. She was punished for talking so much by being allowed only to repeat the last words of others. In the story, she falls in love with Narcissus, who does not return her love, as he only loves himself. She eventually dies of a broken heart and all that remains of her is her voice "which to this day can be heard senselessly repeating the words of others."[46] And what was this nature goddess's name? Her name was Echo. My son and I laughed at the story. It was intriguing to hear an ancient explanation as to why sound bounces back, when you hear your own voice repeated.

Just as the Greek word "echo" means "to sound, to utter sound, to teach by the voice,"[47] the etymology of the word "catechism" means "to sound back and forth."[48] When we catechize our children, we are teaching them through questions and answers to resound the truths of Scripture. Their mimicking is not for "senselessly repeating" words; rather, it is to form their minds so that God's truth reverberates with depth and strength in their souls.

The reason we have the Scriptures in our own language stems from the conviction that doctrine is to be known and understood.[49] We cannot judge whether the teachings we hear are true without the words of Scripture. Martin Luther's Small and Large Catechisms are summaries of the Scriptures. The Small Catechism is ideal to use

---

[46] d'Aulaire, Ingri, and Edgar Parin d'Aulaire. *Ingri and Edgar Parin D'Aulaires' Book of Greek Myths*. Garden City, N.Y.: Doubleday, 1962. 92.

[47] Webster, Noah. *Noah Webster's First Edition of an American Dictionary of the English Language*. Anaheim: Foundation for American Christian Education, 1967 and 1995.

[48] McCain, *Editor's Introduction to the Catechisms, Concordia: The Lutheran Confessions*, 309.

[49] Scaer, David P. *Getting into the Story of Concord: A History of the Book of Concord*. St. Louis: Concordia Publishing House, 1977. 69.

with our children, as Luther describes it as being small, plain and in a simple form.[50]

Through repetition and dialogue, just as we teach our children how to talk, Luther advises us to impress the catechism, word for word, upon our children.[51] This means to teach them the catechism verbatim, and not to worry if terms are not fully understood right away, but simply to learn the words in the rich context they are given. Then,

> after they have learned the text well, teach them the meaning also, so that they know what it means … . Take your time in doing this. For it is not necessary for you to explain all the parts at once, but one after the other. After they understand the First Commandment well, then explain the Second, and so on. Otherwise they will be overwhelmed, so that they will not be able to remember anything well … . After you have taught them this short catechism, then take up the Large Catechism and give them also a richer and fuller knowledge.[52]

Here, Luther is walking us through how to approach catechesis. After our children can answer the Small Catechism questions, we can go back and explain to a fuller extent what the answers mean. We do not need to hurry them through the memorization process. We want to lay a solid foundation on which we can build. After our children have been immersed in the Small Catechism, we can teach them the Large Catechism in order to enrich their understanding.

Our children need the Small Catechism internalized in such a way that it is not just information acquired for Confirmation; rather, the words become part of them for the length of all their days. The Rev. Peter Bender tells how the catechism is both a handbook and prayer book:

> The main goal of catechesis is the creation and sustaining of faith in Christ, and how that faith expresses itself in the Christian life… . Catechesis … involves establishing "a culture of hearing the Word of God and prayer" in both the congregation and home … . [W]hen a "culture of prayer" is established in which the catechism can be learned by heart as one actually meditates upon the text of the catechism, it can begin to shape

---

[50] Luther, Martin. *Enchiridion: The Small Catechism Preface.* In *Concordia: The Lutheran Confessions,* 313.

[51] Ibid.

[52] Ibid., 314.

the way we think. It can also teach us how to listen to God's Word correctly, what to expect from Him in the Sacraments, how to receive the Sacraments for our blessing, how to pray and confess the faith, and how to live in our vocations. This is how the catechism functions as a handbook and prayer book for the Christian faith and life.[53]

Our goal in teaching the catechism is not for our children to reach a point and say, "All right, now I am all finished with the catechism." We all remain students, as Luther himself acknowledged in his Preface to the Large Catechism:

> I act as a child who is being taught the catechism. Every morning — and whenever I have time — I read and say, word for word, the Ten Commandments, the Creed, the Lord's Prayer, the Psalms, and such. I must still read and study them daily. Yet I cannot master the catechism as I wish. But I must remain a child and pupil of the catechism, and am glad to remain so.[54]

We can set the example for our children as we continue to learn and pray the catechism with them. When we respond to what we have read in the Scriptures by repeating back to God what He has spoken to us, we are praying the Scriptures. The Small Catechism is an epitome of the Scriptures. When we take what we learn from the catechism and respond with it to God in prayer, then we are praying the catechism. For example, when we read the Second Article of the Apostles' Creed about Christ, the Son of God, who was conceived by the Holy Spirit and born of the Virgin Mary, we respond in praise and thanksgiving that Christ, true God and true man, became incarnate to save us. We are praying the catechism. This type of meditative and reflective study enables us to appreciate the catechism as a prayer book.

Reciting and discussing the catechism is not merely an intellectual or theoretical exercise; it is intensely practical. As we implement the catechism into our daily lives, we are living like Christians: confessing our sin, which we understand from the Ten Commandments; proclaiming the Gospel to ourselves and others in the Apostles' Creed; using the gift of prayer to speak to our Father; remembering our baptism and returning to it in daily Confession; receiving the forgiveness of sins

---

[53] Fabrizius, *The Lutheran Catechesis Series*, Learn-by-Heart Edition, ix.

[54] Luther, Martin. *Preface to the Large Catechism*. In *Concordia: The Lutheran Confessions*, 353.

from Christ Himself as He speaks through our pastor (Absolution); and eating and drinking the Body and Blood given for us for the remission of sins. We find all this in the catechism, and in such a wonderfully concise summary form for ease of use in nurturing the growing faith of our children.

Our little children grow so quickly, from sitting in bouncy seats and babbling in gibberish to walking and speaking with clarity. As we nurture their physical bodies and their spoken language, so may we nurture the language of their faith. The Rev. Peter Bender teaches:

> Catechesis passes on the language of our holy faith ... . God has His own language for learning how to receive God's gifts in the Divine Service, how to pray, how to confess, and how to live where God has called us. ... The chief reason why the catechism is memorized or "learned by heart" is so that it can shape the faith and understanding of the catechumen and be used by him throughout his life.[55]

Recently a friend inquired as to the date when one of our older children made their "personal decision to become a Christian." At home we talked with our children about the friend's question, its terminology, and its implications. During the discussion, my son considered all this. He sang out, "I believe that I cannot by my own reason or strength believe in Jesus Christ, my Lord, or come to Him; but the Holy Spirit has called me by the Gospel, enlightened me with His gifts, sanctified and kept me in the true faith."[56] My baby boy was growing up. His tonal noises were now articulated words, and he was learning to echo back the truth he had learned in the catechism.

The Small Catechism's Six Chief Parts Through the Eyes of Our Family

The Ten Commandments

Luther's explanation of the Ten Commandments in the Small Catechism tells us how we should fear and love God. He expounds upon each commandment with the things we must shun and the things we ought to do and think instead. The Law helps our children see their sin continually, so they can continually see their need for

---

[55] Fabrizius, *The Lutheran Catechesis Series*, x.

[56] Luther, Martin. *The Small Catechism of Dr. Martin Luther*. In *Lutheran Catechesis*, Learn-by-Heart Edition. Sussex, Wisconsin: Concordia Catechetical Academy, 1998. 13.

Christ. It also teaches them how to love God and love and serve their neighbors, treating others how they themselves would like to be treated (Matthew 7:12).

When we talk about sin in relation to the Law, we help our children recognize what sin is. The other day, when my ten-year-old son hit his sister, we talked about why his behavior was wrong. When asked which commandments he broke in hurting his sister, he replied that he had broken all of them because once one commandment was broken, the whole Law was broken. More specifically, he admitted that he broke the First Commandment, as he was not loving God when he hit his sister; the Fourth Commandment, because he disobeyed his parents who have told him not to hit his sister; and the Fifth Commandment, because he hurt his sister.

Then we talked about what he should have done instead of hitting. He knew that he should have done the opposite of hitting: helping and supporting his sister in all things. My husband often reminds him of this by summarizing simply, "Help, not hurt, your sisters." The Law does not stop there, but rather leads our children to Christ, who came to fulfill the Law perfectly on our behalf.

Christ, our Mercy Seat, covers my son's transgressions. In God's mercy, He clothes all of us with Christ's own perfect righteousness. Thus we can share forgiveness in Jesus with our children, even as we pray with them:

> *O God, the Father, Son, and Holy Spirit, who alone is the true God, and alone is worthy to be held in reverence by men, have mercy upon me. I have not feared, loved, and trusted in You as I should have done. I have put greater confidence in men; I have leaned to my own understanding. Forgive me for the sake of my Redeemer. By Your Holy Spirit remove from me every idolatrous affection. Draw me to You, that I may live in Your fear, trust in Your goodness, and love You with all my heart, with all my soul, and with all my mind; through Jesus Christ, Your Son, our Lord. Amen.*[57]

Apostles' Creed

When our son was two years old, my husband and I would ask him, "Who made you?" He would jump up and down shouting, "One God

[57] Bente, Paul. In *The Lord Will Answer: A Daily Prayer Catechism*. St. Louis: Concordia Publishing House, 2004. 54.

… big God … my God." Now that he is older, his voice joins with all the people of God in this confession of faith: "I believe in God the Father Almighty, maker of heaven and earth."

Luther organized his catechism by the three articles of the Apostles' Creed, addressing the Holy Trinity: God the Father who made us, God the Son Jesus Christ who redeems us, and God the Holy Spirit who calls, sanctifies, and keeps us. In the Large Catechism, Luther explains how the First Article of the Apostles' Creed is presented as a response to the First Commandment,

> It is as if you were to ask a little child, "My dear, what sort of a God do you have? What do you know about Him?" The child could say, "This is my God: first, the Father, who has created heaven and earth. Besides this One only, I regard nothing else as God. For there is no one else who could create heaven and earth."[58]

Luther then summarizes the Second Article, saying that here "the little word *Lord* means simply the same as *redeemer*."[59] In the words of the Creed, we can recite the Gospel with our children, explaining who our Redeemer is and how He has redeemed us.

The Third Article explains the work of the Holy Spirit in bringing us to Christ. The Holy Spirit "has sanctified and still sanctifies us…. He must daily administer forgiveness until we reach the life to come."[60] As we struggle against the world, the devil, and the flesh, we can pray with our children:

> *Grant, dear Lord God, that the blessed Day of Your holy advent may come soon, so that we may be redeemed from this bad, wicked world, the devil's dominion, and be freed from the terrible plague which we must suffer from without and within, from wicked people and our own conscience. Dispatch this old maggot sack that we may finally get a different body, which is not full of sin, inclined to unchasteness and to everything evil, as the present one is, but one that is redeemed from all bodily and spiritual misery and made like Your glorious body, dear Lord Jesus Christ, that we may at last come to our glorious redemption. Amen.*[61]

---

[58] Luther, *Large Catechism*. In *Concordia: The Lutheran Confessions*, 399.

[59] Ibid., 402.

[60] Ibid., 403, 405.

[61] Luther. In *The Lord Will Answer*, 288.

The Lord's Prayer

The other day my son sheepishly asked, "Mom, most of the time when I pray, I just don't know what to say, so I just say the Lord's Prayer. Is that okay?" "Yes," I said, "that is precisely the reason we have this prayer from Jesus, so we know how to pray. Jesus' disciples asked Him to teach them to pray, and He gave us this prayer." In the Large Catechism, Luther explains:

> [The Lord's Prayer] is a great advantage indeed over all other prayers that we might compose ourselves. For in our own prayers the conscience would ever be in doubt and say, "I have prayed, but who knows if it pleases Him or whether I have hit upon the right proportions and form?" Therefore, there is no nobler prayer to be found upon earth than the Lord's Prayer. We pray it daily, because it has this excellent testimony that God loves to hear…. For whenever a godly Christian prays, "Dear Father, let Your will be done," God speaks from on high and says, "Yes, dear child, it shall be so, in spite of the devil and the world."[62]

The Lord's Prayer provides our children with assurance that their heavenly Father hears their prayer. We can teach our children about their freedom in Christ (Galatians 4:6-7), so they might approach the Lord with this prayer any time, day or night.

> *O heavenly Father, blessed God, I am a poor, miserable sinner. I am not worthy to lift up my hands and eyes to You in prayer. But You have commanded us all to pray and have promised to hear us. At the same time, You have taught us the words and the way to pray. Obedient to Your command, and relying on Your gracious promise, I come in the name of my Lord Jesus Christ and pray with all Your holy Christians on earth, as He has taught us to pray. Amen.[63]*

The Sacrament of Holy Baptism

One afternoon my four-year-old daughter jostled her baby doll on her hip as she said, "This baby needs to be baptized." Her twin sister asked, "Baptized?" While still bouncing her baby doll, she replied,

---

[62] Luther, *Large Catechism.* In *Concordia: The Lutheran Confessions*, 411-412.

[63] Luther. In *The Lord Will Answer*, 307.

"Yes, with water in the name of the Father and of the Son and of the Holy Spirit."

Standing together, looking at their dolls, the two girls talked earnestly with each other, noting that *all* the babies needed to be baptized! While eavesdropping on their play, I was struck at the importance these little mothers placed on Holy Baptism.

Luther teaches us that Baptism "delivers us from the devil's jaws and makes us God's own. It suppresses and takes away sin and then daily strengthens the new man. It is working and always continues working until we pass from this estate of misery to eternal glory."[64]

He exhorts us to return to our baptism, to walk in our baptism, to value our baptism as a daily dress, to use our baptism. He sums up our life as a Christian as a daily baptism.[65] How crucial for us to teach our children what Baptism "profits, gives, and works."[66]

We might pray this prayer of gratitude daily with our children:

> *Lord, my God, my gracious God, I thank You for what You have done to me in Baptism! You have regenerated me. You have given me forgiveness of sins, and thereby that righteousness which is valid in Your sight. You have delivered me from death and the devil, and given me eternal salvation. You have granted unto me the Holy Spirit, who works and sustains faith and a new spiritual life within me. O my God, in the possession of such grace let me live and die, and awaken and live forever. Amen, for Christ's sake! Amen.*[67]

Confession

When my son was three years old, we took him to a playground at the park. While on the equipment, he began treating his daddy very disrespectfully. We prompted him to admit that he was wrong, but he said, "I forgive you" to my husband. He had confused this pronouncement with the desired request, "Will you forgive me?" Remaining with the pronouncement, but with the unabashed honesty of a child, he then turned his head to the side and muttered, "But I don't really."

We all need to be taught what true confession means and how to confess our sins to one another. We are deluded if we think that we

---

[64] Luther, *Large Catechism*. In *Concordia: The Lutheran Confessions*, 431.

[65] Ibid., 430-431.

[66] Ibid., 425.

[67] Zorn, C.M. In *The Lord Will Answer*, 359.

have no sin to confess, as we sin all the time, continually, even in ways beyond our perception. In order to see these sins, we must look at our lives in relation to the Ten Commandments. We confess our sin to those we sin against. We confess before our pastors the sins that are particularly troubling us.[68]

Following confession we receive absolution, the forgiveness of sins. Luther's Small Catechism includes a general form of confession so we have a framework to follow during private confession. We may pray this prayer:

> *O God, heavenly Father, I confess to You that I have grievously sinned against You in many ways, not only by my actions, but also by my thoughts and desires, which I cannot fully understand, but which are all known to You. I earnestly repent and am heartily sorry for all my many offenses against You. I pray, be gracious to me, a poor miserable sinner! Out of Your goodness have mercy on me, and for the sake of Your dear Son, Jesus Christ, my Lord, forgive my sins, strengthen me in love toward You and in service to my neighbor that all I do may be pleasing in Your sight and bring praise to Your name; in Jesus' name I pray. Amen.*[69]

The Office of the Keys

One evening, as we read together from Exodus the story of the plagues on Egypt, our children sat enraptured with their minds full of images: a blood-filled river, frogs, gnats, flies, and locusts covering the land, dead cows lying around, bodies covered in boils, hail falling from the sky, days of darkness, and even the death of the firstborn. We talked about how these things came about, and we learned that "the Lord performs His works by His Word ... . Moses was speaking God's Word the way God gave it to him to speak; God Himself was speaking."[70] This story helped us understand that a pastor is God's spokesman.

We teach our children through the Office of the Keys that the authority a pastor has to forgive or retain the sins of others is given to him from Christ.[71] We hear the voice of our pastor forgiving us of our sin, but it is actually Christ Himself speaking these reassuring words to

---

[68] Luther, *Small Catechism*. In *Concordia: The Lutheran Confessions*, 341.

[69] *Lutheran Book of Prayer*. Edited by Scot A. Kinnaman. St. Louis: Concordia Publishing House, 2005. 96.

[70] Bender, Peter. *The Lutheran Catechesis Series*. Second ed. Vol. Old Testament Catechesis, Catechist Edition. Sussex, Wisconsin: Concordia Catechetical Academy, 2005. 35.

[71] John 20:22-23.

us. God serves us through our pastor's certain words of forgiveness in Christ. Luther provides this clarification:

> I do not worship my pastor, but he tells me of a Lord whose name is Christ, and makes Him known to me. I will be attentive to listen to his words as long as he leads me to this Master and Teacher who is the Son of God.[72]

The Sacrament of the Altar

Last year my oldest child told me, "Sometimes, when I have communion, I imagine Jesus with a crossbow, shooting arrows into both of Satan's eyes when I eat the bread. Then when I drink the wine, I imagine Jesus shooting an arrow through the devil's mouth and up the back of his skull." Our son's vivid imagination is not so far off. In the Sacrament he receives forgiveness of sins, and Satan's accusations are silenced in that forgiveness. As Chrysostom wrote:

> If the devil merely sees you returning from the Master's banquet, he flees faster than any wind, as if he had seen a lion breathing forth flames from his mouth. If you show him a tongue stained with the precious blood, he will not be able to make a stand; if you show him your mouth all crimsoned and ruddy, cowardly beast that he is, he will run away.[73]

We can teach our children that the Sacrament of the Altar not only fights the devil's attacks, but also provides for our own need of life and forgiveness. "Here in the Sacrament you are to receive from the lips of Christ forgiveness of sin. It contains and brings with it God's grace and the Spirit with all His gifts, protection, shelter, and power against death and the devil and all misfortune."[74] Luther calls this Sacrament the "food of souls," as in this nourishing partaking of Christ's Body and Blood, the new man is strengthened, faith is refreshed, and forgiveness is gained.[75] With Ambrose, we can assure our children, "Because I always sin, I always need to take the medicine" of the Body and Blood of my Lord.[76]

---

[72] Luther. In *The Lord Will Answer*, 377.

[73] Chrysostom. In *Daily Readings from the Writings of St. John Chrysostom*. Minneapolis: Light and Life Publishers, 1988. 16.

[74] Luther, *Large Catechism*. In *Concordia: The Lutheran Confessions*, 439.

[75] Ibid., 434-435.

[76] Ambrose. Quoted in the Augsburg Confession. In *Concordia: The Lutheran Confessions*, 49.

Parents may wish to teach their children to memorize a prayer such as this:

> *Lord God of mercy, at the table You prepared in the face of my enemies I give You thanks for the body and blood of Your Son, the pledge of my salvation; for the Word by which You give forgiveness; for Your promises by which You give me life. May the gifts of Your heavenly banquet fortify me against the Evil One, strengthen me in the face of the world, overcome my selfishness. Help me to live as one who hungers for Your grace, who thirsts after righteousness, who longs to taste of Your goodness, that I may sit at Your table at the marriage feast when the heavenly Bridegroom comes to take His holy bride to Himself. Amen.*[77]

Far Beyond Confirmation …

We need not close our catechisms after confirmation instruction! Each of the Six Chief Parts provides sufficient daily study for a lifetime. Even so, we find still more in the catechism to teach and pray with our children.

Daily Prayers

Through the Morning Prayer, Evening Prayer, and others throughout the day, we find gifts to remind us of our dependence upon God at all times and in all things. The psalmist gives us a structure for praying as he says, "Evening and morning and at noon I utter my complaint and moan, and he hears my voice" (Psalm 55:17). Prayer is God's gift to us. He gives us cues from the daily order and rhythm of His creation,[78] and He exhorts us to pray to Him.

> *We thank You, Lord God, heavenly Father, for all Your benefits, through Jesus Christ, our Lord, who lives and reigns with You and the Holy Spirit forever and ever. Amen.*[79]

Table of Duties

God serves our neighbor through our children's callings and through our own. The Scripture passages under the Table of Duties are arranged topically by vocation for clear reference. Luther ends this

---

[77] *Lutheran Book of Prayer,* 1970. Quoted in *The Lord Will Answer,* 412.

[78] Engelbrecht, *The Lord Will Answer,* 447.

[79] Luther, *Small Catechism.* In *Lutheran Catechesis* Learn-by-Heart, 34.

section with a little rhyme, "Let each his lesson learn with care/And all the household well shall fare."[80] Each morning before beginning our lessons or chores for the day, a family might pray this simple prayer:

> *Heavenly Father, Creator of heaven and earth, it is out of Your love and wisdom that You gave me work to do and fitted me in body and mind to do this work. And yet my sinful will too often dreads the workday and casts about for other things to do. But You, O God, have called me to this work. Forgive me my sin. Strengthen me by Your Spirit that I may see that my place of work is a field of Your service to my family, my fellow worker, and my neighbor. Give me joy in my vocation, and make me glad and grateful for the strength to serve You; through Jesus Christ. Amen.[81]*

Christian Questions with Their Answers

My husband likes to use these questions on Saturday evening to direct our hearts on what will take place in the Divine Service the next morning. These twenty questions and answers focus on the Sacrament of the Altar. For anyone who does not desire the Sacrament, Luther exhorts this person to do this:

> First, he should touch his body to see if he still has flesh and blood. Then he should believe what the Scriptures say of it in Galatians 5 and Romans 7. Second, he should look around to see whether he is still in the world and remember that there will be no lack of sin and trouble, as the Scriptures say in John 15-16 and in 1 John 2 and 5. Third, he will certainly have the devil also around him, who with his lying and murdering day and night will let him have no peace, within or without, as the Scriptures picture him in John 8 and 16; 1 Peter 5; Ephesians 6; and 2 Timothy 2.[82]

These are sobering words. As we fight in constant struggle, we are reminded that this present world is not our eternal home. The devil, whom Luther liked to describe as never sleeping, is constantly seeking to obliterate our faith. For these reasons, we are thankful to eat and

---

[80] Ibid., 36.

[81] *Lutheran Book of Prayer*, 208.

[82] Luther, *Small Catechism*. In *Lutheran Catechesis* Learn-by-Heart, 40.

drink the Body and Blood of our Lord Jesus Christ for the forgiveness of sins, life, and salvation. We can pray:

> *Lord Jesus Christ, our only comfort, our hope, our righteousness, our strength and sure defense, we beseech Thee, kindle in our breasts a fervent desire, hunger, and thirst for that eternal food of the soul — Thy true body and blood — that we may gladly and frequently receive the glorious Sacrament in true realization of our sins and strong reliance upon Thee, unto the strengthening and assurance of our souls, until at last, life's pilgrimage ended, we come to Thee in the true Fatherland, to see Thee face to face, and abide with Thee through all eternity. Amen.*[83]

Teaching the Holy Scriptures

> *Lord Jesus, when parents brought their children to You so that You could touch them and bless them, You said, "Let the little children come to Me" (Matthew 19:14). I thank You for giving my child to me to raise according to Your Word and for bringing him to Yourself through the waters of Holy Baptism. Thank You for forgiving all of his sins, for rescuing him from death and the devil, and for giving him eternal life as You promise in Your Word…. Please bless me, and give me wisdom to teach my child Your word of truth and life, and help him to learn the joys of your forgiveness.*[84]

Rachel Whiting reflects on the great duty and privilege of teaching the God's Word to our children.

Teaching the Holy Scriptures
Rachel Whiting

God's Words Are Power

As the automatic double-doors opened, a strong gust of wind caught my three-year-old son and me by surprise. While I pushed a shopping cart full of groceries, my son sat perched in the shopping cart seat when we felt the heavy gusts. The wind stirred up leaves, and we

---

[83] Loehe, Wilhelm. *Seed-grains of Prayer: A Manual for Evangelical Christians*. Kansas City, Kansas: Emmanuel Press, 2010. 57.

[84] *Lutheran Book of Prayer*, 192.

looked at each other with wide eyes. As swirls began to blow wildly, my son raised his plump, little arm, extending it with his hand flat out, and said with authority, "Be still, be still."

In my heart, I laughed as I thought about his simple trust. He knows the words of Christ are *that* powerful. My son gave me a peek at the picture in his mind with Jesus, the Word of God, standing strong and mighty, speaking to the wind and sea, and they obeyed His voice. The gust of wind was strong, but Jesus Christ has all power.

Truly, God's Word is powerful, and Christ, the Word incarnate, has all authority in heaven and earth. What a privilege to talk with our children about the Word while sitting, walking, lying down, and rising — all throughout the day.[85] When my children were very small and would plop themselves down in my lap with a Bible storybook in hand, it was so easy to cuddle up and read the often simplified story. As they began to grow, I knew that my children could delve more deeply and learn more about the Bible. It was here, in a desire to *really* educate my children in the Scriptures, that I almost lost sight of the power and purpose of God's Word.

Fill-in-the-Blanks?

In teaching the Bible to my children in a more academic way, I nearly lost my focus. I began to focus too heavily on teaching the facts of the Bible: names of people, order of events, references, dates, and places on maps. While I correctly viewed this information as the nuts and bolts of Bible knowledge for the sake of biblical literacy, all of a sudden the exciting Bible stories were being reduced to multiple choice and fill-in-the-blank answers! I wanted my children to know basic Bible facts; yet when I noticed how my young children exhaled deep sighs when I said that it was Bible time, I felt it was time to re-evaluate.

In overly dissecting biblical texts, I had begun taking away from my children the experience of being immersed in a story — the story of Jesus Christ. In my zeal to have my children know Bible content, I had forgotten the purpose of Scripture. The words of Jesus rang in my ears: "You search the Scriptures because you think that in them you have eternal life; and it is they that bear witness about me"(John 5:40). I was looking at the Scriptures in an overly intellectual, academic way, as if the more my children's Bible knowledge grew, the more their faith would grow. The location of the land of Edom, near where Moses lifted

---

[85] Deuteronomy 6:8.

up the serpent on the pole, may not be a crucial element in helping my children understand what it means to "look" to Christ. Bible knowledge, full of references and dates, cannot become the entirety of being "filled with the knowledge of his will in all spiritual wisdom and understanding and increasing in the knowledge of God" (Colossians 1:9b-10). Yet biblical knowledge is important.

Jesus Christ, true man and true God, tabernacled among us. As incarnate God, He entered the world that He had made. He subjected Himself to time, entered into history, and He walked on the earth in specific geographical locations. He set his feet in real rivers, walked in actual towns, preached on a certain hillside, and prayed in a particular garden. I want my children to know these places, dates, and times, but I want them to remember why. Jesus Christ was heard, seen, and touched in space and time *for us* (1 John 1:1). His genealogy consists of real historical people. This is not dry knowledge but thrilling reality. All of these truths can bring to us the real, physical context through which Christ came to us men for our salvation (Nicene Creed).

A Simple Breath

The Scriptures are breathed out by God (2 Timothy 3:16), and as God breathed life into Adam, the Word is used by the Holy Spirit to breathe eternal life into us. Christ upholds the universe by the word of His power, He creates and sustains faith, as His words are spirit and life (Hebrews 1:3, John 6:63). God is at work, through His Word, by the Holy Spirit (1 Thessalonians 2:13). Just as the Holy Spirit hovered over the face of the waters in the beginning when the Word created all things, so He descends over the waters of Holy Baptism, making us a new creation in Christ. The Holy Spirit continues to work through the Word and the Sacraments, as a sacrament is an element that has been joined to the Word.[86] The Word is living and active (Hebrews 4:12). It is not idle and will accomplish the purpose God had in speaking it (Isaiah 55:11). In the *Formula of Concord*, we learn:

> By His Holy Spirit, through the Word, when it is preached, heard, and pondered, Christ will be effective and active in us, will convert hearts to true repentance and preserve them in the true faith … . He [the Spirit] also will protect them in their great weakness against the devil, the world, and the flesh. He

---

[86] Luther, *Large Catechism*. In *Concordia: The Lutheran Confessions*, 432.

will rule and lead them in His ways, raise them again when they stumble, comfort them under the cross and in temptation, and preserve them for eternal life.[87]

I had overcomplicated the simple message of Scripture for my small children. The purpose of the Scriptures is to reveal Christ to us. When I open the Scriptures with my children, I am taking them to where Christ is found, and Christ is coming to them.[88] As theologians throughout time have noted, all of the Scriptures work together with the same scarlet red thread running through them, as the blood of Jesus and the forgiveness of sins is both prophesied and fulfilled. Some parts of the Scriptures are more difficult to understand than others, but the crucial message of who Jesus is and what He has done for us is simple and clear. We must instruct, but we must not obscure.

What Does it Mean to Grow Our Children in Faith?

We cannot equate growing in faith with growing in the knowledge of facts! The Apology of the Augsburg Confession states: "Faith is not just knowledge. But it is willing to receive or take hold of those things that are offered in the promise about Christ. God wants us to believe Him and to receive from Him blessings. He declares this to be true divine service."[89] I want my children to have "a faith that believes, not merely the history, but also this effect of the history: we have grace, righteousness, and forgiveness of sins through Christ."[90] Luther does not envisage the spiritual life as a process of self-development, but as a process of reception from the triune God. He explains:

> The process of reception turns proud, self-sufficient individuals into humble beggars before God. … If we attempt to gain eternal life with God through rational speculation and spiritual self-development, we will commit spiritual suicide. Those who use their reason and intellect to make a ladder for their devotional ascent into heaven will, like Lucifer, plunge themselves and others into hell instead.[91]

---

[87] Formula of Concord. In *Concordia: The Lutheran Confessions*, 605.

[88] Kleinig, John W. *Grace Upon Grace: Spirituality for Today*. St. Louis: Concordia Publishing House, 2008. 101, 102.

[89] Apology of the Augsburg Confession, *Article V (III)*. In *Concordia: The Lutheran Confessions*, 116.

[90] Ibid., 43.

[91] *Luther's Works*. Word and Sacrament I. Vol. 35. Philadelphia: Muhlenberg Press, 1960. 121.

Even as we teach biblical facts, we can approach or conclude a text with prayer and meditation, teaching our children to receive what God is giving them through His Word. The Rev. Dr. John Kleinig defines meditation as "the exercise of faith in Christ and His performative Word, for faith receives what Christ gives to us through His Word. We receive, as we believe."[92] Luther explains how this meditation looks:

> All the words and stories of the gospels are … sacred signs by which God works in believers what the histories signify… . We meditate properly on the gospel, when we do so sacramentally, for through faith the words produce what they portray. Christ was born; believe that he was born for you and you will be born again. Christ conquered death and sin; believe that he conquered them for you and you will conquer them."[93]

Luther explains this further:

> When you … read or hear how Christ comes here or there, or how someone is brought to him, you should therein perceive the sermon or the gospel through which he is coming to you, or you are being brought to him. For the preaching of the gospel is nothing else than Christ coming to us, or we being brought to him. When you see how he works, however, and how he helps everyone to whom he comes or who is brought to him, then rest assured that faith is accomplishing this in you and that he is offering your soul exactly the same sort of help and favor through the gospel.[94]

This form of reading and meditating, with open ears and hands wanting to receive what God gives us through His Word, through Christ by His Holy Spirit, is very different than wanting to master only Bible details, facts, or worse, "trivia." We teach names of the books of the Bible and other essential details for essential biblical literacy; but we also teach the entirety of Holy Scriptures to nurture faith. Faith receives the promised mercy of God in His Word, and this is the work of the Holy Spirit.[95]

---

[92] Kleinig, *Grace Upon Grace*, 102.

[93] Ibid.

[94] Ibid.

[95] Apology of the Augsburg Confession, *Article IV (II) Justification*. In *Concordia: The Lutheran Confessions*, 89.

Panting for Life

As parents we can be comforted, beyond all else, to know that God is at work in our children through His Word (1 Thessalonians 2:13). In our regular home routine, after breakfast we might hear a Scripture reading and then discuss this reading with help from a catechetical curriculum.[96] We might listen to the Bible selection from a dramatized audio or take turns reading a few verses aloud. My children enjoy using a felt set to reenact the stories we are learning. After we discuss the questions and answers in the curriculum, we close with a meditation on the passage studied, and our meditation focuses our attention on what God is giving us. This sitting, listening, and receiving from God's Word prepares us for the Divine Service on Sunday. We anticipate God serving us with His Word and Sacrament.

What God gives us through His Word cannot be seen with our eyes, but His words go into our ears and fall upon our hearts. The Spirit is described as moving like the invisible wind, and the Spirit works through the Word where Jesus Christ has revealed Himself (John 3:8). We want our children to know the love of Christ that surpasses knowledge (Ephesians 3:19). While we can perhaps more easily raise little champs at Bible trivia, we want our children to say with the psalmist, "As a deer pants for flowing streams, so pants my soul for you, O God" (Psalm 42:1). Paraphrased by one of my children in a prayer journal: "I am panting for life, for You, like a dog who pants, because he is thirsty and tired from running." Luther explains this verse, saying, "As a deer with anxious and trembling eagerness strains toward a fresh flowing stream, so I yearn anxiously and tremblingly for God's Word, Absolution, the Sacrament, and so forth."[97]

May our children pant for God, because He creates, sustains, and strengthens their faith through His Holy Spirit by the power of His Word, which is at work in them. He feeds their growing faith with all the treasures and richness in His Word, in His Son, Jesus Christ, as "all the promises of God find their Yes in him" (2 Corinthians 1:20). May the Word incarnate give our children His grace, mercy, hope, love, comfort, peace, forgiveness, salvation, sanctification, righteousness, true food and true drink[98], with eternal life ... all from God's own fatherly kindness toward us in Him.

---

[96] See resources from the Concordia Catechetical Academy.

[97] Luther, Martin. *A Brief Exhortation to Confession*. In *Concordia: The Lutheran Confessions*, 653.

[98] John 6:55.

Law and Gospel in the Home

To rightly distinguish Law and Gospel is the most difficult and highest Christian art ... . It is taught only by the Holy Spirit in combination with experience.[99] — *C. F. W. Walther*

Homeschooling father, the Rev. Christian Tiews provides these introductory thoughts for our consideration.

How do we parents apply Law and Gospel in homeschooling? We parents must keep in mind that we too are sinners — just like our children — sometimes perhaps even having to swallow our pride and admit to our kids that we messed up. But then we grab hold of the Gospel, remembering that Jesus Christ forgives not only our children, but us parents too, as we stumble along, doing our best to rightly distinguish Law and Gospel in raising our homeschooled children. As C. F. W. Walther notes:

> In the end, when Christians have learned to make the proper practical use of the proper distinction between Law and Gospel, they join St. John in saying, "God is greater than my heart. He has rendered a different verdict on people who sin, and that applies also to me." Blessed are you if you have learned this difficult art. If you have learned it, do not imagine yourselves perfect. You will always be no more than beginners at this art. When the Law condemns you, you must immediately lay hold upon the Gospel.[100]

From a mother's perspective, Rachel provides these reflections on Law and Gospel in the home.

Law and Gospel in the Home
Rachel Whiting

A Boy's Prayer
"Lord, please forgive my sin and help me to be good. Help me to ... be good ... tomorrow. Amen." These were the words my son spoke to God in a defeated sigh before he went to sleep. It had been a long day, full of both accidental mishaps and intentional sins. For example, during our morning chore of putting away the dry dishes, my son accidentally

---

[99] C. F. W. Walther. *Law and Gospel — How to Read and Apply the Bible.* St. Louis: Concordia Publishing House, 2010, Thesis II. 2.

[100] Ibid., 52.

broke five dishes while distractedly doing a little dance. His dog had gone without water for most of the day. He failed to complete his math lesson without numerous reminders. He had repeatedly provoked his sisters, apologized, and asked forgiveness for stirring up strife all throughout the day. Yes, the words my son uttered before going to sleep seemed appropriate! Yet as I walked down the hall, something was unsettling in his request to "be good."

The Two Kingdoms

I mulled over why I could possibly be bothered by such a request. Not one ounce of my son's good behavior could ever secure or maintain his good standing before God, for he had already been forgiven and had been granted Christ's perfect, imputed righteousness. Was this clear to him?

Because of the Holy Spirit, my son has the desire to obey the Law in love and service to his neighbor. As within all Christians, daily he struggles between the desires of his sinful nature and the desires of the new man in Christ, as these war against one another.[101]

Of course, I want my son to have good behavior manifested in love and service to others, but if he looks at himself as wanting to be "good," was he also looking to become acceptable to God based on what he does here on earth? I wanted to assure my son that his life in Christ is not based on his goodness; rather, goodness is given to him on account of Christ's perfect righteousness on his behalf.

Some say doctrine does not matter. Some say doctrine is far too "heady" for a child (or his mother). Yet as my son's mother, I am duty-bound to know the doctrine of the two kingdoms, the doctrine of Law and Gospel, the doctrine of justification, and the doctrine of imputed righteousness. These Lutheran distinctives shape my parenting. The left-hand (temporal or secular) kingdom informs civil righteousness and daily discipline. The right-hand (spiritual or eternal) kingdom frees me to forgive, as I have been forgiven. Both kingdoms are made evident in the Holy Scriptures and described in the Lutheran Confessions, and both kingdoms are realities here and now for the Christian. As a mother, raising a little boy who is trying to "be good," how vital for him to learn to distinguish these two kingdoms. How vital for him to understand the accusation of the Law and to live in the forgiveness of the Gospel in Jesus Christ. "The law was given through Moses; grace and truth came through Jesus Christ" (John 1:17).

---

[101] Romans 7.

To Mix Law and Gospel Is to Confuse

When the Israelites were set free from their slavery in Egypt, delivered through the Red Sea and sanctified by God despite their wilderness wanderings, they wanted to go back to slavery to satisfy their fleshly desires.[102] It seemed easier to return to Egypt and be comfortable than to continue to trust in God to provide for them. We can relate to their temptation, as the world, our own flesh, and the devil beckon us away from trusting in God.

After hearing the Law proclaimed to them, in vain the Israelites cried out, "All the words that the Lord has spoken we will do" (Exodus 24:3). We hear the Israelites saying this, and we see the futility of our own promises reflected in theirs. God's Law is holy; yet we do not fulfill all obedience before God. The Law instructs us; yet we take comfort in the assurance that Jesus came not to abolish God's law, but to fulfill it on our behalf.

Did I hear my own voice saying internally, "All the words that the Lord has spoken I will have my son do"? Was I confusing the Law and the Gospel in my parenting? More questions arose: Did the Law have a more prominent place than the Gospel in our home? Did I give my son a frighteningly wearying "goodness-before-God gauge," whereby he saw himself seemingly up or down in his status before God, depending on how well he behaved? Was I confusing the kingdoms? Had I confounded civil righteousness with spiritual righteousness? Did my fear of having a disobedient son make me hold to the Law for his goodness, instead of focusing on the Spirit's working through the Gospel?

The Law will never give my son sanctification. C. F. W. Walther states: "The attempt to make men godly by means of the Law, and to induce even those who are already believers in Christ to do good by holding up the Law and issuing commands to them, is a very gross confounding of Law and Gospel."[103]

The Law Has No Power to Work Righteousness in Us

"The Law paints the portrait of the life of goodness and blessing, but it is absolutely powerless to create and bestow this life," as the Rev. John Pless explains.[104] The hymnwriter declares this:

---

[102] Bender, *The Lutheran Catechesis Series*, 40.

[103] Walther, C. F. W. *Proper Distinction Between Law and Gospel*. St. Louis: Concordia Publishing House, 1991. 381.

[104] Pless, John T. *Handling the Word of Truth: Law and Gospel in the Church Today*. St. Louis: Concordia Publishing House, 2004. 108.

Salvation unto us has come
By God's grace and favor;
Good works cannot avert our doom,
They help and save us never."[105]

We seek to conduct ourselves decently as citizens here on earth, serving our neighbors in our vocations and upholding God's law and rules established by the authorities in this kingdom under God. As Luther said, "It belongs to the civil authority … to keep the peace, so that our young people are brought up in the fear and discipline of God."[106] We benefit from instruction in such matters, and we are molded as our parents discipline us in the nurture and admonition of the Lord. In the kingdom of the left hand, we have been given nurturing yet firm means by which my son will be raised as a good citizen.

Yet the Law will never give my son spiritual righteousness. If I ever tell my son that he can earn a goodness of his own, then this is most certainly not the Gospel. A "gospel" that is conditional on us leaves us in the bondage of our sin, as turning to our obedience in the law into no gospel at all.[107] The Rev. John Pless paraphrases Walther in this manner: "The Law never finds righteousness; it only confirms unrighteousness. The Gospel never finds righteousness; it only gives and bestows righteousness."[108] The Law serves to mortify our old man, not make him better.

Furthermore, the Law will never give my son redemption. I must not hold before my son God's holy Law with the expectation that as a Christian he can perform perfect obedience to it and thereby obtain favor with God. If I do this, my son will be driven either to an arrogant despising of God's mercy if he falsely believes he keeps the Law with perfection, or to a hopeless, sighing despondency when he knows he does not. Where, then, is our hope?

The Gospel Is the Power of God Unto Salvation

God sustained the Israelites in the wilderness. We remember the Passover meal, the water from the Rock, the bread from heaven. We remember the serpent on the pole, the sacrifices for sin, the blood

---

[105] *Lutheran Service Book.* 555:1.

[106] Luther quoted in Pless, *Handling the Word of Truth*, 125.

[107] Ibid., 113.

[108] Walther, C. F. W. In *Handling the Word of Truth*, paraphrased from *Proper Distinction between Law and Gospel*, 381.

sprinkled on the ark of the covenant. We remember the mercy seat which covered the Ten Commandments. Through the entirety of the Holy Scriptures, we see that Christ is our "righteousness, sanctification and redemption" (1 Corinthians 1:30)!

In Jesus Christ, all our sin is removed from us "as far as the east is from the west" (Psalm 103:12). In Him alone, our sin is absolved, we are forgiven, and His mercies are new every morning. Christ our advocate lives to make intercession for us every day and night, even as we come to Him with our original sin and actual sin again and again. He forgives. Through the Body and Blood of Christ in the Sacrament, He gives us Himself again and again saying, "Given and shed for you, for the remission of your sin."[109]

When my own head hits the pillow at night, I am reminded of unconfessed sins. I ask God to forgive me. For the sake of Christ, He does. I know I am forgiven. My own soul's hope is in the righteousness Christ has placed on me, not in the hope that I will be good the next day. I remember my baptism into Christ, where my old man drowned and I consider myself dead to sin, knowing that it is no longer I who live, but Christ who lives in me (Romans 6; Galatians 2:20). I can go to sleep knowing I am not judged on the basis of performance, because I have been united with Christ's death and resurrection, and my life is hidden with Christ (Colossians 3:3). "In peace I will both lie down and sleep; for you alone, O Lord, make me dwell in safety" (Psalm 4:8).

The message that Christ has accomplished it all for you might sound dangerous, and for some the worry is that the forgiven child will then just do whatever he wants. Indeed, the Apostle Paul encountered such an argument, because he, too, proclaimed full forgiveness and freedom in Christ. But when we proclaim this to our children, we give our children true hope and His peace. With His Word, He restores their souls.

Balm for Our Souls

Since hearing my son's bedtime prayer, I talked with him about all these things. As Christians we are citizens of a temporal kingdom where rules and consequences serve important purposes. When my son chooses to disobey, loving discipline is enforced and privileges are lost. As Christians, we are also citizens of heaven (Philippians 3:20). My son's life in Christ is never based on his own personal goodness; rather, it is certain because of the imputed goodness of Christ. My son

---

[109] Luther, *Small Catechism*. In *Lutheran Catechesis*, Learn-by-Heart Edition, 12.

is forgiven for Christ's sake, and he can rest joyfully in this promise.

I shared these verses with my son: "Preserve me, O God, for in you I take refuge. I say to the LORD, 'You are my Lord; I have no good apart from you'" (Psalm 16:1). He said, "Oh, Mom, I really like that verse! That verse is true!"

Christ is our righteousness. This is a balm to our souls. It is the truth that has set us free from the delusion that we can, even as Christians, earn any merit before God. We are naked and undone in our sin, and even our seemingly "righteous" deeds are as filthy rags before Him (Isaiah 64:6). Jesus takes our sin and covers us in the rich, thick, complete robe of His perfect righteousness (Isaiah 10). Walther explains:

> The Gospel does not require anything good that man must furnish; not a good heart, not a good disposition, no improvement of his condition, no godliness, no love either of God or men. It issues no orders, but changes man. It plants love into his heart and makes him capable of all good works. It demands nothing, but it gives all. Should not this fact make us leap for joy?[110]

The Proper Role of Law and Gospel in the Home

In training my children, I communicate that the Law is holy and good. We need the Law to reveal our own sin to our innately self-righteous minds. The Law instructs us how to live in harmony with one another and how to serve our neighbor. Luther tells us:

> Christ set us free from the curse, not from the obedience, of the Law …. God wants us to keep the Commandments with total commitment and diligence; but not to put our trust in it when we have done so; or despair if we have not. See to it, then, that you distinguish the two words rightly, not giving more to the Law than its due, otherwise you lose the Gospel. Likewise you should not look at the Gospel or build thoughts upon it as though the Law had collapsed. Rather, let each of them remain in its own circle and sphere.[111]

My children need to hear the condemnation of the Law. When one of my children lashes out in violent hitting and does not care what is right or wrong, I am learning to hold the Law as a mirror, so he can see

---

[110] Walther, *Proper Distinction Between Law and Gospel*, 16.

[111] Luther, Martin. Quoted in Pless, *Handling the Word of Truth*, 124-125.

what sin looks like. Or when a child is telling lies and has no qualms about it, I want the Law to press down on this child. The Holy Spirit works through God's Word of Law to slay and expose the old nature, so the good news of the Gospel can heal, granting forgiveness.

My children need to hear the comforting words of the Gospel. When my child feels the weight of his sin, heavy and bearing down, then the Holy Spirit has already worked through the Law and through my child's conscience, where the Law is written. Then my child needs Christ's voice saying, "Come unto Me, all you weary and heavy laden, to find rest for your souls" (Matthew 11:28).

When our children come to us and confess a sin, we must not condemn them further, scolding them in how bad it was to do such and such. We can tell them freely that they are forgiven, because Christ died for all sin, including the sins being confessed and the sins we are not aware of.

The Law is not to be merely outwardly obeyed, in what we do with our hands, but also inwardly, in the thoughts and intents of our hearts. When my children were little, it was easy for them to see that the wrong things they did with their bodies were sinful: biting, hitting, talking rudely, kicking one another. But the sins that could not be seen with their eyes or committed with their hands and feet, like hatred and envy, seemed safely concealed from view.

I remember one day my son asked me if God knew what he was thinking. When I answered that He knows all things, even his thoughts, my son's eyes became really big, as his face filled with dread. "He does? Oh, no!" He felt terror at this realization that the deep sins of his heart and mind were laid bare before God.

We can assure our children that Jesus always obeyed inwardly, in the deepest part of His being. We hold before them Christ's righteousness on their behalf, because He always loved, feared, and trusted His Father above all things. Jesus always lived to do His Father's will for us. We can remind our children that when they hear their pastor speak the words of absolution in the Divine Service, he is speaking in Christ's stead. Our children hear Christ's own words of forgiveness to them. Mercifully, so do we.

Good Works Are God's Good Works

The good works that God has prepared beforehand for my son to do will flow from him, as Luther explains, "We confess that good works must follow faith, yes, not only must, but follow voluntarily, just as a good tree not only must produce good fruits, but does so freely."[112] Yet even these good works will not make him good, as "the good works of believers are imperfect and impure because of sin in the flesh, nevertheless they are acceptable and well pleasing to God … through faith for Christ's sake."[113] As the Rev. John Pless explains, "Faith does not save by making us do works that are worthy of salvation. Faith saves by apprehending the Savior. He alone is the source of all good works in the Christian life."[114]

God does not need our good works, as we are saved on the basis of Christ's works.[115] But our neighbor sorely needs our good works of love and service to them.[116] My son has been set free in Christ to love and serve others, even though these works do not establish a personal goodness. They simply serve his neighbor in love.

Lessons Learned

My son's sighing prayer awakened me to a realization: My parenting must address both kingdoms more distinctly. In the temporal kingdom, my duty is to cultivate obedience, instill respect, uphold the rules, and discipline in love. In the spiritual realm, I must not delude myself that the nagging demands of the Law will produce good fruit, nor should I discourage a child who seeks to be good. But I never want to encourage a child to seek his own "goodness" before God, rather than trusting fully in the promises of God for him in Christ Jesus.

In Christ, we are no longer under the Law, but under grace (Romans 6:14). Our good works as Christians are only good in that they are sanctified by faith in Christ. Jesus Christ has, indeed, become to us "our righteousness and sanctification and redemption" (1 Corinthians 1:30).

While we attend to both kingdoms as parents and teach Law and Gospel, the overarching atmosphere of our homes can be filled with the rich and glorious promise of forgiveness in Jesus Christ. This forgiveness covers us and our children. We can share this with our sighing children and restore their troubled consciences. Through the Gospel, we can reassure our children of the promised peace, hope, life, and salvation given to them freely in Jesus Christ.

---

[112] Pless, *Handling the Word of Truth*, 66.

[113] Formula, Solid Declaration, *Article VI: Good Works*. In *Concordia: The Lutheran Confessions*, 561.

[114] Pless, *Handling the Word of Truth*, 65.

[115] Veith and Moerbe, *Family Vocation*, 29. See Romans 4.

[116] Ibid.

Praying as a Family

He regards the prayer of the destitute,
and does not despise their prayer. — Psalm 102:17

Rachel Whiting invites us to ponder prayer within the context of family life.

Praying as a Family
Rachel Whiting

Children of God

One day in the car when my son was five years old, he spoke to his younger sister in the backseat. I overheard as he, the elder brother, was taking it upon himself to explain the world to what he considered a naive mind.

With a confident tone, he asked her, "Do you know how God sees Daddy and Mommy?" His little sister looked at him in wonder, as if her brother held all the mysteries of the universe. My son explained, "He sees them like they are little children, just like us. He sees all of us like little kids, even Daddy and Mommy."

In simplicity, how true this is, because God does see us as His dear children in Christ Jesus. As Jesus told Mary after His resurrection, He was ascending to His Father and to her Father — and to our Father (John 20:17). As God's children together, our days can be ordered together in prayers of praise, confession, intercession, and thanksgiving.

Prayer: God's Gift to Us

The faith that the Lord gives to us through His Word and Sacraments brings us to life from the dead (Ephesians 2:5). Brought with power from "the domain of darkness" into the kingdom of Jesus Christ (Colossians 1:13), as new creations we use our mouths to speak to God. "O Lord, open my lips, and my mouth will declare Your praise" (Psalm 51:15). Our tongues are not loosed because God needs us to pray to Him; rather we depend on Him, and prayer is God's gift to us. We pray to our Father, even as He knows all things and has given us all things in Christ (Romans 8:32).

Often we do not know what to pray, but the "Spirit Himself intercedes for us" (Romans 8:26), and Christ has given us the Lord's

Prayer.[117] As parents and as Christians, we are privileged to cast our anxieties upon the Lord, because He cares for us (1 Peter 5:7). Scripture tells us that "in everything by prayer and supplication with thanksgiving let your requests be made known to God. And the peace of God, which surpasses all understanding, will guard your hearts and your minds in Christ Jesus" (Philippians 4:6-7).

Voices Joined in Unison

One evening our family was invited to eat dinner with another family from our congregation. Before the meal was served, our hosts asked us to join with them in Daily Prayer: Early Evening (*LSB* 297). As the voices of the parents blended with the voices of their two young daughters, they prayed in unison:

> *Joyous light of glory:*
> *of the immortal Father;*
> *heavenly, holy, blessed Jesus Christ.*
> *We have come to the setting of the sun,*
> *and we look to the evening light.*
> *We sing to God, the Father, Son and Holy Spirit:*
> *You are worthy of being praised with pure voices forever.*
> *O Son of God, O Giver of life: the universe proclaims*
> *Your glory.*[118]

The words and their meanings held such a bounty of beauty and truth woven together, I already felt like my soul had been fed a plenteous feast. The name of this prayer is "Phos Hilaron: O Gladsome Light," and it was originally written in Greek in the third century.[119] I yearned for my family to know this beautiful prayer and many more. We turned to this treasure: the *Lutheran Service Book*.

Family Prayer

We find a variety of services in the *Lutheran Service Book* under the Daily Office. Our family receives great guidance by relying on different offices at various times (Matins, Vespers, Morning Prayer, Evening Prayer, and Compline). On a more regular basis, we use the shorter devotion of Daily Prayer for Individuals and Families.

---

[117] Matthew 6.

[118] *Lutheran Service Book*, 297. See also Phos Hilaron set to music, *LSB* 244.

[119] Campbell, Andrew A. *Living Memory: A Classical Memory Work Companion*. Shelburne Falls, Massachusetts: Quidnam Press, 2008. 86.

Practices may differ over time, but praying as a family binds us together in our faith, as we individually and collectively call on the name of the Lord. Currently, our family gathers for the Close of the Day (*LSB* 298) before bedtime. For the Scripture portion of this, my husband reads a selection from the historic One-Year Lectionary and reads from the Higher Things "Reflections" devotional, adapting the content for the ages of our children.

In the mornings, to open our homeschooling day, I loosely follow the format of Morning Prayer with the children as part of our Bible study together. Sometimes we say the Noon Prayer when the morning has an engagement.[120] Our pastor encourages us to pray the same psalm every day for a week. We also have our special family traditions that we incorporate into the evenings according to the seasons of the Church Year.

Prayer: A Gift Amid Obstacles

Family life brings obstacles to family prayer, but the gift is always available to us. We find reassurance not in our practices, but in His willingness to welcome us at any time, as a father welcomes his dear children. Many times we plan on Daily Prayer: Early Evening at the dinner table after our meal, and the hymnal bravely sits on the edge of the dinner table, where it is in danger of getting spilled on. Then a child accidentally falls backward from tipping his chair, and we completely forget about prayer. Or someone spills a drink all over the table and his clothing, and in the chaos of wiping up the mess and changing the child's clothes, closing prayer time is overlooked.

Our family is most consistent with Close of the Day, yet even then not as often as we might wish. Sometimes we gather all six of us together, and then someone has to use the bathroom. Sometimes there is fighting between children sitting beside one another. But despite the difficulty in getting family prayer started and the hardship encountered to even finish, the forms of prayer serve an important place in our home.

Quiet

The quietness of prayer with spoken and heard words assists our otherwise distracted and hurried souls. We live amid cultural and

---

[120] Concordia Publishing House now offers *Lutheran Service Book*: Daily Prayer Cards, containing the *Daily Prayers for Individuals and Families*. The eight fold-out cards, especially when laminated, are wonderful for use with children.

personal obsessions with clattering noise and compelling images. The time of sitting still as a family prepares us for receiving God's gifts in the Divine Service on Sunday mornings. Scot Kinnaman, editor for the *Treasury of Daily Prayer*, reveals these benefits when he says:

> Christians live their lives from Sunday to Sunday... . Strengthened in faith and prepared by means of God's holy gifts, we leave the Divine Service to live out our daily lives, our vocations, in relationship to God and to our neighbor. Our daily prayer, our daily devotions, are filled with the echo of what we received in the Divine Service. Our daily prayer prepares us for the coming Sunday when we will again be in the presence of God in the Divine Service.[121]

Guiding Our Children in What Is Good for Them

Sometimes when my husband calls the family together for prayer, there arises a dull expression over one of the children's faces. This same silent protest, "Oh, Dad, do I have to?" appears on their faces when they glance down at the spinach on the plates placed before them. In response to forlorn expressions at the dinner table, we normally say something like, "You may not feel like eating that, but it is good for your body. It will help you be healthy." So it is with praying together as a family. If needed, we remind our children that prayer is good for their souls and healthy for their faith. In prayer we correctly acknowledge our utter dependence upon God for all things.

On Being Flexible

With growing children, our routine at home continues to change, but having a scheduled time in the day to gather together as a family helps us develop the habit of family prayer. Joining together after evening baths has worked especially well for our family. We gather together in the living room, where a crucifix hangs on the wall.

Over time, we have added new elements in family prayer. Sometimes we light candles, remembering that Jesus is "the light of the world" (John 8:12). Candles "symbolize God's active faith-creating and faith-sustaining presence among His people."[122] Usually we use an

---

[121] Kinnaman, Scot A. *Treasury of Daily Prayer*. St. Louis: Concordia Publishing House, 2008. xvi.

[122] See the study note for Genesis 1:3. *The Lutheran Study Bible: English Standard Version*. St. Louis: Concordia Publishing House, 2009. 12.

order from the *Lutheran Service Book,* but we also incorporate other prayer books and devotional readings.[123]

We include the music of our faith. Sometimes we listen to the *Evening and Morning: Music of Daily Lutheran Prayer* CD when praying various services together. We have also sung hymns along with other CDs. Sometimes we sing while my son plays a hymn on the piano. We especially enjoy listening to a particular recording with many prayers, canticles, and the psalms chanted.[124] Often we select a single hymn from the current season in the Church Year.

Helpful Hand Motions

With twin four-year-olds, we find hand motions helpful. When we move our hands while giving expression with our lips, this seems to personalize objective truth and help focus minds and hearts. The Rev. Dr. Burnell R. Eckardt reminds us that "it is not the mere repetition of sounds out of the mouth which helps faith, but diligent meditation on the words of the faith. ... [R]ubrics are offered only in the hope of encouraging such attentiveness."[125] If rubrics are found to be helpful for your family, there are many that can be learned.[126]

Making the sign of the cross is an ancient and treasured means of remembering our baptism "in the name of the Father and of the † Son and of the Holy Spirit." This can be included at various times and in many places. The *Lutheran Service Book* recommends making the sign of the cross upon ourselves during the name of our triune God and during the Words of Institution over the bread and wine. This activity focuses our attention on Jesus' words and helps us apprehend the very personal words "for you."[127] Luther also recommends making the sign of the cross upon rising and lying down.[128] In regular activities and

---

[123] Mayes, Benjamin T. G. *The Brotherhood Prayer Book.* Kansas City, Kansas: Emmanuel Press, 2007. Kinnaman, *Treasury of Daily Prayer. Lutheran Book of Prayer.* St. Louis: Concordia Publishing House, 2005. Cameron, Bruce A. *Reading the Psalms with Luther: The Psalter for Individual and Family Devotions.* St. Louis: Concordia Publishing House, 2007.

[124] See *The Brotherhood Prayer Book*: Audio CD. Emmanuel Press.

[125] Eckardt, Burnell F. *Every Day Will I Bless Thee: Meditations for the Daily Office.* Sussex, Wisconsin: Concordia Catechetical Academy, 1998. xv.

[126] Refer to any of these resources:
Eckardt, *Every Day Will I Bless Thee,* xv. Piepkorn, Arthur Carl, and Charles McClean. *The Conduct of the Service.* Fort Wayne, Indiana: Redeemer Press, 2006. Lang, Paul H. D. *Ceremony and Celebration.* Fort Wayne, Indiana: Emmanuel Press, 2012.

[127] *Lutheran Service Book,* 162.

[128] Ibid., 327.

times of doubt and fear, we are comforted that the Lord has called us by name, and we are His.[129]

My children have especially enjoyed using hand motions for the Lord's Prayer. We learned these motions from *Every Day Will I Bless Thee*:

At "Our Father ..." the hands are folded palm to palm, the position of repose, since to call God our Father ought to bring contentment.

At "Hallowed be Thy name," the head is bowed, in reverence for the holy name of God.

At "Thy kingdom come," the hands are slightly parted, as if to receive.

At "Thy will be done ..." the hands are again folded palm to palm, as at first, in the recognition that God's will is good and ought therefore be accepted with contentment.

At "Give us this day ..." the hands are laid one upon the other, both palms upward, just above the waist, as if a beggar asking alms.

At "Forgive us ..." the hands are laid palms upon the breast, one atop the other, a position of modesty, acknowledging our naked sinfulness before God.

At "Lead us not into temptation; but deliver us from evil," the sign of the cross is made, as it is well to do in the face of temptation or evil.

At the conclusion, the hands are again folded palm to palm as at first, thus concluding a threefold expression of contentment toward the Triune God.[130]

The Blessing of Compline

Luther says that here on earth we "carry the old Adam about our neck ... and have the devil around us."[131] Within our families, perhaps more obviously and more frequently than anywhere else, we sin against God and each other. We hurt one another. Yet God has placed us together in a family, and we can all come together in His mercy by confessing our sins and receiving forgiveness. The service of Compline has been especially helpful for my family. In Compline we confess our sins before God and one another.

---

[129] Isaiah 43:1.

[130] Eckardt, *Every Day Will I Bless Thee*, xvi.

[131] Luther, *Large Catechism*. In *Concordia: The Lutheran Confessions*, 420, 421.

God daily and richly forgives us our sin. He has also put the words of forgiveness on our lips. Paul directs the Colossian Christians to forgive "as the Lord has forgiven you" (Colossians 3:13) … . [A] confession of sin should be followed by an Absolution: "For Jesus' sake I forgive you your sin." … The outcome of the words of Christ's forgiveness is praise both with lips and life as we "do everything in the name of the Lord Jesus, giving thanks to God the Father through Him" (Colossians 3:17).[132]

As simultaneous sinners and saints, we await the Last Day. We look for His return, certain of His calling. No matter the time or day, each of us within our homes can pray individually or together with earnest desire for our eternal Savior, "Come, Lord Jesus" (Revelation 22:20).

Teaching and Singing Hymns: For the Mouths of Babes

Music, like reading, has ever been a powerful means both for holding or leaving a given path.… We can sing ourselves out of Lutheranism and Christianity as well as we can read ourselves out of them. Our chorales … are a treasure. If we hope to retain this treasure, it will avail us nothing to have it in print; it must be learned by the children.[133] — Music Reader for Lutheran Schools

In the congregation, day school, and the home, hymns must be learned by our children. We share the thoughts of individuals in these various settings.

From Martin Luther Grammar School in Wyoming, the Rev. Paul Cain, headmaster/pastor, shares these tips on teaching hymns:
One of the most effective ways I've found to teach a hymn, song, psalm, or canticle to people young and old is called "Call and Response." It works especially well with those who do not yet read well or those who cannot read at all. I sing or say a line and ask them to repeat it back to me. After working our way through a hymn stanza, we can then try to sing the entire

---

[132] Baker, Robert C. *Lutheran Spirituality: Life as God's Child.* St. Louis: Concordia Publishing House, 2010. 108.

[133] Grundmann, J., Schumacher, B. *Music Reader for Lutheran Schools.* One-book course. St. Louis: Concordia Publishing House, 1933.

stanza together. Further time can be spent in comprehension of the text or unique musical elements. Then we sing again heartily.

In Idaho, Rachel Pollock shares hymns with her three boys ages 6, 8, and 10 in their church, at home, and when traveling:

We begin each day with Luther's Morning Prayer, and then we sing a hymn together. Usually this hymn is selected from the Church Year, working slightly ahead. For example, in October we sing a hymn for Reformation or All Saints' Day. We sing the same hymn every day for an entire month.

At lunchtime we sometimes have devotions together as a family. We follow an order of service from the Treasury of Daily Prayer. *Throughout the day we listen to music while we do chores or drive to activities. My boys ask for* For All Seasons CDs *with organ music. My husband and I enjoy the* Kantorei CDs.

At night we sing as part of our bedtime routine. After the boys are ready for bed, we sing the Kyrie, recite the Creed, sing the Lord's Prayer, and sing our hymn for the month. We might also sing "I Am Jesus' Little Lamb" and "Now the Light Has Gone Away." Then we recite Luther's Evening Prayer.

Kelly Rottmann, homeschooling mother of three boys, offers this narrative on teaching hymns from her Missouri home.

Teaching and Singing Hymns
Kelly Rottmann

Hymns for Our Children
"Garbage in, garbage out." I first heard this phrase in seventh-grade computer class. I learned to create simple computer programs with various commands, and my computer teacher taught us this phrase as a reminder. The computer can only do exactly as it is programmed to do. One faulty command or keystroke, "garbage in," will throw off the whole computer program and, with predictability, will produce "garbage out." Imperfect input yields undesirable results.

In the same way, condoning a flurry of faulty habits and an indulgence in worldly enticements (1 John 2:15-17) opens a door to unhelpful outcomes or even unbelief. Once destructive patterns are established, it is hard to undo them. What is our alternative?

The hymns of our faith offer young minds a powerful change. Through Lutheran hymnody, children are taught God's wonderful plan for salvation, and this counteracts worldly programming in at least three ways. First, hymns keep one mindful of St. Paul's admonition to think about excellent and praiseworthy things, most notably the message of salvation through Christ's death and resurrection. Secondly, hymns are effective tools for driving away the devil, and they bring peace to those who sing them. Lastly, Lutheran hymns remain abiding, timeless confessions of faith, offering truth to all generations, including children.

Each season of the Church Year offers new habits, new practices, and new hope. Few church seasons affect our children so deeply as Lent. The Lenten hymn "Lamb of God, Pure and Holy" is ideal for teaching children "whatever is honorable, whatever is just, whatever is pure, whatever is lovely" (Philippians 4:8). Its repetitive lyrics, soothing melody, and slow tempo appeal to children. This is important, because the penitential season of Lent can be troubling and sad for children due to its focus on Christ's suffering and death. "Lamb of God, Pure and Holy" gently portrays a loving, selfless Christ who suffers and is scorned, while offering hope with its prayer-filled lyrics:

> All sins Thou borest for us,
> Else had despair reigned o'er us.[134]

Children are soon able to sing this hymn from memory, and this provides them with reassuring words for a lifetime.

Comforting words, borne in the heart from habit, are of utmost importance to children living in a fallen world, where the "devil prowls around like a roaring lion, seeking someone to devour" (1 Peter 5:8). The world, the flesh, and the devil will bombard our children with "garbage" through varying venues. Carnal love songs and immoral images on television entice with empty promises filled with empty pleasure. Defective programming can fill children's hearts and minds with uncertainty and despair.

Through hymnody, children receive powerful tools for rejecting the "garbage" of this world, even as they are taught the valuable message of salvation in its place. "On My Heart Imprint Your Image" (*LSB*, 422)

---

[134] *Lutheran Service Book*, 434.

gives examples of Lenten words that grant what Luther calls "a calm and joyful disposition."[135] Even though this hymn is brief, it is an effective reminder for both child and demon alike of the crucified Christ's saving power. Power is immediately obvious, because of the hymn's strong baptismal focus in its initial lyrics:

> On my heart imprint Your image,
> Blessed Jesus, King of grace,
> That life's riches, care, and pleasures
> Never may Your work erase;
> Let the clear inscription be:
> Jesus, crucified for me,
> Is my life, my hope's foundation,
> And my glory and salvation!

Every time children sing these lyrics they are reminded of their life-giving Holy Baptism into Christ, and they can receive the sign of the cross both upon their foreheads and their hearts. Sin, death, and the devil take flight whenever this hymn is sung. This gives children everlasting peace and joy in an everlasting means for confessing their faith.

Confessing our Christian faith through our hymnody is not a new idea. For Johann Sebastian Bach, pious Lutheran and unsurpassed composer, confession of faith and glorification of God provided beautiful contributions to Lutheran hymnody. In the Lenten hymn "O Sacred Head, Now Wounded," Bach composes a setting that solemnly portrays Christ's crucifixion. He then beautifully conveys the grateful sinner's earnest plea for steadfast faith until death. This hymn captivates children of all generations because Bach gives it a rhythmic "living pulse,"[136] making the music as timeless as the Gospel message itself. Poignant confessions of faith in Lenten hymns like this one teach children to sing reverently with thankfulness and praise. Together with the communion of saints, we respond to God, and we sing unto Him a new song (Psalm 33:3).

Lutheran hymnody teaches children music with integrity. As new creations in Christ, children are newly programmed with hymns in very human and spiritual ways to receive the joyous new song of

---

[135] Brondos, Joel A., comp. *No Greater Treasure: Foundational Readings in Luther and Melanchthon on Education*. N.p.: Lulu, n.d., 142.

[136] Smith, Jane Stuart, and Betty Carlson. *The Gift of Music: Great Composers and Their Influence*. 3rd ed. Wheaton, Illinois: Crossway Books, 1995. 35.

Easter. The risen Savior is "my life, my hope's foundation, and my glory and salvation!"[137] From the start of the Church Year to its end and back again, we give our children excellence in "input" when we teach them to sing our Lutheran hymns.

---

[137] *Lutheran Service Book*. 422.

OUR HERITAGE: CHRISTIAN EDUCATION

While I am careful to keep the priority order of theological first and educational second, I see "classical Lutheran education" as a natural and logical expression of good theology and good educational theory and practice wrapped into one. A family does well to focus primarily on the principles for the spiritual upbringing of their children as they homeschool, and secondarily on the type of education they choose. However, I truly believe that the natural next step for those seeking an education that supports their children spiritually leads to classical education. This may occur in steps. It took several years of homeschooling for me to realize what classical education was and that it really was the most natural educational model in support of the faith I was so eager to pass on to my children. — Susan Knowles, homeschooling mother

What Is Christian Education?

While the liberal arts tradition may be rejected in neighborhood schools, home educators become uniquely poised to recover this great tradition within their own homes. Cheryl Swope offers these thoughts on historic Christian education.

What Is Christian Education?

Cheryl Swope

Historic Christian education is the tradition of the liberal arts and sciences designed both to *inform* and *transform* a student by inclining him toward truth, goodness, and beauty in the context of the Christian faith. St. Augustine serves as our forerunner in preserving the liberal arts in a Christian framework.

Begun in ancient times, formalized in the medieval period, broadened during the Reformation, and battled but preserved throughout the ages, "classical Christian education" seeks to cultivate wise, eloquent, self-examined human beings who pursue truth and live their lives in noble service to others, fully forgiven in Christ.

In his foreword to *Lutheran Education: From Wittenberg to the Future*, Dr. Gene Edward Veith writes, "The Lutheran education tradition … consists of a liberal arts education — a broad, humane curriculum, rich in the classics, and open to truth even from non-Christian sources — combined with Christian catechesis."[138] The liberal arts cultivate the student's mind and character with academic rigor, formative content, and tools for learning; Christian catechesis instructs in matters of the soul through the Holy Scriptures, historic confessions, liturgy, and hymnody. Historic or classical Christian education is taught with the Great Books, music, art, and ideas of Western civilization. The Seven Liberal Arts and the Small Catechism's Six Chief Parts serve to equip a child for dual citizenship in both the earthly realm and the heavenly kingdom.

What Are the Liberal Arts?

The Seven Liberal Arts include the three arts of language (Trivium) and the four arts of mathematics (Quadrivium). "Liberal" derives from the Latin word for "free," as these arts were designed so free men could think about great ideas. In contrast, the "servile" arts ("hands-on," "practical daily living skills") prepare solely for menial labor. The liberal arts enable an individual to live, to study, to think, and to serve others in any vocation. These liberal arts prepare for the liberal sciences: moral, natural, and theological. All incline the student toward truth, goodness, and beauty.

---

[138] Korcok, Thomas. *Lutheran Education: From Wittenberg to the Future.* St. Louis: Concordia Publishing House, 2011.

The Three Arts of Language (Trivium)

Grammar — all that is foundational in language

Grammar includes learning letters, reading, and spelling; beautiful penmanship, crafting sentences and paragraphs; developing a rich vocabulary. Grammar is taught initially by imitation — copying excellent writing of others, reading and hearing good literature — and especially through the study of Latin. The disciplined study of the ordered Latin grammar enhances the knowledge of the student's own native grammar and vocabulary, strengthening the student's mind, and offering access to a great literary heritage. For thousands of years, Greek has also assisted in teaching the arts of language and provides the foundation for reading classic literary works.

Dialectic — analysis of language

Analytical thinking, logic, and argumentation comprise Dialectic. The student of Dialectic learns to identify false statements and illogical premises, whether in his own thinking or in the assertions of others. Logic helps to organize a student's mind and prepare a student for public discourse. Informal logic is taught through simple cause and effect with consequences and moral lessons, such as those found in Aesop's Fables. Formal logic is taught as the student's mind matures.

Rhetoric — eloquence, beauty, and persuasion with language

Rhetoric enables the student to write and speak with eloquence. Ancient Roman orator Quintilian urges the use of excellent speech even with very young children (*Institutio Oratoria*, Book One). When parents and teachers read poetry aloud, they bring beautiful examples of language to their children. Early skills and exercises taught in Grammar and Dialectic provide the foundational and analytical elements of language. Formal rhetoric enhances language for excellence, beauty of expression, and persuasion.

The Four Arts of Mathematics (Quadrivium)

The Quadrivium cultivates in the student an appreciation for and wonder in the patterns, order, and beauty of the world in which he lives. Through the Quadrivium, as with the Trivium, the teacher's purpose is to incline the child toward that which is significantly true, good, and beautiful. This approach to the Mathematical Arts contrasts sharply with starkly utilitarian, economic questions, such as, *If I will never use this in my daily life, why learn it? If I will not need this to "get a job," why study this?*

As with all liberal education, the Quadrivium teaches foundational content with a formative impact on the student himself. The Mathematical Arts — far more than isolated bits of knowledge for economic gain — command a strong presence in the classical curriculum. These arts can be understood as follows:

Discrete quantity or number
  Arithmetic — theory of number
  Music Theory — application of the theory of number

Continuous quantity
  Geometry — theory of space
  Astronomy — application of the theory of space[139]

What Is Catechesis?

In ancient times it was called in Greek catechism (i.e., instruction for children). It teaches what every Christian must know. Therefore, we must have the young learn well and fluently the parts of the catechism or instruction for children, diligently exercising themselves in them, and keep them busy with these parts.[140] — Martin Luther

As referenced in an earlier narrative, Martin Luther's Small Catechism divides the teaching of the historic Christian faith into these Six Chief Parts: Ten Commandments, Apostles' Creed, Lord's Prayer, Sacrament of Holy Baptism, Confession, Sacrament of the Altar.

Comfort in the Lutheran Doctrine of Vocation

Parents and educators can find the task of teaching overwhelming. *How can I do all of this?* With classical education's emphasis on academic rigor and high levels of structure, teachers may grow weary; however, when we remember the important "why" of classical Lutheran education, the daily "how" can become less daunting as we find a growing number of excellent resources to support us in our task. See Appendix D for recommended publishers and curricula.

---

[139] Sister Miriam Joseph. *The Trivium: The Liberal Arts of Logic, Grammar, and Rhetoric.* Philadelphia: Paul Dry Books, 2002. 3.

[140] Luther, Martin. *The Large Catechism of Martin Luther.* Radford, Virginia: Wilder Publications, 2008. 9.

As parents and teachers, we can take heart and remember that God Himself works through us, in spite of our weaknesses, to accomplish His good purposes in our children.

> God has chosen to work through human beings, who, in their different capacities and according to their different talents, serve each other. ... The ability to read God's Word is an inexpressibly precious blessing, but reading is an ability that did not spring fully formed in our young minds. It required the vocation of teachers. ... By virtue of our creation, our purpose in life is to do good works, which God Himself "prepared" for us to do. We are "God's workmanship," which means that God is at work in us to do the works He intends.[141]

Summary: Christian Education

The liberal arts tradition cultivates wisdom, eloquence, and virtue for earthly citizenship; Christian catechesis teaches that only the Holy Spirit grants faith in Christ Jesus, and in Him alone is righteousness for heavenly citizenship. Classical Christian education combines the liberal arts with Christian catechesis to cultivate the formative benefits of the liberal arts, while nurturing the child in the historic Christian faith. Christian virtue includes humility, as the child who studies Latin or Greek is not to think of himself more highly than the child who does not have such privileges; instead, he may thank His heavenly Father for a strong education given from God's own divine fatherly goodness and mercy. All learning is subservient to the Holy Scriptures.

> [T]each them, first of all, the Ten Commandments, the Creed, the Lord's Prayer, etc., always presenting the same words of the text, so that those who learn can repeat them after you, and retain them in the memory.[142] Luther exhorted: Above all, the foremost reading for everybody, both in the universities and in the schools, should be Holy Scripture — and for the younger boys, the Gospels. [143]

Classical Christian education seeks to develop in students self-knowledge, tools for learning, the ability to contemplate great

---

[141] Veith, Gene Edward. *God At Work: Your Christian Vocation in All of Life.* Wheaton: Crossway, 2002. 14, 38.

[142] Luther, Martin, *Luther's Small Catechism, with Explanation.* St. Louis: Concordia Publishing House, 2005. Preface.

[143] *Luther's Works.* Treatise of 1520 "To the Christian Nobility." Vol. 44, 205.

art, music, literature, and ideas; and an understanding of the world in which he lives — all for the love and service of others. Above all, Christian education inclines a child toward truth, goodness, and beauty, fulfilled fully and eternally in the person and work of Jesus Christ for us.

Building Character Through Literature: A Father's Perspective

A story is a special thing.
The ones that I have read,
They do not stay inside the books.
They live inside my head.[144]
– Marchette Chute

Rachel Whiting's husband Todd shares candid thoughts in this narrative on the power of reading books together in the home.

Building Character Through Literature
Todd Whiting

The Story Takes Hold

As a kid, I did not like to read. In fact, truth be told, I hated reading. I only read books when forced. I was a fidgety, active child, unwilling to sit still long enough to focus my attention on words written on a page. So in my childhood and youth I missed out on reading. Even when I was read to, usually I was not listening. Yet, unbeknownst to me, a seed for the love of reading and stories was sown within me when I was in fifth grade. This seed would not sprout and bear fruit until many years later, but it was buried deeply at this time.

My fifth-grade classmates and rowdy, rough group of boys in the '80s. Playing army in the woods and down by the creek was a regular pastime. While in class I tended to just stare out the window, daydreaming of outdoor adventures to my heart's delight. Yet, during reading time, the eyes of my mind and heart were strangely captivated by one book my teacher read aloud. My mind became fixed on accompanying a boy named Billy. I began to share in his pains and triumphs.

---

[144] Szekeres, Cyndy. *A Small Child's Book of Cozy Poems.* New York: Scholastic, 1999. 25.

What made the book *Where the Red Fern Grows*, by Wilson Rawls, so special to me was not any one specific character or event in the book per se; rather it was that we were all there, our whole class, together in this faraway place in the mountains in Oklahoma. Mimicking scenes became the highlight of recess. Incidents from the book replayed in my mind as I laid my head down to sleep.

The years passed, and it was not until I was well into my teenage years that I began to see the value of reading and to understand the transformative power of stories. Perhaps the hyperactive energy of my youth was beginning to wane and I could sit still. Perhaps the carefree child was being left behind, and as I saw the concerns of adulthood upon the horizon, an escape into a book held more appeal than reality. Whatever the circumstance, the time was right for the planted seed to grow.

I began to read and read voraciously, as if making up for lost time. One of the first books I read was Saint Augustine's *Confessions*. Augustine interpreted a child's chanting as a divine message to him, but for me the mantra seemed to apply to everything: "Take it and read, take it and read."[145] I read widely in fiction and in theology.

Today, as a father, I am determined to impart my great love of reading and stories to my children. For many years, I have been in the habit of reading aloud to my children in the evenings. A few years ago, I read *Where the Red Fern Grows* to them. While my two younger children were already asleep in their beds for the night, I read this story to my two older children. I read the book aloud in its entirety … almost.

The evening we were very near to finishing *Where the Red Fern Grows*, we knew clearly in our minds what had happened the previous night. We were enjoying being re-submerged into the story, as I read aloud to my wife and two older children. We felt the suspense in the air as we anticipated a turning point in the book. But suddenly I received a message from work and was sent off into the "real world" to dig into an issue that needed my immediate attention. Well, the kids would not be interrupted, so my wife continued where I had stopped and read aloud to them. While I sat working one room away, I heard my wife's voice become choked as she strained to get her words out. Then I peeked into the room and saw the three of them sitting together on the couch, all of them weeping.

While I could see them crying, I knew for sure that they could not see me. In fact, from their perspective, I was not anywhere to be found.

---

[145] Augustine. *Confessions.* Harmondsworth, Middlesex, England: Penguin Books, 1961. 177.

I was not there with them in their pain, to feel this deep sadness. While I missed experiencing this moment with them, I watched and found again what I had learned in fifth grade: Reading aloud is an enriching, shared experience that binds the reader and the listeners together. My family shared in Billy's pain as he lost Old Dan and then Little Ann. My family even received a foretaste of the pain that they will experience one day when our own family dog will die.

Three Contexts for Reading

There are three general contexts for reading. We can read a book silently on our own, and the impression of the story remains private to us. We can read a book on our own and then come together with others who have also read the same book, and we can discuss the story with one another. Lastly, we can read a book aloud with a group of people and experience the story together during the actual reading of the book.

In silent reading, one takes a journey to a faraway land through time and space to enter a book alone. If a part is confusing, no one is there to offer an interpretation. No one prevents private indulgences in error of understanding. No one assists with discussion of themes or to share as a companion in the emotions of a devastating tragedy. Unless one can articulate the story with a certain level of thoroughness and depth, the experience remains personal and private.

Being a part of a book club can make reading more of a shared experience. Everyone reads the same book and then gathers together to discuss what was read. Your companions hear the same story and travel to the same place. You have friends to discuss the book's characters, plot, and themes.

A group of guys from my church formed such a group. We enjoyed getting together in the evenings as we gathered in a circle around an outdoor fire. With headlamps and flashlights we compared notes and read excerpts from the books we were reading together. One of the books we read was the *Iliad*. Many of us, including me, had not read it before, but when it was complete, we all agreed that the book embodied something that was missing in our formative years. After taking the journey into battle and being there on the battlefield as Homer described it, we all sensed an increased awareness of how our own culture viewed manhood. In our group discussions we contemplated what type of men we should be to our sons.

Often my son will read a book and come to me afterward saying, "Dad, you've got to read this book! If you can't read it on your own, can you read it aloud to everyone in the evening?" My son wants his experience in what he read to become part of my experience, so we can relate together about places we have both gone and people we have both met. I do my best to read what he requests of me, whether aloud or privately. Recently I read *Hittite Warrior*, by Joanne Williamson, at my son's request. When I was finished, we talked about the story.

The experience of individually reading the same book as others and coming together to discuss it is beneficial in connecting with a book and other readers, but reading aloud to a group can be even more significant and bonding. Listeners enter the book hand in hand, all at the same time. Together you explore the author's characters and imagination. Together you are transported to another world. Reading aloud together is a profoundly powerful shared experience.

Leading My Children in Shared Experiences

Like a family hike in the woods or a family drive together on a road trip, being together on a journey is a shared adventure. Whatever comes your way during this time together, you are not alone. Shared experiences strengthen the family as a unit. In *Books That Build Character*, William Kilpatrick points out:

> Just as good stories help to create an emotional bond to goodness, family reading strengthens the family bond. Shared reading draws families together. It provides mutual delight and builds emotional bridges. It establishes intimacy between parent and child in a way that few other activities can match.[146]

When I read aloud to my children, I become their leader as I take them on an adventure. I guide them through the story as we share in the joys, pains, trials, and struggles of the narrative. The nature of reading aloud gives a parent the opportunity to help children process the experiences in a book. When Dr. James Taylor gave a lecture on the "Transforming Power of Stories," he explained how an experience happens too quickly and is difficult to organize in one's mind, but stories suspend

---

[146] Kilpatrick, William, and Gregory Wolfe. *Books That Build Character: A Guide to Teaching Your Child Moral Values Through Stories*. New York: Simon and Schuster, 1994. 27.

things, putting a frame around an experience and giving it a form.[147]

As a story is painted on the canvas of my children's minds, I can pause my reading and give all of us a chance to stand back and look at the painting as a whole. Often when reading a story aloud, I come across something that causes me to pause and look up. I have time to reflect with my children. We may stop reading and discuss a storyline or sort out a section we may not have understood. We can go back and reread and relive the story, at our own pace. While reading as a family, often one of my children will say, "What does that mean?" "Do you know what that reminds me of?" or "Can you believe that so-and-so did that?" The questions come with more frequency depending on the story. I can stop to answer their questions. Sometimes we stop just to revel in absurdity, as we laugh together while reading books like *Mr. Popper's Penguins* or the original *Doctor Dolittle* series.

Stories Read Aloud Shape Character

All stories, whether fictional or nonfictional, can affect the listener. The stories I read aloud to my children seem to make an impression upon their imagination and form their character with more precision than the reading they do on their own. Reading aloud can have a lasting impact. As our children immerse themselves in stories and characters, their minds are given a moral storehouse to pull from for real-life experiences.

Keeping the Imagination Alive

Children seem to have an easier time entering an author's world than adults do. The reality of their world and the world in the story may even become mixed up in the mind of a child. Once when my son was two-and-a-half years old, my wife randomly asked him what he was thinking. He replied, "Pooh and Caleb. If Pooh comes to my house, I'll eat his honey." Pooh Bear seemed as real to him as his little playmate Caleb. When my son was four, he asked, "If I go to England, will Narnia be there?" As children grow, the lines of reality become more clear. But as they grow, we want the ability to be immersed in the "realness" of a story to remain intact.

I learned early with my children that over-analyzing a story or over-moralizing can actually have the opposite of the desired effect. Taylor

---

[147] Taylor, James. "Transforming Power of Stories." CiRCE conference, Charlotte, North Carolina, 2002.

advises caution with discussion questions that make a story seem like a math problem; they can be deadly to the understanding of a story.[148] Kilpatrick explains how "children are motivated far more by what attracts the imagination than by what appeals to reason.... [T]heir behavior is shaped to a large extent by the dramas that play in the theaters of their minds."[149] We want to enable the magic of a story to impress itself on our children, while gently guiding them on the moral lessons to be learned, without turning the story into a clearly defined teaching lesson. In the book *Tending the Heart of Virtue*, Vigen Guroian states:

> Mere instruction in morality is not sufficient to nurture the virtues. It might even backfire, especially when the presentation is heavily exhortative and the pupil's will is coerced. Instead, a compelling vision of the goodness of goodness itself needs to be presented in a way that is attractive and stirs the imagination. A good moral education addresses both the cognitive and affective dimensions of human nature. Stories are an irreplaceable medium for this kind of moral education — that is, the education of character.[150]

Moral lessons are best left buried in a story for a child to extract, through very minimal coaxing if necessary. The moral lessons in bravery, sacrifice, and courage that my book club unearthed from the *Iliad* would never have had the same effect on me if they were extracted and presented alone in a lecture on manhood. They had to exist in the story, in the blood, in the dirt, and in the pain. As Flannery O'Connor said, "A story is a way to say something that can't be said any other way.... You tell a story because a statement would be inadequate."[151]

Empathetic Reading

As my children listen to a story, they are essentially climbing into the mind of the author. They begin to wear the author's characters like clothing. They embrace certain characters and despise others. As my children hear the feelings and thoughts of literary figures, they relate with them experientially. Dr. Gene Edward Veith describes this in the outset of *Reading Between the Lines*, his wonderful book on reading

---

[148] Ibid.

[149] Kilpatrick, *Books That Build Character*, 21.

[150] Guroian, Vigen. *Tending the Heart of Virtue: How Classic Stories Awaken a Child's Moral Imagination.* New York: Oxford University Press, 1998. 20.

[151] Ibid., 17.

literature:

> The ability to imagine what it would be like to experience
> what someone else is experiencing, to project ourselves into
> someone else's point of view, can be crucial to moral sensi-
> tivity. When we read a novel, we are ushered into the point of
> view of various characters and are gladdened by their victo-
> ries and saddened by their tragedies. Reading provides mental
> training for empathizing with real people.[152]

We could sit our children down and talk about the characteristics
of a good friend in a list fashion, or instead we can read them a story
that will capture their imaginations, affecting both mind and heart.
In *Charlotte's Web*, by E. B. White, and *The Wind in the Willows*, by
Kenneth Grahame, friendship and sacrifice are painted with bright,
beautiful colors that remain in the mind even after the book is closed.
When my daughter served me dessert the other night, she said, "I am
just like Mary and Laura, Dad. Do you remember how they always
chose the best and biggest portion to give their father?" She had
picked up on the admirable trait of preferring others before yourself
from Laura Ingalls Wilder's *Little House on the Prairie* series.

Reading can be vicariously instructive, as characters reveal various
points of view, disclose good or bad decisions, and exhibit admirable
or dishonorable characteristics. While sitting in his living room, a child
can experience the good, the bad, and the ugly. When my children
feel the pain and triumphs of a story, their own character is affected,
as if they had personally and actually lived through the drama in a
story. They are given a mental exercise that carries over into real life.
When my son takes his dreaded medicine, we chant, "Fight the White
Witch," a metaphor for him to summon the courage to vanquish the
evil-tasting drink. When he takes the first swig, we cheer. Swallow after
swallow, he conquers the foe for his own good. As Kilpatrick explains,
"The dramatic nature of stories enables us to 'rehearse' moral decisions,
strengthening our solidarity with the good."[153]

Play: Vicarious Escapade

Children, who are already in the process of figuring out who they
are, easily "try on" characters for size. Their impressionable natures

---

[152] Veith, Gene Edward. *Reading Between the Lines: A Christian Guide to Literature.* Wheaton: Crossway Books, 1990. 31.

[153] Kilpatrick, *Books That Build Character,* 24.

enable them to personify characters in their creative role-playing. As my children head out the door to play, I enjoy asking, "Who are you?" The expression on their faces seem to say, "Why are you asking me that question? Isn't it obvious by looking at me?" My son replies that he is Reepicheep, Prince Caspian, Eomer, or Robin Hood. My daughter might say that she is Lucy or Lady Galadriel. My children experiment with characters, relate to how it feels to be them, and practice how the characters dealt with adversity. C. S. Lewis wrote:

> But in reading great literature I become a thousand men and yet remain myself. Like the night sky in the Greek poem, I see with myriad eyes, but it is still I who see. Here, as in worship, in love, in moral action, and in knowing, I transcend myself; and am never more myself than when I do.[154]

Moral Imagination

I love to watch my son as I run our collie/Aussie shepherd mix around the perimeter of our property. My son, usually disguised as a literary character, often walks in a dignified manner with his head held high. With a look of determination in his eye and a sword tucked into his belt, he sways with a wide steady gait. He removes his sword, taking up a stance to fight. His sword swings madly at the thin air as he screams out a guttural sound.

That is what I see. In my son's mind, much more takes place. With an imagination strengthened by stories, he swings his sword to fight the hideous Orcs. He battles the hatred of Saruman. He attempts to save Middle-earth. As an onlooker, I continue running with our dog, but I become more alert; if "Aragorn" mistakes me for an Orc, I am doomed. I smile, because my son is doing more than playing; he is practicing courage in the face of evil.

Other times, he wears an oversized vest with cut-off pants and a satchel around his neck. He walks wearily, as if he does not know how much longer he can carry on. He is Frodo and the ring he bears is growing heavier and heavier to carry. He is rehearsing perseverance in faithfully fulfilling his calling despite feelings which war against the task before him.

One afternoon I watched my son grip his staff with a long beard blowing in the wind. He wore a bathrobe, never minding the 95-degree heat, because he was the wizard Gandalf. My son stepped slowly, as if contemplating how to be wise.

---

[154] Ibid., 40.

The literary works of J. R. R. Tolkien and others empower my children's moral imagination. Kilpatrick explains the power of narrative: "The story gives him a chance to live along with the characters, to keep company with them, and, in doing so, to experience what they experience and learn what they learn."[155] Through a character, my children act out what they have vicariously experienced during our family times of reading aloud.

Literature and Character

Whether simple or profound, good stories impact us. When my son was small, I read the *Little Bear* series, by E. H. Minarik and M. Sendak, to him. I asked him why he liked hearing the stories over and over again; he said, "Because Little Bear loves Father Bear."

Not all stories come from published authors. My son enjoyed my own impromptu "Mouse in the Shirt" bedtime stories. I shone a small flashlight beneath my shirt and pretended that the light was a tiny storytelling mouse. The mouse told stories to my son and daughter. The mouse's make-believe characters, Jim and James, wrestled with the consequences of their bad decisions. I remember my children looking up from their beds, with the wheels of their minds turning. Questions about the stories revealed that, in their imaginations, the mouse-story characters had become far from fictional.

Even as adults, when we read, we encounter characters that we relate to, aspire to, dislike, and even loathe. We see whom we want to emulate, like Faramir from *The Lord of the Rings*, and whom we would want to be the opposite, like Fyodor Pavlovich Karamazov from *The Brothers Karamazov*. We can recognize vice and virtue more quickly in real life when we have witnessed these in literary figures. I have learned to allow my children to attach themselves to their favorite characters, even if I find it hard to relate to why a connection was made. After reading through the majority of *The Lord of the Rings* trilogy, my son surprised me by announcing that his favorite character was the simple brave companion of Frodo Baggins, his gardener, Samwise Gamgee.

Meeting characters in a story can be enlightening. Sometimes characters reveal things about ourselves that we did not know, even characteristics that we are ashamed of. My children related to *Pinocchio*, by Carlo Collodi, when my wife read the unabridged version aloud to them. Pinocchio laments the fact that he is so prone

---

[155] Ibid., 30.

to disobey. Though he tries and tries to be good, he utterly fails every test he is given. His selfish desires rule over him. Pinocchio continually places the fault for his errors on others, and he lies because he finds it so much easier than telling the truth. In self-revelation, my son said to my wife soberly, "Mom, that sounds just like me." Then Pinocchio finds redemption from his wretchedness in a mysterious transformation in ocean water and in being forgiven of his misdeeds. The wooden puppet, made in the image of a boy, becomes a loving flesh-and-blood boy at the end of the story and is united with his maker, his father, whom he now loves selflessly.[156] Similarly, children find hope in the redemptive story of Narnia's Edmund, as he goes from being a traitor to a hero due to Aslan's sacrifice of himself.

Getting Started on Reading Aloud

If your family is more accustomed to watching images on a screen than creating them in the chambers of their minds, the adjustment to listening to stories read aloud requires retraining. This can take some time. Yet the effect is worth the work. Plopping our children down in front of a screen will not reap the same rewards as having them wrestle with characters and stories that penetrate their minds. Dr. Veith advises, "Turning off the television and picking up a book is a good beginning."[157]

If you are not practiced in reading aloud, it can be a bit rough at first. You may find reading aloud awkward. Even the resonance of your own voice may sound unfamiliar. Your speech may be choppy, and your listeners may show frustration as you struggle out of your unpracticed monotone "robot" mode. You also may be distracted and find your mind prone to wandering, especially as you begin to get into a story. Just keep reading. Give yourself a comfortable amount of time to read aloud. Begin with short sessions and gradually increase to one hour, as your family becomes more acquainted with the rewarding experience of listening together.

It may feel a chore to begin a new book after completing one, but it is also exciting. It takes time to get into a new story, especially if the setting changes dramatically. For example, it is an adjustment to transition from the Great American Plains to the land of Middle-earth. If, after an ample section of the beginning of a new book is read and the

---

[156] Guroian, *Tending the Heart of Virtue*, 40-61.

[157] Veith, *Reading Between the Lines*, 27.

children are not getting lost in the story, this is a sign to put the book aside to possibly try to read it again at a later time. Conversely, if when you stop your reading for the evening, you hear groans of complaint, this is a good sign that the book you all have embarked upon is a worthwhile journey. It can be culture-shocking to enter back into one's own life after escaping into a story.

If you decide to begin reading aloud, what will you read? Here are some authors that we have enjoyed as a family: C. S. Lewis, J. R. R. Tolkien, George MacDonald, Hans Christian Andersen, Laura Ingalls Wilder, A. A. Milne, E. Nesbit, E. B. White, the d'Aulaires, L. M. Montgomery, … and the list could go on. (See Appendix E for recommended children's literature.)

God Speaks Aloud: The Best Book of All

Sometimes a child's baby book will include a page entitled, "A Letter from My Parents." In my son's baby book, there is such a page. When my son was a few months away from turning two years old, my wife and I wrote on that page, "We desire to develop your imagination through hearing stories. We want you to love books and to love most of all God's Book. We want you to love stories, to one day love most of all the greatest story ever told — God's sending of His Son."

The most profound read-aloud that our children can experience is the Word of God being read aloud at home and during the Divine Service of Word and Sacrament. In the Divine Service, God is serving us with His Word and Sacraments. During the Old Testament Reading, we remember what Paul teaches in the New Testament: "Now these things happened to them as an example, but they were written down for our instruction, on whom the end of the ages has come" (1 Corinthians 10:11). And: "For whatever was written in former days was written for our instruction, that through endurance and through the encouragement of the Scriptures we might have hope" (Romans 15:4). During all the readings, the Holy Spirit works with transformative power as our faith is strengthened and our minds are renewed (Romans 12:2). Through the power of Christ's words of forgiveness, we are absolved of our sin. Through the Word combined with earthly elements, we taste and see that the Lord is good as we feast on His Body and Blood.

As Christians we all gather as one body — the rich, the poor, the weak, the strong, the young, the old — all sinners with ears divinely opened to hear the words of life. In the story of Christ's redemption, we have all become real characters, as through Christ's very real incarnation, life, death, and resurrection, He has placed us within Himself, within His own story of our redemption. In this true story, we are affected as new life and continual grace are bestowed. Collectively, as Christ's bride, we the church are united in this shared experience. And it is not only we who dwell on earth who join together in the Divine Service, for angels, archangels, and all the company of heaven are present as well.

The Lost Art of Memorization

Rachel Whiting explores the impressive impact of memorization on a child's academic instruction, character development, and childhood enjoyment:

The Lost Art of Memorization
Rachel Whiting

Years ago when my husband read aloud Laura Ingalls Wilder's *Little House on the Prairie* books in the evenings, I was impressed at the amount of content Mary and Laura had memorized. They were able to recite memorized pieces aloud for the benefit of themselves, their classmates, and their family. The family viewed recitations as a valued and edifying activity. Enjoyable family time in the Ingalls home was spent with a roaring fire, music, and recitations of memory work. In our modern world, especially in some educational circles, memorization has become a lost art of ill repute.

Of course, Laura Ingalls Wilder lived at a time when information was scarce, and books were not readily accessible. By contrast, one might think, "Why memorize anything at all, with the World Wide Web at our fingertips? If we cannot remember something, we type a phrase of it into Google!" But do such quick, pragmatic searches for information affect our children in the same deep, lasting, and intimate ways as memorized words?

Why Memorize?

Memorization and recitation enable a child to know a selection deep within them. Over time, memorized works may even affect one's personality and character. "Memorization is the complete form of internalization, and the best way to intimately know something is to know it so well you can communicate it effectively, fluently, even artistically to another."[158]

It is enriching in more ways than one to have a selection memorized. Words flow like the sound of music when poetry is on one's tongue. The practice in enunciating rhythmic and rhyming language builds confidence that carries over into general communication skills and other disciplines. I have found the following insight true for my own children:

> Frequently, the sense of accomplishment that accompanies the memorization of poetry builds linguistic and even academic confidence and spills over into other areas. Like performing a piece of music, memorization and artistic recitation of poetry requires a certain level of perfection which only conscientious effort and consistency can bring. If a student memorizes a long poem and can recite it flawlessly, he will believe that he can learn anything, be it math processes or facts from history. "By heart" learning not only strengthens the mind, it also strengthens the heart and spirit of the child.[159]

How to Memorize and Recite

In the desire to equip and nurture my children's minds, memory work is a regular part of our studies. My children memorize all sorts of information: math facts, English grammar definitions and lists, Latin vocabulary, conjugations and declensions, states, capitals, and countries, lists of presidents, Greek gods, biblical books, apostles, tribes, and kings. This type of information is normally memorized within the context of the subject it pertains to when we come across it in our studies. In memorizing poetic and scriptural works, we use a system called Memory Work Binder, modifying it slightly to make it work for our family.[160] This system has given us a valuable tool to systematically review memorized material while we learn new material. We use tabs in a three-ring binder that guide us. A new piece to memorize is placed under the *daily* tab, while memorized works are practiced under *weekly* and *monthly* tabs to promote mastery and retention of material.

The way we approach memory work is very simple: we listen,

---

[158] Pudewa, Andrew. *Linguistic Development Through Poetry Memorization*. Locust Grove, Oklahoma: Institute for Excellence in Writing, 2005. 5.

[159] Ibid., 3.

[160] Campbell, Andrew A. *Living Memory*, 12-13.

speak, read, and write the piece we are working on memorizing.[161] Often I write a selection on a white board or chalkboard. I erase words and phrases and see if they can recall the words in the missing spots. We repeat the line being worked on till it is mastered and then move on to the next. Copying by hand also helps cement a piece in their minds. My kids enjoy the practice of speaking aloud a selection, figuring out where to put emphasis, and learning to pause at punctuation.

Hiding God's Word in Our Hearts

Memory work is personal and practical, as once a piece is memorized, a child carries it with him wherever he goes.[162] As Christians we know the immense value of having Scripture internalized, as we aspire to say with the psalmist, "I have stored up your word in my heart, that I might not sin against you" (Psalm 119:10). When my son was nervous to go to his first soccer practice of the season, he keep repeating in the car on the way there, "When I am afraid, I put my trust in you" from Psalm 56:3-4. There is great comfort in memorizing Scripture.[163]

Memorizing and reciting creeds, canticles, hymns, and prayers encourages fuller participation in the liturgy during family prayer at home and in the Divine Service of Word and Sacrament at church. Internalizing and confessing the Apostles' Creed and Nicene Creed are essential. Although usually spoken corporately, these creeds are a personal expression of "I believe." Memorized canticles, songs taken from Scripture, cause my older children to perk up, as they hear the words they have learned to sing by heart in the Venite, Te Deum, Benedictus, Nunc Dimittis, and Magnificat. It is the same way with hymns they have memorized. Their faces light up when the hymn begins. We see this with memorized prayers, which are helpful in developing the habit of prayer. The prayers found in Luther's Small Catechism give framework for our days. My children have enjoyed learning prayers in both English and Latin.[164]

---

[161] Ibid., 9-10.

[162] Ibid., 8.

[163] Here are some passages that have been a blessing to my children: Exodus 15:1-12; Deuteronomy 5:16; Psalm 23; 34:13; 141:3; 116; 119:11, 105; Proverbs 6:16-19; 12:18; 15:1; 16:21, 24, 32; 17:22; 18:9,10; 25:28; 26:18-19; 27:2; Matthew 5:1-20; 6:19-21, 24; 7:12; Luke 2:8-15; John 3:16; 14:6; Romans 6:3-4; 8:31-39; 1 Corinthians 13:4-8a; Galatians 5:22; Philippians 2:14-15; 4:8; Colossians 3:20; Titus 3:5-7; James 1:19; 1 John 1:8, 9.

[164] My older children have memorized: The Lord's Prayer/Pater Noster, Table Blessing, Doxology/Gloria Patria, Holy, Holy, Holy/The Sanctus and Benedictus. These prayers can be found in *Living Memory: A Classical Memory Work Companion*, by Andrew Campbell, 49-51.

Learning Poetry and Poetic Language

The art of memorizing and reciting poetry offers children varied personal benefits, such as enjoyment, inspiration, self-confidence, articulation, presentation skills, and a sense of accomplishment, just to name a few.[165] Poetic language also influences our children's writing and language skills. Shortly after memorizing Robert Louis Stevenson's poem "The Wind," my seven-year-old daughter began her own poem: "O wind that is howling/O wind are you prowling/Prowling upon me/And over the sea."

Poetry can grow with our children. The poems my younger children have memorized are appropriate to their age. As they grow, the complexity, seriousness, and depth of meaning of memorized poetry can grow as well.

Memorizing whimsical poetry is an engaging way to increase vocabulary:

There Was an Old Person Whose Habits, by Edward Lear

There was an Old Person whose habits,
Induced him to feed upon Rabbits;
When he'd eaten eighteen,
He turned perfectly green,
Upon which he relinquished those habits.[166]

Poetry can help us appreciate the seasons of nature:

Stopping by Woods on a Snowy Evening, by Robert Frost

Whose woods these are I think I know.
His house is in the village, though;
He will not see me stopping here
To watch his woods fill up with snow.[167]

(Three more verses follow, ending in the famous lines, "And miles to go before I sleep./And miles to go before I sleep.")

---

[165] Many poems that my children have learned are from *Linguistic Development Through Poetry Memorization, A Mastery Learning Approach*, by Andrew Pudewa, from the Institute for Excellence in Writing.

[166] Lear, Edward, and Vivien Noakes. *The Complete Verse and Other Nonsense*. New York: Penguin Books, 2002. 165.

[167] Frost, Robert, and Susan Jeffers. *Stopping by Woods on a Snowy Evening*. New York: Dutton, 2001.

Memorizing poetry can help focus on the seasons of the Church Year:

Our God upon a Donkey, by Chad Bird

Our God upon a donkey rides.
His glory in our skin he hides.
Beneath his feet are garments strewn,
And branches from the trees are hewn.
A sweet reverse of Eden's shame,
As unclad Adams laud his name.[168]

Poetic language can inspire creativity. My son enjoys dressing in various costumes. When he is acting like a dwarf, he possesses the words to sing as he traipses on paths in the woods:

The Dwarves' Song, by J. R. R. Tolkien

Far over the misty mountains cold
To dungeons deep and caverns old
We must away ere break of day
To seek the pale enchanted gold.

The dwarves of yore made mighty spells,
While hammers fell like ringing bells
In places deep, where dark things sleep,
In hollow halls beneath the fells.[169]

(There are eight more enchanting verses to this poem.)

Poetry can teach literary devices:

The Eagle, by Alfred Tennyson

He clasps the crag with crooked hands;
Close to the sun in lonely lands,
Ringed with the azure world, he stands.

The wrinkled sea beneath him crawls;
He watches from his mountain walls,
And like a thunderbolt he falls.[170]

---

[168] Bird, Chad. *The Infant Priest: Hymns and Poems*. Chad L. Bird, 2013. 38.

[169] Tolkien, J. R. R. *The Hobbit*, or *There and Back Again*. Boston: Houghton Mifflin, 1997. 14, 15.

[170] Ferris, Helen Josephine. *Favorite Poems: Old and New*. Garden City, N.Y.: Doubleday, 1957. 291.

Memorized selections can also become a gift for someone. What a surprise for their father to hear the children sing "O Come, All Ye Faithful" in Latin:

Adeste fideles,
Laeti triumphantes,
Venite, venite in Bethlehem!
Natum videte,
Regem angelorum.

Venite, adoremus!
Venite, adoremus!
Venite, adoremus Dominum![171]

(My older children memorized the first three of eight verses to sing for him.)

Memorizing a poem one comes across in reading can be a fun way for the book's storyline to remain with a child, such as this one from *The Wind in the Willows*:

The Song of Mr. Toad, by Kenneth Grahame

The world has held great Heroes,
    As history-books have showed;
But never a name to go down in fame
    Compared with that of Toad!

The clever men at Oxford
    Know all that there is to be knowed.
But they none of them knew one half as much
    As intelligent Mr. Toad![172]

(There are three more humorous stanzas to this poem.)

Poetry can provide rhythmic words even during illness:

The Land of Counterpane, by Robert Louis Stevenson

When I was sick and lay a-bed,
I had two pillows at my head,
And all my toys beside me lay

---

[171] *Lingua Angelica Song Book: Christian Latin Reading Course*. Louisville: Memoria Press, 2001. 9.

[172] Grahame, Kenneth. *The Wind in the Willows*. New York: Bantam Books, Inc., 1982. 175.

To keep me happy all the day.
And sometimes for an hour or so
I watched my leaden soldiers go,
With different uniforms and drills,
Among the bed-clothes, through the hills;
And sometimes sent my ships in fleets
All up and down among the sheets;
Or brought my trees and houses out,
And planted cities all about.
I was the giant great and still
That sits upon the pillow-hill,
And sees before him, dale and plain,
The pleasant land of counterpane.[173]

Poetry can even make chores more enjoyable. When my older children start to sing this song while doing their kitchen duties, I laugh and remind them not to do what the song actually says!

Chip the Glasses and Crack the Plates, by J. R. R. Tolkien

Chip the glasses and crack the plates!
    Blunt the knives and bend the forks!
That's what Bilbo Baggins hates—
    Smash the bottles and burn the corks!

Cut the cloth and tread on the fat!
    Pour the milk on the pantry floor!
Leave the bones on the bedroom mat!
    Splash the wine on every door!

Dump the crocks in a boiling bowl;
    Pound them up with a thumping pole;
And when you've finished if any are whole,
    Send them down the hall to roll!

That's what Bilbo Baggins hates!
So, carefully! Carefully with the plates![174]

Poetry has enriched our family by providing inside jokes and the delight of language. The older children call their daddy "Jonathan Bing," if he lounges in his pajamas on a Saturday morning.

---

[173] Stevenson, Robert Louis, and Tasha Tudor. *A Child's Garden of Verses*. Chicago: Rand McNally, 1981. 22.
[174] Tolkien, *The Hobbit*, 12.

Jonathan Bing, by Beatrice Curtis Brown

Poor old Jonathan Bing
Went out in his carriage to visit the King,
But everyone pointed and said, "Look at that!
Jonathan Bing has forgotten his hat!"

Poor old Jonathan Bing
Went home and put on a new hat for the King,
But by the palace the soldier said, "Hi!
You can't see the King; you've forgotten your tie!"

Poor old Jonathan Bing,
He put on a beautiful tie for the King,
But when he arrived, Archbishop said, "Ho!
You can't come to court in pajamas, you know!"

Poor old Jonathan Bing
Went home and addressed a short note to the King:
"If you please will excuse me, I won't come to tea;
For home's the best place for all people like me!"[175]

With the wink of an eye during a child's birthday or special holiday meal, we remind one another not to be a "Jonathan Blake."

After the Party, by William Wise

Jonathan Blake
Ate too much cake,
He isn't himself today;
He's tucked up in bed
With a feverish head,
And he doesn't much care to play.[176]

(Three more stanzas reveal all the different foods he ate, explaining why he is "not at his best today.") Playful activities can also be enriched through poetry:

The Swing, by Robert Louis Stevenson

How do you like to go up in a swing,
    Up in the air so blue?

---

[175] Pudewa, *Linguistic Development through Poetry Memorization*, 26.
[176] Ibid., 23.

Oh, I do think it the pleasantest thing
    Ever a child can do![177]

(There are two more delightful verses to this poem.) Finally, poetry can be useful for utter silliness. When I read this poem to my children, they requested to memorize it.

There Once Was a Puffin, by Florence Page Jaques

Oh, there once was a Puffin
Just the shape of a muffin,
And he lived on an island
In the
      bright
           blue sea!

He ate little fishes,
That were most delicious,
And he had them for supper
And he
      had
         them
            for tea.[178]

(Three more verses go on to describe how lonely the Puffin is as he has no one to play with; then the fish suggest he stop eating them and have them for playmates instead. "So they now play together/In all sorts of weather/And the Puffin eats pancakes/Like you and like me.")

Finally, bath time at the end of the day is more enjoyable with a poetic song!

The Bath Song, by J. R. R. Tolkien

Sing hey! for the bath at close of day
That washes the weary mud away!
A loon is he that will not sing:
O! Water Hot is a noble thing!

---

[177] Stevenson and Tudor, *A Child's Garden of Verses*, 22.

[178] Berquist, Laura M. *The Harp and Laurel Wreath: Poetry and Dictation for the Classical Curriculum*. San Francisco: Ignatius Press, 1999. 26.

O! Sweet is the sound of falling rain,
And the brook that leaps from hill to plain;
But better than rain or rippling streams
Is Water Hot that smokes and steams.[179]

(Two more upbeat stanzas follow.)

The Joy of Recitation

My older children enjoy practicing the art of elocution as they rehearse their memorized works. The children's poetry recitations have been a tremendous blessing to us as parents. When the grandparents visited last, we all enjoyed the time together as the older children took turns reciting their memorized pieces. With poise and confidence, my children spoke as if on a stage instead of standing in our living room. It was a rollicking good time. One may not even detect all the benefits that slip secretly in with the intricacies of beautiful, delightful language patterns. The child receives so much without directly noticing it.

A Lost Art Is Found

During the recitation, my older children shared words that they had wrestled with as they diligently worked to memorize them, but as they spoke, the words flowed freely and sounded like their own. And in fact the words had become their own, because they were memorized and were now a part of them. I was reminded of the days in the *Little House on the Prairie* books and I was thankful that the art of memorization and recitation was no longer lost, for it has found a home in mine.

---

[179] Tolkien, J. R. R. *The Fellowship of the Ring: Being the First Part of The Lord of the Rings.* Boston: Houghton Mifflin, 2002. 100.

The Joys of Latin and Greek

Just as many families discover lost methods of teaching through homeschooling, so homeschoolers discover lost subjects to teach! Recovering the strongest elements of education is more attainable now than ever because of the availability of clear, teachable resources. With "open-and-go" programs such as *Prima Latina, Latina Christiana I, First Form Latin*, and *Elementary Greek*, parents with no formal training in Latin and Greek can now both teach and learn classical languages with their children! Traditionally, Latin is taught first, then Greek.

Homeschooling father in Oklahoma, the Rev. Christian C. Tiews offers his thoughts on teaching Latin and Greek within our Lutheran homeschools.

The Joys of Latin and Greek
The Rev. Christian Tiews

"Why Latin? It's a dead language!" "Learn Spanish instead!" they cry. Well, learning Spanish *is* a fine thing. It opens up your mind to another culture, is useful as America's population becomes increasingly Hispanic, etc. But if Spanish is a good tool like a pocket knife, then Latin (or Classical/Biblical Greek) is like the Swiss Army knife with a *dozen* different tools — that is, classical languages give you an entire toolbox in your pocket.

What are the benefits of learning these ancient and supposedly "dead" languages? The benefits are numerous. First, Latin and Greek teach you how grammar works. This includes English grammar! Latin and Greek lay a foundation for learning and understanding language. Second, they help improve memorization and increase your English vocabulary. Third, and historically understood as the primary benefit, the classical languages uniquely open the door to the history, culture, and writings of antiquity. Latin provides access to the Vulgate, the Latin translation of the Old and New Testaments, while Biblical Greek equips you to read the New Testament in the original language. Both languages school you in logic and provide the gateway to essential classical literature. Finally, Latin and Greek teach mental discipline. These languages even help improve SAT scores. In 2006, Latin students averaged 672, whereas the average for all students was 503 (*www.memoriapress.com/articles/why-study-latin*).

Until only about three generations ago, Latin was standard fare in American high schools, so almost *everybody* learned Latin! Now we have even more resources to teach Latin and Greek. Consider *Latina Christiana* (for gradeschoolers), *Latin in the Christian Trivium* (middle school), and *Wheelock's* (for middle school to high school students). Several months ago I started teaching Biblical Greek to six homeschooled students and three adults, who are all extremely excited to learn how to read the New Testament in its original language. We use *Basics of Biblical Greek*, by Mounce, as our textbook and workbook. If you feel ready to learn both Latin and Greek but must choose only one, begin with Latin.

Let me offer an illustration of why the grammar-first approach is so important for learning languages, and especially Latin and Greek: Grammar could be compared to a large wall-mounted bookcase in a library. First you need to assemble the bookcase (that is, learn the grammar) board by board, so you can fasten it to the wall. Only *then* can you place books in it (i.e., the vocabulary). Without your "grammar bookcase," you will never understand how the various books (vocabularies) interconnect and where to place them. English (or Spanish) grammar is relatively easy and requires less grammar than other languages. However, if we do not learn how English grammar *works*, this becomes an obstacle.

Conversely, the former Latin and/or Greek student might come to realize that not only were the classical languages a strong preparation for understanding language, but they also assist the pastoral vocation. When I studied five years of Classical Greek and nine years of Latin in a humanist *Gymnasium* (prep school) in Germany, I never dreamt that one day I would use those great treasures for the pastoral ministry. Nor did I realize that I would have the privilege of passing those treasures down to those coming after me.

Let us not forget Luther's words: "We will not long preserve the Gospel without the (original) languages. The languages are the sheath in which this Sword of the Spirit is contained.... If through our neglect we let the languages go (which God forbid!), we shall ... lose the Gospel."[180]

Shall we let the classical languages die? I am reminded of a recent comment by my fourteen-year-old son: "Who says Latin and Greek are dead? I use both languages all the time!"

---

[180] Luther, Martin. Vol. 45 of *Luther's Works*. American Edition. Philadelphia: Fortress Press, 1962. 360.

For easy-to-teach resources to explore introductory classical languages, or to delve more deeply into Latin and Greek, see Appendix D, page 244.

The Mathematical Arts

The spirit of genuine mathematics, i.e., its methods, concepts, and structure — in contrast with mindless calculations — constitutes one of the finest expressions of the human spirit. The great areas of mathematics — algebra, number theory ... topology, geometry, trigonometry, etc. — have arisen from man's experience of the world that the infinite, personal, Triune, and Sovereign God has created and currently sustains.[181]
— James Nickel

In some homes, language and literacy seem easier to address than strong, faithful instruction in mathematics, music, and science. Few subjects require more daily diligence, time, and attention than the mathematical arts. Cheryl Swope offers thoughts on remembering the Christian context of the mathematical arts to assist our motivation, our purpose, and our perseverance.

The Mathematical Arts in Christian Home Education
Cheryl Swope

Arithmetic has a very great and elevating effect, compelling the soul to reason about abstract number.... . Arithmetic is a kind of knowledge in which the best natures should be trained, and which must not be given up.
— Plato, Republic, VII

What Is Mathematics?
James Nickel writes, "A good definition of mathematics is that it is an abstract formation of ideas suggested by the patterned structure of God's creation."[182] Far beyond our notions of "math" as the tool whereby we balance our checkbooks or eventually land a job in engineering, the mathematical arts reveal God's handiwork in ways many of us have never considered, learned, or taught.

---

[181] Nickel, James. *Mathematics: Is God Silent?* Rev. 2nd ed. Vallecito, California: Ross House Books, 2001.
[182] Ibid.

In *Mathematics: Is God Silent?* Nickel invites readers to ponder these abstractions, as the wonders of mathematics manifest themselves in daily lessons. Similarly, authors Ravi Jain and Kevin Clark explore these ideas in the Quadrivium sections of the *Liberal Arts Tradition*. For millenia, arithmetic was pursued as one of the arts, not as an isolated or utilitarian skill. Jain and Clark explain, "Deeply understanding the necessary connections and relationships among the numbers would have been an essential element of the liberal art of arithmetic."[183] They note that ancient texts possessed "an air of ... wonder that is today missing from elementary mathematics. It is as if the ancients assumed that numbers are bizarre and glorious and investigated them with the vigor of an explorer looking to discover in them some rare treasure."[184] Furthermore, the mathematical arts intended to lead "from wonder to wisdom."[185]

How Shall We Teach Mathematics?

Beginning with the youngest child, we inculcate a simple "number sense" with an awe of patterns. We cultivate a love of order and a knowledge of shapes, time, and distance. We reflect on geometrical designs in tiles on the floor, the patchwork pieces and colors in Grandma's quilt, and the shimmering patterns of stars in the night sky. We count objects on our tables and flowers in our gardens. We measure, we group and regroup, we mark time. We read counting books. We play simple games with cards, dice, and dominoes. We work puzzles, and we create patterns with colored beads for children to copy. In the grocery store, we measure the weight of bananas, and we ask the child to guess how much they will weigh. We count the eggs in a dozen, and we note the difference between "large" and "small" green peppers. At the kitchen counter, we cut apples in "halves," and potatoes in "quarters," and we follow step-by-step directions to create something whole out of smaller parts. In our conversations, we teach the early language of mathematics.

We begin a formal arithmetic program when an early number sense has been cultivated. A Beka, Rod and Staff, and other programs offer nicely sequenced, step-by-step programs with built-in options for flannelboard instruction and other visual techniques to illustrate lessons. In the early formal years, arithmetic facts must be memorized. Although

---

[183] Jain, Ravi and Clark, Kevin. *Liberal Arts Tradition.* Camp Hill, Pennsylvania: Classical Academic Press, 2013. 53.

[184] Ibid., 54

[185] Ibid., 55

this might appear "boring" to adults, the step-by-step approach of arithmetic will ensure the automaticity of operations necessary for later mathematical competence. Even if students seem to prefer more random, "hands-on," or "flashy" math programs if left to decide for themselves, students will appreciate knowing foundational facts and understanding necessary arithmetic concepts later. *Ray's Arithmetic* is another no-nonsense, straightforward favorite among serious home-schoolers for building mastery in arithmetic. Strong foundations in arithmetic are essential for progression in mathematics.

For this reason, formal math lessons, like Latin and music lessons, should be taught at your child's most attentive time of day. Provide daily arithmetic practice later in the day, and continue to build rapid mental calculations with simple games in the car or in the evenings. Brief but consistent daily lessons with regular periods of practice accomplish far more than lengthy but infrequent math periods. Morever, the mathematical arts uniquely provide practice in daily work habits, diligence, and perseverance.

Math Storybooks

In addition to a formal math curriculum, consider reading story-books designed to bring mathematics "alive." While homeschoolers often consider read-alouds for literary purposes, storybooks can assist greatly with the development and understanding of mathematical vocabulary too! Search online for "counting books" as a place to begin in the early years. Quickly expand the search to include "living math books."

For example, when studying the Middle Ages, *Sir Cumference* and the *Dragon of Pi* reinforce your child's math lessons in enjoyable, memorable ways. Consider reading a page or two from non-fiction math encyclopedias, such as those from Usborne or Dorling Kindersley. You can find biographies of mathematicians and scientists, such as *Along Came Galileo* and others by Jeanne Bendick, written for children. Such books help you introduce your child to mathematical terms, vocabulary, and concepts in a delightful context.

Delight

"To teach, to delight, to move" (*docere, delectare, movere*) — attributed to the era of Quintilian and Cicero, later adopted by Augustine, and now the motto of Memoria Press — can become the timeless inspiration for any excellent teacher. Even as you teach systematically from a formal mathematics program, supplemental resources abound to assist you in cultivating delight. Audio CDs, flashcards, wall charts, numberlines, and math facts tables promote memorization, while nightly games and read-alouds, such as those mentioned above, solidify conceptual understanding, enhance mathematical application, and strengthen mental calculations.

As our children grow, we can continue to encourage "math appreciation." Some Lutheran homeschoolers appreciate Harold Jacobs' engaging and humorous books for teaching algebra, geometry, and an appreciation of mathematics. Consider *Mathematics: A Human Endeavor* or *The Joy of Mathematics* in upper grades. See additional resources for teaching math and science in Appendix D.

The study of arithmetic, music theory, geometry, and astronomy — historically grouped as the Quadrivium or mathematical arts — provide far more than we may have received in our own education, but we can give this to our children. From the early years through adolescence, we can introduce our children to wonder, beauty, and a sense of transcendence just as readily through mathematics as in art or poetry.

The mathematical arts support creative work, leading our students to participate in the "maze of the continuous," an apt description given by calculus co-founder Gottfried Leibniz.[186] Whether or not the student ever becomes an architect, a designer, or an engineer, each student benefits from an increased awe of the Creator and a greater understanding of the created universe. As we teach music theory and the other mathematical arts alongside catechesis, perhaps the Church will benefit from well-trained, competent musicians within the greater context of beautiful liturgical music for the sake of the Gospel.

Shepherd of tender youth,
Guiding in love and truth
      Through devious ways;
Christ, our triumphant king,
We come Your name to sing
And here our children bring
      To join Your praise.[187]

---

[186] Ibid., 56.

[187] *Lutheran Service Book*, 864:1.

Our Unity: Working Together in Home, Church, and School

When parents, pastors, and congregations consider the importance of the Christian education of their children, they may come to different conclusions. Some parents ask their congregation to open a Lutheran school. Other parents choose to homeschool and often find much help and support in their congregation. Even in a congregation with a Lutheran school, you may find homeschooling families. Church day school families and homeschooling families should not see themselves as rivals or threats to one another. I see us in a common cause. — Paul Cain

A Common Cause

Pastor and headmaster at Martin Luther Grammar School, the Rev. Paul Cain shares these thoughts on our common cause as Christian educators:

Given the state of the cultural and societal challenges to Christianity in our country right now, we have far more important things to fight, rather than fighting each other. Lutheran Christian educators would do well to join a common cause with those among our own church body and congregations that desire educated, catechized young people and future adults who are winsome advocates for truth, whether the fact that 2 + 2 does, indeed, equal 4, or for the eternal truths of Holy Scripture.

Rev. Cain shares these excerpts from a sermon he preached on the text Matthew 23:1-12.[188]

Our Unity in Christian Education

As Reformation Day nears on the calendar, my heart and mind turn to reform in the Church. We are Lutheran Christians, spiritual heirs of the sixteenth-century Reformation of the Christian Church. Christians are always in need of repentance. The Church, from a local congregation to a regional group of congregations, a church body or denomination, or Christianity as a whole, is always in need of reform.

Christian education has always been important to Lutheran Christians:

- Lutherans like Johann Sturm, Phillip Melanchthon, and Martin Luther revived classical education in their day, founding a proper education on Christ and His Gospel, but also advocating for education for all, including girls and peasants, and a free public Christian education paid for by the state, especially if the head of state was a Christian prince.

- The Jesuits, formed by the Roman Church as a response to the Reformation, famous yet today for their rigorous quality education institutions, patterned their schools and curricula after Lutheran models.

- We know that the Saxon Lutherans left Germany because of problems with unionism and syncretism, but recent scholarship shows that they were even more concerned with the sad state of German schools than with the problems of the state church. In particular, they were troubled by the fact that what was taught in the state schools contradicted the Christian faith that was taught at home and at church.[189]

- When the Missouri Synod was founded in 1847, there were sixteen original Lutheran congregations and fourteen original Lutheran schools.

- In the history of the Missouri Synod, there were more schools than congregations in our church body from the 1870s through the early 1900s.

- Today, we are blessed with two seminaries, ten universities and colleges, and more than 2,300 early childhood centers and preschools operated by congregations and Christian day schools within the Lutheran Church—Missouri Synod. More than 129,000 children, ranging in age from infant/toddler to five years of age, are involved

---

[188] "Christian Education." Reformation Sunday, Immanuel Lutheran Church, Sheridan, Wyoming. Proper 26A, 30 October 2011.

[189] See *Lutheran Education: From Wittenberg to the Future*, Thomas Korcok, St. Louis: Concordia Publishing House, 2011.

in these early childhood programs. Additionally, our congregations operate 945 elementary schools which serve 107,000 students.[190]

- Martin Luther Grammar School was accredited this summer by the Consortium for Classical Lutheran Education. Other Lutheran schools are becoming accredited through CCLE's accreditation process.

Christian education is important to Lutherans. And it all begins with the Fourth Commandment.

The editors of the *Reader's Edition of the Book of Concord, Concordia: The Lutheran Confessions*, provide a very helpful introduction to the Fourth Commandment in Luther's Large Catechism:

> Commandments four through ten describe relationships with our fellow humans. Here Luther's understanding of "vocation" is apparent. Vocation comes from the Latin *vocare*, meaning "to call." God calls everyone to certain roles, or stations, in life. In this commandment, Luther describes our duty before God to honor father and mother, that is, to respect authority. God instituted all forms of authority as an extension of parental authority, for our good. There are various parental authorities, or "fathers," in our lives, including pastors, teachers, and government officials.

The editor's notes offer further insight into the life of good works to which Christians are called.

> We should not regard 'Church work' as more holy than the other things in life that we routinely do. Rather, all callings and stations in life serve God and are opportunities for us to obey God's commandments and to serve our neighbor. The key observation Luther offers is this: faith is what makes a person holy. Faith alone. Good works serve God by serving other people.[191]

As a congregation that sponsors a Christian school, sometimes we need to state and restate the obvious: parents are given to be the first teachers of their own children. Parents are to have primary authority and choice over the raising of their own children, not the state. Parents are given to feed, clothe, and shelter their children. Parents are to

---

[190] 2014-2015 LCMS school statistics are as follows: Total number of schools (2,111), early childhood centers (1,190), elementary schools (842), high schools (85). Total number of students (156,722), early childhood (61,705), grades K-8 (80,145), grades 9-12 (14,872).

[191] McCain, *Concordia: The Lutheran Confessions*, 370.

educate their children. But the most important education a parent can give is the discipline and instruction of the Lord.

Paul teaches this in Ephesians 6:1-4: "Children, obey your parents in the Lord, for this is right. 'Honor your father and mother' (this is the first commandment with a promise), 'that it may go well with you and that you may live long in the land.' Fathers, do not provoke your children to anger, but bring them up in the discipline and instruction of the Lord."

This is a divine responsibility. Education in this life prepares one for family, work, and leisure. Christian education is a preparation for this life *and* the life to come. As you consider the education of your children or grandchildren, or if you are still thinking about your own education, ask yourself this about any educational opportunity or choice: "Will this school, teacher, or career encourage my faith in Christ, or destroy or discourage my faith in Christ?"

Luther's day had problems much like our own. He says as much in his treatment of the Fourth Commandment:

> Here again the sad plight arises that no one sees or hears this truth. All live on as though God gave us children for our pleasure or amusement and servants so that we could use them like a cow or an ass, only for work. Or they live as though we were only to gratify our lewd behavior with our subjects, ignoring them, as though we have no concern for what they learn or how they live. No one is willing to see that this is the command of the Supreme Majesty, who will most strictly call us to account and punish us for it. Nor does anyone see that there is so much need to be seriously concerned about the young. For if we wish to have excellent and able persons both for civil and Church leadership, we must spare no diligence, time, or cost in teaching and educating our children, so that they may serve God and the world. We must not think only about how we may amass money and possessions for them. God can indeed support and make them rich without us, as He daily does. But for this purpose He has given us children and issued this command: we should train and govern them according to His will. Otherwise, He would have no purpose for a father and a mother. Therefore, let everyone know that it is his duty, on peril of losing the divine favor, to bring up his children in the fear and knowledge of God above all things [Proverbs 1:7]. And

if the children are talented, have them learn and study something. Then they may be hired for whatever need there is.[192]

What did Luther say? "[W]e must spare no diligence, time, or cost
in teaching and educating our children, so that they may serve God and
the world." Amen. God, strengthen our courage to that end.

We have need for faithful Lutheran Christians in every godly
vocation, from husbands and wives as parents, to laborers, educators,
and public servants. There will always be a need for faithful men to
heed the call to the Office of the Holy Ministry.

Dealing with sin is not a matter of training, discipline, or education.
If you train a sinner, you get a trained sinner. Discipline a sinner and the
result is a disciplined sinner. Educate a sinner, and you get an educated
sinner. A sinner forgiven in Christ is still a sinner, but that sinner is
now also a saint. Training, discipline, and education cannot accomplish
that! Only Jesus' saving work can do this! "Be kind to one another,
tenderhearted, forgiving one another, as God in Christ forgave you"
(Ephesians 4:32).

Jesus prays "that they all [all Christians] may be one" (John 17:21a).
Jesus asserts in the same prayer, "Sanctify them in the truth; Your
word is truth" (John 17:17). This is the same plea St. Paul makes in 1
Corinthians: "I appeal to you, brothers, by the name of our Lord Jesus
Christ, that all of you agree, and that there be no divisions among you,
but that you be united in the same mind and the same judgment"
(1 Corinthians 1:10).

Let us honor Luther and Walther and our spiritual fathers and
mothers in the faith across all time and space by submitting, in humble
faith, to our one true Rabbi, Teacher, and Instructor, Jesus, the Christ,
our Savior and the Eternal Word of "our Father who art in Heaven." In
the name of Jesus. Amen.

The Common Cause of Lutheran Education: Christ at the Center

To continue the discussion on Lutheran education, Brennick
Christiansen, homeschooled K-12, a graduate of Concordia University–
Chicago, and now a classical Lutheran schoolteacher, echoes the above
thoughts and shares his own:

In all Lutheran education, whether the day school or more intimate
homeschool, the ultimate "why" of education shows the purpose of any

---

[192] Luther, *Large Catechism.* In *Concordia: The Lutheran Confessions,* 378.

and every subject as pointing ultimately to Christ and supplementing theological study, the overarching master to the rest of the academic disciplines. Arithmetic, chemistry, and physics display God's masterful creation of the universe. Music, literature, and other arts exhibit the beauty God gave mankind to enjoy and express. Engineering, business, and law depict God's gift of order, organization, and systemization.

As he matures, the student finds himself reading Scripture to maneuver through the contemplation of controversial topics, such as evolution and abortion. The Christian student discovers that all areas of study both stem from and reinforce the truth of theology. Found nowhere else, theology offers and studies the climax of and unifying point for all learning: God himself taking on human flesh, so that his death and resurrection might bring for sinful flesh the forgiveness of sins and eternal life.

How Pastors Assist Homeschoolers

With the acknowledgment that Christian instruction begins in the home and must become firmly planted over time, Cheryl Swope shares the ways Lutheran pastors have assisted her family over the years, including all of the following:

- providing hymn selections, lectionary readings, and liturgy settings before Sunday morning,
- offering daytime or early evening Bible classes, reading groups, and midweek services,
- greeting children by name on Sunday mornings,
- inviting older children to participate in adult religious instruction,
- acknowledging and praying for the dedication of all who enjoy the vocation of teacher, including homeschooling parents,
- sharing with families new books for teaching church history, apologetics, and doctrine,
- being available for and encouraging private confession for parent and child.

A Common Cause: Summary

From New York, homeschooling mother Susan Knowles adds to the above thoughts with some summarizing comments:

While some state laws define boundaries in educational relationships differently than others, supporting the role of parents as primary caregivers and instructors of their children is the same for our churches, regardless of the state in which they are located. Churches can support parents in the light of the Gospel, encouraging them in providing an environment for their children that properly discerns Law and Gospel and that bears appropriate fruit in their lives, with faith toward God and love for neighbor. On the church's part, the varying levels of support given to families by a congregation can range from Sunday religious instruction to various forms of weekday religious instruction, to instruction in Lutheran day schools, and these are all appropriate and loving ways of supporting families in their God-given roles to the glory of God. When churches focus on this central mission, they encourage and empower parents to take on the role God has given them in relation to their children's education no matter what mixture of educational opportunities the parents choose. And the whole church benefits.

You Are a Blessing to Your Pastor

The Rev. Erik Rottmann offers these meditations for homeschoolers.

How Your Homeschool Can Help Your Pastor and Congregation

The Rev. Erik Rottmann

Homeschooling requires audacity. At least, many people will think of you as audacious. You have dared to assume that you are in a better position to educate your child than all professional educators combined. In so assuming, you pose a threat to someone else's assumptions, professional commitments, and ego. Perhaps you have already noticed a rocky relationship between homeschool and public school. The churchly implication of your "audacity" might surprise you. After briefly describing this implication, I will list some ideas to help your homeschool keep a positive relationship with your church family.

Not only have you assumed you are the best teacher for your child, but you have also made a multi-year commitment to proving your assumption true. The primary cause of your success will not be your educational background, your curricula, or your creativity. You will succeed because of time spent with your child. In the same way that "love covers a multitude of sins" (1 Peter 4:8), time likewise covers a host of educational weaknesses. Time is the main reason no one can educate your child more effectively than you.

Here is the surprising implication: the phrase "no one" in the previous sentence includes your pastor. Your assumption must include him. Even in matters of the Christian faith, the time advantage remains yours. Your pastor has already learned from experience that parents teach more about faith (or unbelief!) than he is able to teach:

- It is difficult for your pastor to impress the importance of worship upon a confirmation student whose father has provided a lifetime example of refusing worship.

- Your pastor can more readily draw catechetical examples from Bible stories if his students have heard the Bible stories "from infancy" (2 Timothy 3:15).

- Instruction in prayer will not seem foreign or strange to the child who has already learned the basic habits of prayer.

He might not yet realize it, but *you became a source of joy and blessing to your pastor the moment you decided to homeschool your child.* Home education in the faith is not a matter of doing the pastor's job for him. It is a matter of no longer requiring your pastor to do your job for you.

Recall Luther's repeated phrase at the head of each chief part in the Small Catechism: "As the head of the family should teach it in a simple way to his household." For at least two generations, our educational culture has overlooked these words in favor of allowing pastors, parochial school teachers, and Sunday School teachers to carry the main load of teaching the faith. Your homeschool might help set the stage for a cultural change.

Not everyone in your congregation will immediately notice the benefits of homeschooling the faith. Here are some things you can do to help:

1. Teach in concert with your pastor. Seek his input when making selections from the vast ocean of available religious curricula. If possible, draw from his Sunday sermon during homeschool chapel. Discuss Sunday School and confirmation class with your children. Encourage your children to reflect your congregation's piety, rather than to stand distinct from it.

2. Teach Bible stories! Bible stories! Bible stories! Starting with illustrated Bible stories read aloud in the mornings or at bedtime, move toward the independent reading of the Scriptures. Make the Bible stories a regular part of life. In addition to teaching Bible stories as analogies and examples for family conversations, prepare your children for your pastor's confirmation class by connecting Bible stories to the Small Catechism. For example, Naboth's vineyard (1 Kings 21) wonderfully illustrates the Ninth Commandment, "You shall not covet your neighbor's house." (See Appendix C for suggested Bible story books.)

3. Guide your children toward the nobility of quiet service to neighbor. Homeschooled children frequently develop a know-it-all reputation. No, they are not smarter than their peers. Generally speaking, homeschooled children simply have mastered more material in a shorter time. It is also possible that they have developed superior social skills. People will notice these things. You can accomplish the twofold success of 1) instilling humility in your child and 2) keeping a positive relationship with your congregation. You can do this by teaching — in word and in deed — that the fundamental purpose of any talent or acquired skill is love for neighbor. Our Lord's words might apply even to the high-quality education of the homeschooled child: "Everyone to whom much was given, of him much will be required, and from him to whom they entrusted much, they will demand the more" (Luke 12:48). It might take a while for your children to grow into realizing this, but the very best uses of their abilities will be found in the ways they serve and interact with their family, peers, and fellow Christians.

4. Focus on the big picture. Homeschoolers tend to sing the praises of homeschooling. Unfortunately, these praises often include a funeral dirge for public and even parochial education. Such messages can create resentment for parents who are unable or unwilling to homeschool. Rather than narrowly implying that everyone should homeschool, take a more expansive approach. Encourage other parents to remain directly involved in their child's education, no matter where the child goes to school.

An illustration: My wife and I carpooled with another family in the congregation while our children attended a neighboring Lutheran school. When we decided to homeschool, the other family felt a terrible crisis. "Pastor," the father exclaimed, "we simply cannot homeschool our children!" After assuring these fine Christian parents of my continued high regard for them, I encouraged them to remain attentive to their children's education, which they did. Both of their children later became excellent examples of public-school success.

5. Keep a good sense of humor. Homeschool or not, everyone can fall into the trap of taking themselves too seriously. When I tongue-in-cheek refer to my family as "homeschool freaks," people laugh. They also feel a little less suspicious. With time, communication might begin.

Beyond Our Own Kitchen Table

"We thank Michael for his gift of six dollars and forty-nine cents," the KFUO announcer spoke through our kitchen radio one morning. While other monetary donations dwarfed his little gift, my six-year-old boy beamed at the wonder of participating in something larger than himself. He had contributed to the proclamation of the Gospel through Lutheran radio.
— Cheryl Swope

Beyond Our Own Kitchen Table: Missions and Service
Cheryl Swope

Even as we teach our children within the walls of our homes, we find many occasions to reach further, so our children can serve others. We tuck their handwritten Scripture verses into cards for grandparents or into get-well notes to neighbors. We encourage words of thanks to the child's pastor and organist following the end of the Divine Service. We include our children's coins in our church envelopes, or we allow them to contribute with their own envelopes. We reflect out loud, in front of our children, on the necessity and miracle of our receiving the Gospel of Jesus Christ in Word and Sacrament every Sunday.

We can incorporate opportunities for service into our school lessons. We can post world maps or find countries on the globe as we study world geography, and we can pray for people who live in the nations we study. We can share details of world cultures and religions through books such as *Children Just Like Me*, from Dorling Kindersley. We can find organizations within our own Lutheran Church—Missouri Synod to support missions in these nations. Children may select a particular mission of interest. The physical plight of other children seems to appeal especially to children, so we might consider adopting causes that assist with providing school books, meals, or coats, along with books and the Gospel message.

One example, the Lutheran Heritage Foundation, *www.lhfmissions.org*, is especially well suited to homeschoolers' support, because LHF provides children's books such as *A Child's Garden of Bible Stories* in many languages. The LHF newsletter features photos and stories from various parts of the world. These features can be read aloud, marked on world maps, and accompanied with moments of prayer. We can create our own combined history, geography, and missions class each year.

Our children can serve locally in our own congregations. Whether in small, personal ways or as part of larger mission efforts, our children live as baptized members of the holy Christian church, and we can invite them to rejoice with those who rejoice and weep with those who weep. Our children can bake snacks for the adult Bible class, participate in the support of missionaries or seminarians, join the ladies' group for quilting, or volunteer when the choir seeks new members. In smaller congregations, our children's eagerness may even help to allay fears of older members who might worry that their own efforts will not be passed on to the next generations.

When we serve in our congregations, we can explain to our children that, to the greatest extent possible, we will seek to join with such efforts long-term. We do not stop serving on a whim, nor due to minor inconveniences, lest we discourage others who have served so faithfully, long before we arrived. If our children cannot participate regularly or actively, but prefer to raise money behind the scenes, we can ask our pastor or congregational president to explain the many uses of our children's financial contributions, so our children can see the need for their efforts, no matter how small. We can remind our children that even small works are prepared for our children by God Himself.

To help illustrate this truth, one of our family scrapbooks includes a photo given to us long ago by one of our neighbors. In the photo, our little Michelle, then only about six years old, wore pigtails and stood by her bicycle with a basket of colorful homemade necklaces. Upon learning of the devastation caused by a hurricane, she had begun selling these necklaces up and down our street to raise money for the hurricane survivors. Michelle's coin purse, full of donated money, spoke far more to the love and generosity of our neighbors than to my daughter's handiwork, but the photo reminded us of the sacrificial love for others granted by God to our baptized children. We can nurture this in our children, as we direct our family's gaze beyond the ample food and drink that God supplies every day to our own kitchen tables.

Such conversations can occur throughout the day. We can guide our children's thoughts to compassion, even when we share the great literature of Western civilization. In *Reading Between the Lines*, Dr. Gene Edward Veith observes, "Literature increases our perception … . The discipline of reading can help us to be more aware of our surroundings, more sensitive to the people and events we encounter, and more alert to their significance and value." He shares this example, "Nineteenth century Londoners saw poor children every day swarming throughout the streets, but most never gave them a second thought. When they read Charles Dickens' *Oliver Twist*, however, they noticed those children, and they were moved to compassion and to action."[193]

Options for service abound. Within our own congregations, prayer concerns are announced, and our children can become attentive to these. We can pray about the individuals in our homes. We can visit the sick and dying mentioned by our pastor on Sunday mornings.

A few years ago, one of our robust elders began to suffer visibly from the effects of cancer. He became quite frail, as the disease progressed rapidly and aggressively. When doctors could do no more, our elder rested in a hospital bed inside his country home. Like so many others in our small Missouri congregation, when we entered the home we brought chicken and potato salad. My children saw the growing bounty in the family's refrigerator. They also noticed that our elder's family members sat in the living room, pale and wearied by the long, repetitive days of watchfulness. My children soon witnessed the mutual consolation of Christians.

Invited to the large room where the man slept, we sat in chairs placed just for the purpose of gathering around him. We listened quietly, as our elder's wife slowly described the poignant events of the past few days. My children asked about the distant family members pictured on the walls, and at times we heard cheerful stories of the past. In truth we did little, but we were there.

Before we left to drive back over the long gravel roads, we asked if we could all gather to pray. We stood around the white bed where our weakened elder slept gently, his sallow face moving only slightly with almost imperceptible breathing. His family stood with us, sharing small

---

[193] Veith, *Reading Between the Lines*, 122.

but grateful smiles, when we asked if we could pray the Lord's Prayer. My children bowed their heads.

In that moment, I remembered, as if in a flashback, a joyful image of this man rising in "his" pew at church, as he once stood to sing his favorite hymn, *I Know That My Redeemer Lives*.

> He lives and grants me daily breath;
> He lives, and I shall conquer death;
> He lives my mansion to prepare;
> He lives to bring me safely there.[194]

With the somber humility that attends a deathbed, my children and I joined with the family to pray the prayer our friend had prayed thousands of times, "Our Father, who art in heaven, hallowed be thy name … ." We left with tears in our eyes, knowing we would never see him alive again.

Days later, before we left our house for the funeral, my daughter slipped off to her room. She appeared with a poem and asked for a frame. Michelle inserted her written thoughts into the frame and presented them to our elder's wife of more than fifty years. Michelle entitled her poem, "In Memoriam."

In Memoriam

> As the larks sing sweetly on
> Over hill and yon
> Day is done, battle won
> Still he singeth on.

> At close of day, the way is o'er
> At the bend awaits:
> Jesus, Lord, Protector,
> Savior — meets us at the Gate.[195]

Finding Support

For the body does not consist of one member but of many … . God arranged the members in the body, each of them, as he chose. If all were a single member, where would the body be? As it is, there are many parts, yet one body. — 1 Corinthians 12:14, 18-20

---

[194] *Lutheran Service Book*, 461:7.

[195] Swope, Michelle. *Through Time's Looking Glass: A Book of Poetry*. Louisville: Memoria Press. 2014.

Often, especially in the early years, homeschooling families express feelings of isolation or even loneliness. When we reach outside our homes to serve others, these feelings may dissipate. Our children learn much through such moments of service. Some homeschoolers find support through collaboration in day-to-day teaching efforts, group field trips, co-ops, conferences, and other group activities. Search "Homeschool ____" with the name of your state or province to find opportunities for service and support.

You may also appreciate one or more of these options:

- Start a local get-together with Lutheran homeschoolers in your own state or region. Find a congregation to provide regular Matins or Vespers for your group. As you attend, consider contributing to the congregation's building fund or general fund to support the efforts. Your children might assist with weekly clean-up, gathering of bulletins, or ushering for these services. Meet monthly, quarterly, or annually.

- Join the Consortium for Classical Lutheran Education (CCLE), which embraces homeschoolers in its annual summer conference with home-school gatherings, programming for children, and sessions on Lutheran homeschooling. Participate in the free, online discussion group created just for Lutheran homeschoolers. See *ccle.org*

- Partner with a Lutheran day school. Call your local Lutheran school and ask about flexible options such as joining choir or instrumental music groups, drama or sports, standardized testing or field trips, specific classes, or chapel services.

- Enroll in Wittenberg Academy's online classes, and instantly receive a community of Lutheran parents and educators.

- Partner with a Lutheran college or university for dual enrollment during the high school years.

- Look for Facebook groups just for Lutheran homeschoolers, or join "Martin Loopers" online discussion group.

- Read Sister, Daughter, Mother, Wife, a blog for encouragement with Lutheran women's vocations *www.sisterdaughtermotherwife.com*.

- Join the Sturm "yahoogroups" listserve, named for Reformation era educator Johann Sturm

- Consider "Sisters of Katie Luther," a new group established for women, *SteadfastLutherans.org*.

Sometimes people ask whether the broad-based Classical Conversations is a Lutheran group. It is not, although these communities may be hosted by Lutheran congregations. This group is not to be confused with CCLE, the Consortium for Classical Lutheran Education, which is a Lutheran group for homeschoolers, classroom teachers, and anyone interested in Lutheran education.

Homeschooling families share their experiences with cooperative learning in various settings, including their own congregations:

From Illinois, Korey describes her experience homeschooling girls, ages 5, 7, and 8:

We began homeschooling and enrolled with Classical Conversations. We absolutely adore CC. I worked for twelve years as a DCE [Director of Christian Education] before homeschooling. I was quite nervous to begin, but our school year was such a success, over the first summer my daughter said she missed school. She added, "I like doing school at home with you as my teacher, Mommy."

Michelle in Virginia shares this:

With three children, ages 9, 11, and 15, we attend a Latin-Centered Curriculum (Memoria Press) co-op where my older children study Latin, Greek, science, classical studies and humanities, drama, and music. We came to Lutheranism after we started down the homeschooling path. Now we attend a very strong Lutheran church where I am learning with my children.

In Kansas, Kasey and Heather homeschool their three children, ages 1, 4, and 7. Heather writes:

Our church has a homeschooling co-op where we learned about the Consortium for Classical Lutheran Education. I am very grateful for all Lutheran support systems for classical educators!

Kristen add this from Washington:

I have one son, 14, and a daughter, 7. We attend a co-op in our area that has connected me with excellent Latin, logic, and writing teachers. With more support, our pastor introduced my son to Koine Greek, which developed a deeper interest in the New Testament and formed a lasting bond.

This Wyoming family appreciates a nearby Lutheran school:

My husband and I have two children (10, 11), both with Autism Spectrum Disorder. Homeschooling works well for my children. We attend Mount Hope Lutheran Church, where the Classical Academy welcomes us to attend daily chapel, special speaker events, and field trips.

Sarah shares these thoughts from Florida:

My daughter struggles with oral communication. We knew that practicing communication with peers and adults, both formally and informally, would be essential for our shy lady. Now that we are near the end of our second year of Classical Conversations, I've come to value the entire structure, organization, and content of these community days. While Classical Conversations communities are sometimes hosted at Lutheran churches, it is a "Christian" and not a Lutheran organization. While the statement of faith is similar to a creed and, as a Lutheran Christian, I agree with much of it, I do not subscribe my name to it. When seeking structured community learning — whether with an established homeschool group, a co-op, or just another family in your congregation — look for excellent pacing, organization, and the social support especially valuable to new homeschooling families. As for my little lady, last week she gave a beautiful and articulate retelling of the Prodigal Son for her presentation on the topic "God's Love."

Susan Knowles adds this, as she recently partnered with a Lutheran university for her son's home education:

We appreciate the dual-enrollment options through Concordia University — Wisconsin. Classes such as accounting, computer science, and economics help us with state-driven high school requirements, while simultaneously securing very affordable college credits.

Lutheran families voice appreciation for the growing resources and support offered through the Consortium for Classical Lutheran Education.

From Kansas, Eric and Karianne offer encouragement to attend conferences for Lutheran homeschoolers:

When we were relatively new to homeschooling, we had three young children and we had not met a single other Lutheran homeschooling family. My husband and I attended our first classical Lutheran education conference (CCLE) in Houston, and we were thrilled to meet other classical Lutheran homeschoolers.

From Colorado, Nate and Joanna add:

We are blessed with three children (ages 7, 12, 13). We, too, appreciate CCLE's online group, ClassicalLutheranHomeschoolers, ccle.org.

Similarly, Nick and Lydia express gratitude for online support:

Nick serves in the military, and I stay at home with our five children (ages infant, 2, 3, 6, 7). We appreciate ClassicalLutheranHomeschoolers online, "a wealth of information just an email away!"

From Minnesota, Bill and Natalie write:

With two boys (7, 10), we especially appreciate CCLE's literature list with good suggestions for every age.

Charles and Elizabeth, parents of boys (8 and 16), share their favorite homeschooling resources:

Many of our favorite homeschooling materials are from Concordia Publishing House, and we also appreciate high school online from Faith Lutheran School in Plano, Texas. We learned of this at one of the annual CCLE summer conferences!

Familial Support

Sometimes support comes from within our own extended families! Kelly Rottmann shares this narrative example:

Grandparents in Home Education
Kelly Rottmann

In the Holy Scriptures, the Apostle Paul writes to Timothy, "I am reminded of your sincere faith, a faith that dwelt first in your grandmother Lois and your mother Eunice and now, I am sure, dwells in you as well" (2 Timothy 1:5). From this single mention of Timothy's grandmother, home educators are reminded of the potential resource in their own children's grandparents.

Often we think of grandparents' help during our children's youngest years, but grandparents can be particularly helpful during the high school years. Elective courses required for graduation offer perfect opportunities for grandparents to teach. An enthusiastic grandparent can teach, whether skilled in carpentry, gardening, balancing the household budget, regional history, archaeology; quilting, knitting, or pie baking. Help student and grandparent prepare short-term goals together, outline and shop for needed materials, and plan desired outcomes. Directly involve the student in the process of planning.

Recently our son, Aaron, had the opportunity to complete three home economics electives with his grandparents. Advanced preparation was needed, because each elective required a one-week visit to each grandparents' home. We decided that Aaron would complete his reflective papers at home the following week after his visit. All together, each elective took a total of three weeks to complete.

Aaron and his grandparents chose and agreed upon specific projects for meal preparation, sewing, and knitting. Lists of materials were made and purchased. Careful instruction paired with cookbooks, project patterns, and real-life experiences became sufficient for meeting the learning goals of this particular elective.

For each project, Aaron would learn about the basic tools and terminology associated with it. Each grandparent would teach specific skills outlined beforehand with a procedure for evaluation. When a skill was taught and mastery was demonstrated, the teacher checked this off the list.

In addition to spending invaluable time with his grandparents, Aaron's struggle to knit may have been the most valuable part of this elective! Aaron expressed the humbling reminder of one's need for patience, perseverance, and communication when attempting new tasks. Aaron also voiced appreciation for his grandparents' skills and wisdom. These were the unwritten, hoped-for goals we had in mind for our son. Our unwritten goals support some of the main goals of a classical Christian education; that is, to nurture students so that they become able to "ask questions, and find answers about the meaning, purpose and value of things."[196] For this we owe our thanks to grandparents!

Mutual Benefit: Homeschoolers and Lutheran Day Schools

How to Locate an Unexpected Partner for Home Education: A School

While homeschool communities and co-ops can be beneficial, introducing your children to orthodox Lutheran school teachers

---

[196] Hein, Steven A. et al. *A Handbook for Classical Lutheran Education: The Best of the Consortium for Classical and Lutheran Education's Journals*. Fort Wayne, Indiana: CCLE Press, 2013, 7.

may be even more desirable. This may occur within your congregational Sunday School program, through online classes with Lutheran teachers, or within the context of a strong Lutheran day school.

Whether for part-time enrollment or extracurricular benefits, in the initial contact with a day school, you may find a heartier welcome when you offer tuition, fees, or even volunteer assistance (e.g., working as a teacher's aide, providing clerical or janitorial assistance) in exchange for opportunities the school may offer. When you inquire about services for your child, simultaneously request ways to become a blessing to the work of the school.

The following list comprises just a tiny sampling of schools welcoming homeschool families in various ways. Even if you do not live near these schools, you might appreciate learning of their services as possible suggestions for other Lutheran day schools nearer to your home:

- **Bethany Lutheran School** in Overland Park, Kansas
  bethanyschool.net

  Consider this as a possible model. Bethany Lutheran School offers a Homeschool Academy within the Lutheran Day School!

- **Immanuel Lutheran School** in Mayville, Wisconsin
  admissions@immanuelmayville.com

  "Homeschool families are welcome to join us for specific classes throughout the week. We offer Saxon math instruction, Spalding Language Arts instruction supplemented with Shurley grammar, Latin and German instruction, Music, and Art. All are welcome to join us for weekly chapel services, and homeschool families are invited to participate in field trips throughout the year."

- **Immanuel Lutheran School** in Roswell, New Mexico
  ilcroswell.org

  Begun as a "hybrid" classical Lutheran school, homeschooled students may join currently for 3-day or 5-day classes in Latin, math, history, writing, science, singing in chapel, and much more.

- **Immanuel Lutheran School** in Sheboygan, Wisconsin
  immanuel-school.com

  Flexible enrollment is offered preschool through 8th grade in core classes, science classes with labs, athletics, music, choir, band, field trips, standardized testing, art, and more.

- **Faith Lutheran School** in Plano, Texas
  flsplano.org

  Enroll in daily or part-time classes K-12, or select live, online classes to participate from anywhere in North America!

- **Martin Luther Grammar School** in Sheridan, Wyoming
  sheridanmlgs.blogspot.com

  Participate in Latin classes, education with technology, field trips, daily liturgical chapel, and more.

- **Messiah Lutheran School** in Keller, Texas
  mlcatexas.org

  Enroll in part-time or full-time classical education opportunities ranging from age 2 on up. Enjoy a classical Christian literature-based preschool. School-age children can participate in arithmetic, Latin, English grammar, and upper-level classes with Socratic discussion. The school offers enrichment activities such as the fine arts, archery, sports, and more.

- **Mount Hope Lutheran Classical Academy** in Casper, Wyoming
  (307) 234-6865

  All homeschoolers are welcome! Attend daily chapel, field trips, or special sessions with speakers

- **St. Paul Lutheran School** in Brookfield, Illinois
  spbrookfield.org

  "Homeschoolers are welcome to attend our chapel, our classes such as science or Latin, and more. At SPLS, we have made some effort to have the same subject (e.g., reading and math) at the same time for all classes, which might help a family with children in different grades. A homeschooling parent might be willing to assist by setting up labs. Homeschoolers are always welcome to access our online resources, standardized testing opportunities, textbook loan program, fine arts or physical education classes, field trips, and enjoy participation in service projects."

- **Zion Lutheran Church and School** in Nampa, Idaho
  zionlutherannampa.com

  "Zion Lutheran invites homeschooling families to participate in classes, in the mid-week summer Vesper services with potluck supper beforehand, in year-round mid-week Bible study on the first and third Wednesday mornings, and in Friday Matins services. We welcome all."

Tips for Lutheran Day Schools

For more information on cooperative learning between school and home, the Rev. Joel Brondos, headmaster/pastor of St. Paul Lutheran School in Brookfield, Illinois, shares his thoughts on how Lutheran day schools can assist and include homeschooling families. He lists nine ideas for Lutheran school headmasters, pastors, and teachers to consider.

Lutheran Day Schools: Inviting and Including Homeschoolers
The Rev. Joel Brondos

1. Online Resources
Allow homeschooler access to online resources. This includes subjects in Moodle, Latin and literature resources and quizzes, Google Apps for Education, and Hapara. Consider minimum subscription costs per student or unlimited usage per family.

2. Standardized Testing
Invite homeschoolers during formal and informal standardized testing, such as STAR Math and STAR Reading online, the Iowa Tests of Basic Skills, and others.

3. Extracurricular Activities
Allow participation in extracurricular activities such as choir, band, chess club, volleyball, basketball, and cross country. There might be a bit of "competitive" spirit here, because some parents might not want a homeschooler receiving more attention in a dramatic production or in a particular sport than a day-schooler receives, but I think if the communicated intent is to promote participation for all children, this may be minimized.

4. Fine Arts and Physical Education Classes
Offer enrollment in fine arts or physical education classes, as these opportunities may be more difficult to duplicate at home. Homeschooling parents might volunteer to teach, supervise, or assist in other ways. This would be a great help to small schools.

5. Lending Library
Consider a textbook or literature loan program. Small schools often have to buy a classroom set of grammar, math, or literature trade books. Homeschoolers could be welcomed to borrow these.

6. Special Presentations and Field Trips
Invite local homeschooling groups to participate in special presentations, such as concerts or speakers, or join in field trips with day-school classes.

Some day schools offer periodic "chamber concerts," where we pay a professional musician to come in and perform a 45-minute concert and explain the history behind the instrument, the composers, etc. Homeschoolers may wish to attend science demonstrations, puppet shows, and other special events.

7. Faculty Opportunities

Extend faculty invitations to homeschooling parents, especially those who have graduated their children. By the time a homeschooling parent becomes a master of so many subjects, the child is grown and off to high school, college, and beyond. These parents could be a tremendous asset to small Lutheran schools, whether as paid teacher assistants or full-time teachers of particular subjects. They might also become a part-time paid liaison between the school and homeschool families.

8. Service Projects

Invite participation in school service projects. The children could all work together in community service or a mission opportunity.

9. Daily or Weekly Chapel

Invite homeschoolers to attend regular chapel services. Some might assist with music, the altar, or simply add to the voices when singing hymns.

PEACE IN PARENTING: THE LUTHERAN DIFFERENCE

Our calling or vocation in life has been cleansed by the blood of the Lamb. Everything we do is holy by faith in Christ. The Christian moves from the call of Baptism in the church to the baptismal call in daily life. The worship of daily life is to love our neighbor through all the offices God gives to us. Thus the office of parent becomes the foundation for every other station of life. Society flows from the family, as do the good works that God has called us to do.[197] — *Daniel Preus*

The Joy of Receiving

How is Lutheran parenting different? Rachel Whiting shares her personal journey and reflections on a biblical understanding of parenthood.

The Joy of Receiving
Rachel Whiting

As a child I would ask Jesus to come into my heart almost daily, but I never felt like it "took." When worship leaders called for "All

---

[197] Preus, Daniel. *Why I Am a Lutheran: Jesus at the Center.* St. Louis: Concordia Publishing House, 2004. 78.

heads bowed and all eyes closed," I would raise my hand to "make" Jesus the Lord of my life.

As a teenager, I would read my Bible to prove my devotion. I "burned" my sins written down on little pieces of paper by throwing them into a fire at camp. I walked the aisles, sang "I Surrender All" many, many times, and I signed little cards to re-dedicate my life to Jesus. The counselors who met me at the end of aisles always seemed so frustrated with me, because I told them I wasn't able to surrender or dedicate my life enough. I was never sure if I had really given my life to Jesus or not. Had I surrendered all? Their answer: Just pray more and give more of yourself to Jesus.

As an adult, I began to substitute a heavily logical system of theology. Some relief came in understanding that I was dead in my sins and that it was God who made me alive. Yet the theology did not end there; I still attended a church with long, technical, works-based sermons. Even the works-based "sacraments" were seen as ineffectual symbols in this system. Despair ruled my life, as my sin was ever before me.

My husband and I visited a new church. As I sat waiting for the service to begin, I glanced at those around me. One question kept running through my mind: "Where are the Bibles?" In other churches, people brought Bibles of different colors and sizes. During the sermons, those Bibles would sit open on their laps as they thumbed through them, pen in hand. So why did I not see this practice in the Divine Service? I could not help being skeptical of people who intended to just sit there during the sermon.

We continued visiting this church. I grew to understand that the focus during the sermon in the Divine Service is on receiving God's Word. The concept of *receiving* from God in church was foreign to me; my background, with its constant efforts to give to God, had taught the reverse. The Divine Service is indeed receiving from God all of these good gifts: His absolution, His peace, His Gospel, His truth, His grace, His washing, His Body, His Blood, His forgiveness of all our sin, and His righteousness. The Apology of the Augsburg Confession states:

> So the worship and divine service of the Gospel is to receive gifts from God. On the contrary, the worship of the Law is to offer and present our gifts to God … . The chief worship of the Gospel is to desire to receive the forgiveness of sins, grace, and righteousness.[198]

---

[198] Apology of the Augsburg Confession. In *Concordia: The Lutheran Confessions*, 130.

How revolutionary! How freeing to look to Christ and to receive His gifts through the Word and Sacraments. Instead of looking to myself or attempting more mustered-up resolutions, I found a welcome balm to my soul.

What did this mean for me as a mother? As I learned more, I felt relief that my children would not have to ride the manmade spiritual roller coaster in futile quests to climb "Jacob's ladder" of spiritual growth.

Yet even after understanding that Jesus is our "ladder," descended to us men for our salvation, we still fight the tendency to think that we must do something. It is our nature in Adam. The hands that grabbed the forbidden fruit still flail in desperation, as if we must take our salvation into our own grasp. Instead, we are to receive with empty, open hands. One day not long ago, my son, raised in the Lutheran church, asked, "Mom, will I still be saved even if I don't get the whole Bible read?" Not only do false teachers speak of forgiveness and salvation as something to be earned, but this expectation is embedded in our own hearts too.

Jesus knows this. He holds before us a little child as our example. And truly, little children are good at receiving. Babies are the best. The helplessness of their state makes them perfect receptors. They are served and helped, and they have no qualms about allowing someone else to do everything for them. They do not demand reason or exercise logic to find holes in what they are told; everything they hear is believable to them. The simplicity of young children's minds and the depth of their imaginations seem to allow them to embrace faith freely, though we know even this is empowered by the gift of the Holy Spirit.

Yet as children grow, so does their desire for independence. As soon as my son became big enough to get into his car seat by himself, fits would occur if I lifted him into it. How offended he was if I ever did something that he felt he had the capacity to do for himself! Age takes away the inclination to receive, unless we combat this with the truth of Law and Gospel for our children.

Young or old, child or parent, as Luther wrote before dying, "We are beggars; this is true."[199] We are all beggars with empty hands, receiving the words of absolution proclaimed to us. We are beggars with deaf ears made to hear the Word of the Lord. We are beggars with hungry mouths opened to the feast spread before us, the Body and Blood of

---

[199] Kellerman, James. "The Last Written Words of Luther: Holy Ponderings of the Rev. Father Doctor Martin Luther, 16 February 1546." Accessed October 17, 2014. *www.iclnet.org/pub/resources/text/wittenberg/luther/beggars.txt.*

our Lord, the medicine of immortality. Like little receptive babes, let us crave the pure spiritual milk of the Word, nursed with what Chrysostom called the "Nipple of the Spiritual Cup."[200] As the Lord Jesus Christ gave Himself for us and He came not to be served but to serve (Matthew 20:28; Galatians 1:4), so He continues to do so in the Divine Service of Word and Sacrament. Our children receive, and we as Lutheran parents receive. In Jesus, we receive full pardon, mercy, and assurance of forgiveness for our sins. Freely forgiven, we forgive. This makes all the difference.[201]

When Our Children Experience Doubt

Your promises are free and do not depend on my worthiness or merit. I can rest in them with the surest faith and trust in Your goodness with my whole heart.[202] — *Johann Gerhard*

As guardians of our children's souls, we respond to our children's questions with our own trust in God's everlasting goodness. In the next two narratives, entitled "Doubting God's Forgiveness" and "Doubting God's Love," Rachel Whiting reflects on matters of doubt and faith within the home.

Doubting God's Forgiveness
Rachel Whiting

At the end of a typical day, homeschooling mothers are often exhausted. This evening was no different. Bedtime rituals for my four children were almost over. My oldest was in his room for the night. Nearby in the prettily decorated girls' room, I knelt by the bedside of my next oldest, an eight-year-old daughter. With prayers said, a song sung, a back rub administered, "I love you's" exchanged, and bedtime kisses given, I rose from kneeling. I began to adjust the cheery blankets over my youngest girls, twins, already asleep across the room. As

---

[200] Chrysostom, *Daily Readings from the Writings of St. John Chrysostom*, 5.

[201] A version of this article first appeared at *www.sisterdaughtermotherwife.com*. Whiting, Rachel. "The Joy of Receiving: My Conversion Story." Sister, Daughter, Mother, Wife, Living Our Vocations as Lutheran Women. July 29, 2014. Accessed October 17, 2014.

[202] Johann Gerhard. *Meditations on Divine Mercy*. St. Louis: Concordia Publishing House, 99.

my older daughter's small, tucked-in frame lay in the darkness, she whispered, "Mom, what is it like to die?"

Now my older two children are infamous for asking loaded questions once they are tucked into bed. Uncertain whether this is truly a stalling technique or a voicing of genuine concerns in the stillness, my husband and I answer their musings. After all, the nature of sleep is a foreboding foreshadow of death, lying still for so many hours. For a child, lying in bed can be as much as half her day, so this question did not seem too unreasonable.

I answered my daughter's question. However, given my own fatigue, I heard this rather cold, matter-of-fact response from my lips, "You stop breathing because your heart stops beating." I caught myself when I realized how harsh this sounded to her. Then, in a more gracious way, I breathed deeply and told her how the Christian's soul leaves his body and is instantly with Christ. The body decays in the earth, yet on the Last Day, Christ will raise that body and rejoin it with the soul for all eternity. My daughter listened in silence. To my surprise, she offered nothing more.

The room was quiet. I tried again to smooth her sisters' blankets, and that is when I heard it. My daughter uttered a loud cry as if in terror, "No, no, no! I don't want to die!" I looked at her, the dark outline of her body shaking up and down. "What if I end up going to hell?" she wailed. "What if I'm not really forgiven? What if there is just one sin that I am not forgiven of?" Terror had seized her conscience. The peaceful, playful bedroom became for her a dark torture chamber.

As she sobbed, I imagined demons perched on her four bedposts with deep toothless grins, smiling down on her, cackling with glee at the doubt tormenting her soul. In the Large Catechism, Luther describes the devil,

> pushing and provoking in all directions. But he especially agitates matters that concern the conscience and spiritual affairs. He leads us to despise and disregard both God's Word and works. He tears us away from faith, hope, and love, and he brings us into misbelief, false security and stubbornness. Or, on the other hand, he leads us to despair, denial of God, blasphemy, and innumerable other shocking things. These are snares and nets, indeed, real fiery darts that are shot like poison into the heart, not by flesh and blood, but by the devil. Great and grievous, indeed, are these dangers and temptations, which every Christian must bear … . So every hour that

we are in this vile life, we are attacked on all sides, chased and hunted down.[203]

Yes, the devil even sneaks under the cover of darkness into our children's cheerily decorated bedrooms. He attempts to nestle between teddy bears and fuzzy blankets, so that he can thrust his poisonous darts of doubt into carefully tended faith. He seeks to lead our precious children from hope to agonizing despair, from truth to his concocted lies, from perfect peace to paralyzing fear. But we are not left defenseless against his blows. Not at all. We have been given the Holy Word of God and the Holy Sacraments.

I sat with my daughter on her bed, and we talked long into the night. Without waking the other girls, I shined a flashlight on the wall to look at the crucifix beside her bed. Seeing Christ hang on the cross, I reminded her that Jesus accomplished her salvation. "It is finished." There isn't one sin that wasn't placed on Christ that my daughter would have to pay for herself, because the blood of Jesus cleanses us from all sin (1 John 1:7). We talked about her partaking of Christ, who is eternal life, when she eats His Body and Blood in the Sacrament of the Altar.[204] She does not need to fear death, because Christ already died her death. When she was placed in Christ at her baptism, all that was His became hers, and all that was hers became His.

My daughter made the sign of the cross, remembering her baptism into Christ. We talked about how she would never perish, but has everlasting life in Him. God, her loving Father, is greater than all, and no one can snatch her out of the Father's hands in Christ Jesus (John 10:28-29)

Breathing deeply, my little girl relaxed under her covers. She found comfort again in Romans 8:38-39, that neither death nor life will be able to separate her from the love of God in Christ Jesus our Lord. We prayed together.

As my daughter began to cling tightly to the Word of God, the faithful sword of the Spirit (Ephesians 6:17), the arrows of doubt were pulled out of her. The Lord cradled her soul and mended her wounds with His truth and peace. She eventually drifted off to sleep, her face resting on her still-moistened pillow.

---

[203] Luther, *Large Catechism*. In *Concordia: The Lutheran Confessions*, 420-421.

[204] Rachel's family attends an LCMS church that practices early communion. The examination of this practice is beyond the scope of this book. For information on the rite of "First Communion Prior to Confirmation," refer to the *Lutheran Service Book Agenda* (03-1177). St. Louis: Concordia Publishing House, 2006. 25-26.

The next morning, as always, God's mercies were new. My daughter asked to mark all the verses that we had discussed the night before. Armed with sticky notes, a highlighter, and a pencil, she wanted to know exactly where these were located in her own Bible. I felt privileged to see my daughter embrace the truth that we "do not live by bread alone, but by every word that comes from the mouth of God" (Deuteronomy 8:3; Matthew 4:4).

This truth regarding the Lord's Prayer instructs us all, even our children:

> No one may go in security and carelessly, as though the devil were far from us. At all times we must expect and block his blows. Though I am now chaste, patient, kind, and in firm faith, the devil will this very hour send such an arrow into my heart that I can scarcely stand. For he is an enemy that never stops or becomes tired.... So there is no help or comfort except to run here, take hold of the Lord's Prayer, and speak to God from the heart like this: 'Dear Father, you have asked me to pray ... .'[205]

"While we live in the flesh and have the devil around us, no one can escape his temptation and lures. It can only mean that we must endure trials — indeed, be engulfed in them. But we say this prayer so that we may not fall and be drowned in them."[206] And lead us not into temptation. But deliver us from the evil one (Matthew 6:13). Amen.

Doubting God's Love
Rachel Whiting

Every time I refolded the cool washcloth, it quickly became warm against her feverish skin. I mumbled, "Lord Jesus, heal my baby." My three-year-old's hot hand touched my face as she complained, "Momma, Je-Je can't heal me." "Oh, yes, He can," I quickly reassured her.

"If Je-Je can heal me, then He won't. He just won't heal me right now. He won't!" As I looked at my daughter's sullen face, I thought about all the Gospel stories I had read to her, stories about how Jesus healed sickness and disease with just a word or a touch. I could see her mind spin, as she wondered why Jesus didn't do that for her, right now.

---

[205] Luther, *Large Catechism*. In *Concordia: Lutheran Confessions*, 421.

[206] Ibid.

Doubting God is the common plight of fallen humankind. The devil, the world, and our sinful nature teach us to demand a "savior" who fulfills our own desires. Of course, he must grant us health and our happiness here and now, and he must prove his love by giving us the experiences that we want. When my young daughter's suffering contradicted her immature beliefs about Jesus, she questioned God's love and care. She was confused about where and how God reveals Himself. She needed to learn that her experience and feelings are not pieces of a puzzle that she assembles with her own hands in a tangible effort to see whether or not God is good and loving.

Our children need to be taught about the true Jesus. Luther wrote in the Smalcald Articles, "God does not want to deal with us in any other way than through the spoken Word and the Sacraments."[207] The Lord comes to us as He promises, and we are not to look for Him outside of where He is found. This is good news! We are not left to grope in the dark, as if we could figure out by what we think or feel whether God cares about our problems. We are assured through His own promises that the Lord lavishes His grace upon us, creating and sustaining faith through His Word.

We can teach our children that Christ Jesus does more than simply teach us. He saves us as He speaks His Word to us. God created the world through speaking powerful words, and He has created faith in our hearts in the same way.

When the Word is read and spoken in the Divine Service, we can help instill a proper awe and reverence in our children. During the reading of the Word in the Divine Service, I like to whisper to my little fidgeting children, "Listen, God is talking to you." They look up at me wide-eyed as I say, "Do you hear Him?" We can encourage them to hold the Word sacred by listening to it.

At home we memorize Scripture passages, canticles, the Small Catechism, hymns, and prayers, and the Divine Service becomes wonderfully familiar. We also memorize poetry and songs. My children love to sing the words, "I was baptized, happy day, all my sins were washed away, God looked down on me and smiled, I became His own dear child." This children's song conveys the comforting, reassuring truth of the Father's declaration that at Christ's Baptism, He was well pleased with His Son, and now He is well pleased with us in our

---

[207] Luther, Martin. *Smalcald Articles*. In *Concordia: The Lutheran Confessions*, 281.

baptism, which unites us with Christ. He spiritually washes us through water combined with His Word.

When moments of crisis come, we need to remind our children that they are baptized children of God. It is in this washing, not in their circumstances, that God has dealt with them. I rejoice to hear my little ones boldly join in the hymn "God's Own Child, I Gladly Say It":

> Satan, hear this proclamation:
> I am baptized into Christ!
> Drop your ugly accusation,
> I am not so soon enticed.
> Now that to the font I've traveled,
> All your might has come unraveled,
> And, against your tyranny,
> God, my Lord, unites with me![208]

Christ spiritually feeds us with bread and wine as we consume His Body and Blood. Our son, our oldest child, has talked with me about how he loves the Sacrament of the Altar. He says, "I just love the wine; it burns as it goes down my throat and I can feel all my sins being burned away." When our children are tempted to look to their feelings as a gauge to determine whether God is for them or against them, we can remind them that in this sacramental meal, Christ's blood is "given and shed *for you* for the forgiveness of sins."[209]

God bestows His assurance through all our senses. He works actively, as we read the Word with our eyes and hear it with our ears. We feel the water of regeneration on our skin in the baptismal font. We touch with our lips and taste with our mouths the Body and Blood of Christ. In the objective Word and Sacraments, coming from outside of us, yet to us, God grants us the promise of forgiveness in Jesus Christ. We must not look to our circumstances or to our feelings when we seek to assess God's love for us. Through His Word and Sacraments, He graciously invades our doubt with the assurance of His love.

Our days as mothers are full of crying children, bloody knees, sibling fights, and sometimes sickness. We have many opportunities to point our children to Christ on the cross. He has taken all fevers, sicknesses, sins, and death into Himself as He incurred His Father's wrath against our sin. What we are going through now — the tears,

---

[208] *Lutheran Service Book*, 594:3.

[209] Luther, *The Small Catechism of Dr. Martin Luther*. In *Lutheran Catechesis*, Learn-by-Heart Edition. 24-25.

mourning, crying, pain, sickness, and death — will all be part of the former things that will pass away. He does not promise to remove our suffering, but to be present with us throughout all trials. He works all things to our good (Romans 8:28). In the midst of it all, despite our own feelings and experiences, let us teach our children and remind ourselves that God loves, washes, forgives, feeds, and keeps us through His gracious Word and Sacraments.[210] God is with us even in our suffering. In all things, God loves us dearly in His Son.

When Our Children Sin Against Us

And forgive us our trespasses, as we forgive those who trespass against us. — Matthew 6:12

Parenting challenges us personally. Often we must set aside our own immature reactions, so that we may respond to our children in ways that will instruct them. In this narrative, Rachel contemplates the implications of her son's words, as she gains renewed appreciation for forgiving those who trespass against us.

When Our Children Sin Against Us
Rachel Whiting

"I don't like you, Mom." The words flowed freely from the mouth of my little boy and caused me instant denial. "What did you say?" He repeated plainly, "I don't like you, Mom." We were standing in the driveway, as he watched his friend leave from a play date. My son was angry to have stopped playing with his little friend, and I became the recipient of his feelings. He was just learning how to speak and had said only a few short sentences. Now this sentence could be added to the short list of his "first" sentences.

How could this be? Yes, he cried and whined and had fits like every small child. I knew he was a sinner since conception; yet never had he revealed this so blatantly. Nor had I felt it so personally. Everything else was growing and developing so remarkably! He had learned how to roll over and then to sit. He learned how to crawl and then to walk.

---

[210] A version of this article first appeared at *www.sisterdaughtermotherwife.com*. Whiting, Rachel. "When Your Child Doubts God's Love." Sister, Daughter, Mother, Wife, Living Our Vocations as Lutheran Women. July 11, 2014. Accessed October 17, 2014.

Yet with this new event, I could see strife blossom in a new way. My young son's enlistment in the war with the world, the flesh, and the devil was now clearly active.

My little boy was brought into this world through the water and blood of my body. He was brought forth again in rebirth through the waters of Holy Baptism by the Blood of Christ. In this cuddly, sweet, young baby boy, an old man of flesh, the Old Adam, had been drowned in the waters of Baptism; moreover, a new man, made in the image of the God-Man Christ, arose. Yet now my son's Old Adam was rearing his ugly head in the fight to dominate and have his way. My little son's sinful flesh could now articulate rebellion in newly acquired words.

Like all new mothers meeting their firstborn, I had been overwhelmed with wonderment at holding new life. Yet this baby, bathed in baptismal water, must still live out his days. The fact is, we are all born for trouble, as sparks fly upward (Job 5:7).

Luther said that "if you live in repentance, you walk in Baptism."[211] Baptism "indicates that the Old Adam in us should by daily contrition and repentance be drowned and die with all sins and evil desires, and that a new man should daily emerge and arise to live before God in righteousness and purity forever."[212] The Large Catechism explains how the new man becomes strong, as the old man is suppressed and decreases. When we repent, we return to Baptism, where the Old Adam is drowned.[213]

Just as our children learn how to walk physically, they must learn how to walk spiritually. Learning how to walk physically does not take very long, whereas learning to walk in Baptism through daily repentance takes a lifetime.

In our families and in our homes, we sin against the Lord and against one another. It is necessary for us to confess our sins to one another and to announce and receive forgiveness. Our days are filled with strivings and failings, but they are filled with mercy. We can close our day in peace.

In our home, our day often ends with Early Evening, Close of the Day, or Compline.[214] The service of Compline is especially helpful, as

---

[211] Luther, *Large Catechism*. In *Concordia: The Lutheran Confessions*, 430.

[212] Romans 6:1-14; Galatians 3:27; Luther, *The Small Catechism of Dr. Martin Luther*, 19.

[213] Luther, *Large Catechism*. In *Concordia: The Lutheran Confessions*, 429-430.

[214] *Lutheran Service Book*, 297, 298, 253-259.

in it we say the following:

> I confess to God, Almighty, before the whole company of heaven and to you, my brothers and sisters, that I have sinned in thought, word, and deed by my fault, by my own fault, by my own most grievous fault; wherefore I pray God Almighty to have mercy on me, forgive me all my sins, and bring me to everlasting life. Amen.[215]

The response from mutual confession is this assurance: "The almighty and merciful Lord grant you pardon, forgiveness, and remission of all your sins. Amen."[216]

From infancy to our death, the war rages against a threefold enemy (i.e., the fallen world, the prowling devil, and our own sinful flesh) till we draw our last breath. But comfort comes to us in the Word and Sacraments, through which Christ actively keeps us in the one true faith.

As our baptized children grow in grace and knowledge, we bring God's Word to them, and we pray for them. The Scriptures compare spiritual growth with the fruit of a tree, which does not appear until after much digging, watering, and pruning with the patient passage of time.[217]

As a mother, it is painful to watch spiritual struggle ensue in our children. It is like the anguish of childbirth, as Christ is formed in our children.[218] We desire to see them walk in Baptism with even greater joy than we had when watching them take their first physical steps! We pray for our children, and we discipline them. Ready with forgiveness, we love our children, because He first loved us. We forgive, because we are forgiven.

The other night, before bed, my son said, "Something is bothering me, and laying heavy on me." "What is it?" I asked. "The other day I was mad at you and I felt like I hated you, and I knew it was wrong to feel like that towards you. I am sorry that I hated you; will you forgive me?" In joy, I whispered back to him, "Yes, I forgive you."

I continued honestly. "I, too, have hated my parents. Remember, Jesus never hated His Father or Joseph, His guardian, or Mary, His mother. His obedience earned for us a righteousness that He gives to

---

[215] Ibid., 254.

[216] Ibid.

[217] Psalm 1:3, Luke 6:43-44.

[218] Galatians 4:19.

us. In His death and resurrection He takes our sin away. We are both forgiven and free in Him."

Through the Lord's Prayer petition that He lead us not into temptation, we pray "that God would guard and keep us so that the devil, the world, and our sinful nature may not deceive us or mislead us into false belief, despair, and other great shame and vice. Although we are attacked by these things, we pray that we may finally overcome them and win the victory."[219] As our children engage in the battles of life, may they cling to the forgiveness of sins in Christ. Let us smile wide into their little faces as we tell them of the conquering, victorious Christ who has "purchased and won us from all sins, from death, and the power of the devil … with His holy, precious blood and with His innocent suffering and death."[220] This truth will set them free.[221]

Christ Is for Sinners

As parents, we learn while we teach. Rachel reflects on God's gracious provision of a merciful Savior, even as she helps her daughter through repeated struggles at home.

Christ Is For Sinners
Rachel Whiting

As I washed the dishes, I felt my daughter's hand on my arm. My eyes turned from the sink full of wet dishes to her eyes full of wet tears. With a quivering voice she said she had to tell me something. It was a sin she had committed. She said that she had not been honest about something she said she had done. I forgave her and reminded her of Christ's forgiveness. We hugged, we prayed, and we continued going about our busy day.

Not long afterward, I was unloading the dryer and heard my daughter's shaking voice: "Mom, can I talk to you?" She felt she had not been completely honest in another situation and requested forgiveness. We talked, we hugged, we prayed again. With thankfulness we praised God for the conviction of the Holy Spirit.

---

[219] Luther, *The Small Catechism of Dr. Martin Luther*, 17.

[220] Ibid., 13.

[221] A version of this article first appeared at *www.sisterdaughtermotherwife.com*. Whiting, Rachel. "Learning to Walk in Baptism: My Child's Old Adam." Sister, Daughter, Mother, Wife, Living Our Vocations as Lutheran Women. May 30, 2014. Accessed October 17, 2014.

While I was cutting up vegetables in the kitchen to make soup for dinner, I heard my daughter's quiet voice again. "Mom, I need to tell you something." She felt she had exaggerated something she had said to a friend. I found her little voice and reddened eyes around every corner in the house, as her confessions continued in this fashion for many days.

Over time, her disposition grew more accustomed to crying than maintaining composure. If her face did not have streaming tears, then it looked forlorn. Smiling became a foreign expression. My daughter concluded she was more prone to sin when in the company of others, so she thought it would be best to be alone. She even said it was better if she just did not talk, because she sinned so much in what she said. She feared her own wretchedness! What was happening to my child? Where was the girl who laughed easily and loudly, who sang *The Sound of Music* soundtrack as she twirled through her day? My husband and I were concerned about her solemnity; yet we did not want to belittle the sensitivity of her conscience.

Our dilemma continued, as my daughter adamantly confessed everything she could think of. She lived with a floodlight upon her soul, yet she felt terror at the idea of any sins buried beyond her perception. "The heart is deceitful above all things, and desperately sick; who can understand it?" (Jeremiah 17:9). I told her, "If only sins that can be named are forgiven, consciences could never find peace. For many sins cannot be seen or remembered."[222] I thought this would help, but then she highlighted in her Bible, Psalm 19:12: "Who can discern his errors? Declare me innocent from hidden faults."

Some of what I said seemed to *reach* her, but much of the time she listened with a blank expression, as if the news was too good and too simple for the scheming complexities of her mind. As the days wore on, her confessions were sounding even more minuscule, like accidents instead of sins. My husband and I became worn out by her continual confessions. We were reminded of the exasperation of Luther's confessor Staupitz when he said to Luther, "Go and commit a real sin."[223] We prayed for wisdom how to parent our daughter.

Our sinful natures take everything that is good and turn it into something perverse. Even the wonderful gifts of repentance, confession,

---

[222] Augsburg Confession. In *Concordia: The Lutheran Confessions*, 50.

[223] McKim, Donald K. *The Cambridge Companion to Martin Luther.* Cambridge: Cambridge University Press, 2003. 265.

and absolution can become twisted into something our sinful natures will revel in, when we try to place salvation into our own hands. We protest the finished work of Christ as we squirm and say, "Just give me something I can do," and we torture ourselves. My daughter found apparent satisfaction in her tears; she could cry them. It seemed she wanted to weep herself a river on which to traverse the path to the kingdom of heaven.

Our Own Past

Before becoming a Lutheran, I would have viewed such introspective turmoil as suitable agony. I thought that constant inner torture provided "proof" that one was a secure and growing Christian. Look inward; find evidence. With contrasting comfort, I have come to appreciate the Divine Service, where we receive the comforting assurance of the Gospel. We look away from self and only to Christ Himself. God's salvation has come to us through Christ's efficacious life, death, and resurrection for us. This gaze outward to His work on our behalf thwarts the destructive tendencies and doctrines of an excessively inward focus. Christ's fulfillment of the Law on our behalf frees us from a frightening despair that might otherwise choke our faith.

When reading *The Hammer of God*, by Bo Giertz, I was reminded that salvation is not dependent upon our own personal improvements in our battle against sin. Nor is security in Christ found in the delusion that we can somehow cleanse our own heart and then commend this purified heart to God. Our cold, calculating flesh clings greedily toward steps to perform or formulas to follow, but true life in Christ looks to Another for a salvation we cannot accomplish ourselves. From beginning to end, Jesus Christ is He who accomplishes our redemption. With holy perfection and sinless sacrifice, He alone is our confidence and our peace.

Unexpected Help for My Daughter

As a mother, I yearned for the Holy Spirit to restore for my daughter the joy of her salvation! I began to understand what Luther intended in his letter to Melanchthon:

> Be a sinner, and let your sins be strong (sin boldly), but let your trust in Christ be stronger, and rejoice in Christ who is the victor over sin, death, and the world. We will commit sins while we are here, for this life is not a place where justice resides. We,

however, says Peter (2 Peter 3:13), are looking forward to a new heaven and a new earth where justice will reign.[224]

We live the only way we as sinners this side of eternity can live, as sinners redeemed in Christ. This does not translate into wanton sinning with a view to grace abounding (Romans 6:1). Yet we know that as Christians, we still sin. Whenever we talk with others, we sin. Whenever we think in isolation, we sin. When we care for others, our caring is tainted. Even when we confess our sin, we may feel we have done something to earn our own forgiveness. We confess with all saints on earth that we live with both original and actual sin, hunted and haunted every day. Thanks be to God, we also enjoy new life hidden in Christ. We are never alone, never dependent on ourselves for faith and life. Our Victor and Advocate ever lives to make intercession for us (Hebrews 7:25). In this world we will have constant tribulation, but we find comfort in Jesus Christ, who has overcome the world for us (John 16:33). I communicated this to my daughter, because I understood her plight.

Before joining the Lutheran church, my husband and I were in the same spiritually dangerous place where our daughter had stumbled. I flashed back to Sunday mornings years ago, when my husband and I found ourselves searching for any reason to not go to the church we attended at the time. A slight sniffle would suffice. We knew this desire was wrong, and in desperation we asked to meet with the church's pastor. We told him that we thought we needed help. We asked if the church could offer the Lord's Supper more often. Looking back, I wince at his response. The pastor sat in our living room, and he looked deeply into our distraught faces. He did not provide comfort to our troubled consciences. Instead, he told us we could not partake of the Lord's Supper more often, because we could not adequately prepare ourselves more often.

We did not realize that his "meal of remembrance" is far different than "Given and shed for you, for the forgiveness of sins." He left us only with the certainty that we had failed yet again. When he left, my husband and I silently bore the heaviness of this new burden. We had already felt shamefully sinful in our lack of desire to attend church, but now we heard that we were too miserable to be fed spiritual food. Our shriveling faith faced starvation.

---

[224] Luther, Martin, referenced by Erika Bullmann Flores. "Let Your Sins Be Strong: A Letter From Luther to Melanchthon Letter No. 99, 1 August 1521, From the Wartburg." Accessed November 22, 2014. *www.iclnet.org/pub/resources/text/wittenberg/luther/letsinsbe.txt*.

Freedom

Today in the Lutheran church, we hear and receive the forgiveness of sins every Sunday. How comforting is the answer to the question in the Small Catechism, "Who receives the sacrament worthily?" With all of our children, we memorized the answer! *"Fasting and bodily preparation are certainly fine outward training. But that person is truly worthy and well prepared who has faith in these words: 'Given and shed for you for the forgiveness of sins.' … ."*[225] We can come to the Altar of our Lord knowing that Jesus Christ died and rose again for us. Our sins — and our very sinfulness — are fully forgiven in Him!

My daughter's torment is relieved in the full forgiveness of Jesus Christ given to her through His Word and Sacraments, apart from her own efforts to rid herself of sin or its effects. Yes, there is a continuing battle, and the inner war will rage till the moment of her death. But she need not drag herself through days of despair. Nor does she need to maintain a forlorn countenance to evidence the struggle! With her gaze turned away from herself and her sin, and turned instead to Jesus Christ and His salvation, my daughter's inner struggle can work for her good. We shared with her this freedom, as found in Martin Luther's words:

In the midst of utter woe
When our sins oppress us,
Where shall we for refuge go,
Where for grace to bless us?
To Thee, Lord Jesus, only!
Thy precious blood was shed to win
Full atonement for our sin.

Holy and righteous God!
Holy and mighty God!
Holy and all merciful Savior!
Eternal Lord God!
Lord, preserve and keep us
In the peace that faith can give.
Have mercy, O Lord![226]

My daughter's tender Shepherd nourishes, sustains, and keeps her in the one true faith. When doubt strikes, she can remember her baptism into Christ, where she has already died, and she can rest in

---

[225] Luther, *Small Catechism*. In *Concordia: The Lutheran Confessions*, 343.
[226] *Lutheran Service Book*, 755:3.

the present life that she has in Christ. All will be fully realized on the Last Day. My daughter hears the words of forgiveness spoken into her ears and tastes in her mouth the Feast of Victory in the Divine Service. Here is sustenance for the heavy-laden, rest for the weary, and strength for all believers.

The Lord is mighty to save and His arm is never too short (Isaiah 59:1a). He has taken hold of us in Christ, whose sacrifice for sin is sufficient for all sins, even the sins of Christians.[227] "What shall I render to the Lord for all His benefits to me? I will lift up the cup of salvation and call on the name of the Lord" (Psalm 116:12). May we take heed to Luther's exhortation:

> So when the devil throws your sins in your face and declares that you deserve death and hell, tell him this: "I admit that I deserve death and hell, what of it? For I know One who suffered and made satisfaction on my behalf. His name is Jesus Christ, Son of God, and where He is I shall be also!"[228]

Stargazing: Reflections on Teaching Our Children at Home

How privileged we are to teach our children at home, even when we may not realize it. Cheryl offers these closing thoughts as a wife and homeschooling mother who graduated twins with significant special needs and developmental delays, after homeschooling from the children's infancy.

Stargazing
Cheryl Swope

My husband and I witness our friends becoming somewhat reluctant "empty nesters," as we see the need to continue teaching our children even beyond their graduation. At 20, neither of our twins can attend college due to their special learning needs and medical challenges, yet both want to continue learning. Over time their difficulties

---

[227] Parton, Craig A. *The Defense Never Rests: A Lawyer's Quest for the Gospel.* St. Louis: Concordia Publishing House, 2003. 37.

[228] Mize, Gaven. "Please Allow Me to Introduce Myself." Alien Righteousness, Justification That's Not from around These Parts. Accessed November 22, 2014. *alienrighteousness.org/author/shepherdsvilleslugger/.*

have increased, so we learned to relax our expectations, but never the quality of our courses or methods. Our son continues studying logic, music theory, history, literature, and other classes at home. He learns slowly, but with Socratic questioning and purpose we see his thinking sharpen.

Our son's medical conditions progress, so he hopes his continued education will strengthen his otherwise weakening mind. We required several years to master introductory Latin, but Michael told me recently, "Latin is so meticulous and systematic, I think it takes my boggled mind and sorts it out." He added, "I want to study Latin forever." His twin sister Michelle chimed in, "Me too." Most of our daughter's academic abilities never progressed to the level of her brother's, but she enjoys beginning elements of each area in the liberal arts, all bathed in truths from theology, the queen of the liberal sciences.

As teachers and parents, we want to help our children love truth, goodness, and beauty. We encourage this through the liberal arts and sciences and the great literature, music, art, and ideas of Western civilization. Each will grasp different aspects. One day we read *The Merchant of Venice* together; my concrete-thinking son understood very little, but Michelle loved Portia's famous speech on mercy. She played Portia in each scene. When Bassanio (reluctantly played by her brother) referenced Troy and Hercules, we recalled our beginning classical studies. When Bassanio noted that outward appearance does not always indicate inward beauty, my son found himself pausing at the wisdom of this insight.

Hours later the same day, my husband located some star guides and gathered the children. Equipped with binoculars and blankets, we all settled in on a big blanket for an early autumn evening of stargazing. On such occasions, we see how all learning comes together in gratifying ways. Lying still in an open field near the woods that night, we marveled at the numerous clusters of stars in our country sky, far more than we could count. My daughter recalled Abraham and God's promise. We rested quietly in this promise's fulfillment in Christ Jesus for us. My husband identified the constellation Aquila. Michelle said she knew from Latin that it would be an eagle. We smiled. My husband pointed out various constellations and the planet Mars. The names of constellations prompted stories from Greek and Roman mythology, and our children know these far better than we do.

As a family that evening, we all relaxed together, captivated by one of those rare moments that instantly beautify family life. When the darkness deepened in the sky, we spotted the Big Dipper low on the horizon. My husband noted the trapezoid shape of its ladle, and my children nodded. He pointed to another constellation, "45 degrees from the bright star overhead." As the children followed his finger, I remembered protractors from our many years of geometry lessons together. We searched the rugged craters of the moon through our binoculars. My son surprised me by noting the half moon's appearance as a "perfect semi-circle, with the diameter bisecting the whole." Then for a moment we fell silent.

As Christian parents, we embrace an education that teaches for this life and for the life that is to come. We strengthen our children's minds through disciplined studies. We give them essential skills and tools for learning. We also nurture their faith. We love and forgive together, as we bring our children to their Savior in Holy Baptism, teach them Bible stories and the catechism, instruct them in Christian doctrine, immerse them in hymns and prayers, and pray for them all their lives. We receive with them daily lessons in humility and dependence upon the One who made us, the One who redeemed us, and the One who set all of the stars in the darkness of the night sky.

That night a fall chill descended under those stars. Snuggling our fragile daughter to keep her warm, I appreciated the richness a beautiful Christian education offers even children such as ours. "O Lord, how manifold are Your works! In wisdom You have made them all." [229]

---

[229] Psalm 104:24. A version of this article first appeared in *The Classical Teacher* magazine, Memoria Press, 2014.

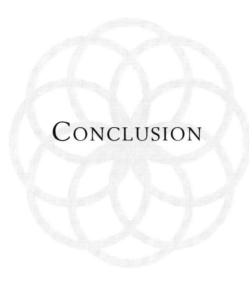

CONCLUSION

May the husband and wife highly esteem each other with sincere love. Bind together with the bond of chaste love the hearts of the pious who are married so they embrace each other willingly and continue in Your holy service. ... May the strong bond of marriage be a holy mystery of the love between Christ and the church (Ephesians 5:32) ... . Bend also the hearts of the children so they show to their parents the obedience owed to them ... . May parents and children worship You, true God, with united devotion in this life so they may praise You in eternal life with united praises. ... The household is a household church, highly esteemed by God and angels. Amen.[230] — Johann Gerhard

Conclusion

Cheryl Swope and Rachel Whiting

The Lord our God is one (Deuteronomy 6:4b). He is our triune God, eternally existing in three Persons, the Father, the Son, and the Holy Spirit. He spoke, saying, "Let us make man in our image" (Genesis 1:27a). Man was made, and it was not good for him to be alone. Woman was made from the man. God bestows children through the union of the man and the woman, and He may give the blessing of

---

[230] Gerhard, *Meditations on Divine Mercy*, 141-143.

children through the beautiful provision of adoption. The plurality and unity of the family reflects the plurality and unity of God.[231]

How bountiful is this picture of the family in reflecting the image of God. Yet how disfigured and corrupt the family became due to the fall into sin! Though designed to speak of the blessedness of God, we blame, we deceive, we neglect. We exhibit our selfishness.

Thanks be to God, His great love does not leave us in the state we put ourselves in! God sent His only Son for our redemption. God grabs hold of us when He unites us with Christ in Baptism, and He sustains us through His own life-giving Word and Sacraments. Oh, the depths of the grace and mercy of God!

Abundant Life

Because of Christ, death is replaced by life. In dying to ourselves to love and serve, there is life at work in others (2 Corinthians 4:12). In losing our life for Christ's sake, we find it (Matthew 10:39b). In these days before the Last Day, the world, our own flesh, and the devil want the old man resuscitated to breathe in curse-laden air, but our new man clings to Christ, who is Life and who has conquered the curse upon us. Jesus Christ is the victor for us. Through the God-breathed word, we have the breath of life.[232] By His grace and merciful forbearance toward us, we serve now as the masks of God in love and forbearance toward one another. Christ came for us to "have life and have it abundantly" (John 10:10).

In the family, and individually, we find reconciliation in Jesus Christ alone. As parents and as children, our sins are forgiven, and our faith is strengthened. We receive Absolution, we hear the preached Word, and we partake of His Holy Supper in the Divine Service. Our gracious Lord provides us with every good gift. He draws us to Himself through Jesus Christ, our very Bread of Life.

As parents we are to provide for the whole personhood of our children. Whatever educational path we follow, the responsibility remains ours. We equip our children for citizenship in temporal and eternal kingdoms, as He enables us to do so. In the development of strong academic skills, knowledge, and eloquence, we give our children the provisions to fulfill their vocations in any area of service. And as we embrace our own vocation as parents, we raise our children for the

---

[231] Fabrizius, *The Lutheran Catechesis Series*, 4.

[232] Ezekiel 37:5, 2 Timothy 3:16-17.

purpose of their being a mask of God to others, as our Lord Christ is hidden in our neighbor.[233]

May you find encouragement in Christ our Lord, who has called you to be parents or grandparents, teachers or pastors. He has not left you alone. Our God, Immanuel, is forever with us (Isaiah 7:14, Matthew 1:23). Though the days and years are filled with real challenges which grow and change with our growing children, Christ our steady Rock is the same, yesterday, today, and forever (Hebrews 13:8). Through joys or tears, triumphs or heartaches, God is working all things together for our good[234] (Romans 8:28). We turn to Him in prayer. The Holy Spirit comforts us. We are reminded, "He who did not spare his own Son but gave him up for us all, how will he not also with him graciously give us all things?" Jesus Christ is our hope now and for an unfathomable, blissful eternity.

When the Lord graciously places a child into our lives, He gives to us an *eternal treasure*. As we teach this child, we can assure him above all else that in Christ, life forever has been won.

> *Little children, come to Me,*
> *For My kingdom is of these.*
> *Life and love I have to give,*
> *Mercy for your sin.*
>
> *In the water, in the Word,*
> *In His promise, be assured:*
> *Those who are baptized and believe*
> *Shall be born again.*
>
> *Father welcomes all His children*
> *To His fam'ly through His Son.*
> *Father giving His salvation,*
> *Life forever has been won.*[235]

---

[233] Matthew 25:40; Veith and Moerbe, *Family Vocation*, 11.

[234] Romans 8:32

[235] *Lutheran Service Book*, 605:1-3.

APPENDICES

A. Home Education Laws and Organizations

HSLDA.org – Home School Legal Defense Assn. – U.S.

HSLDA.ca – Home School Legal Defense Assn. – Canada

NATHHAN.com – National Challenged Homeschoolers Associated Network – special needs

NHERI.org – National Home Education Research Institute

Wrightslaw.org – special needs in home and school

B. Homeschooling Supplies

<u>Writing</u>
Electric pencil sharpener
Sturdy pencils with good erasers
Composition books
Mechanical pencils

<u>Drawing and Art</u>
Prismacolor pencils
Sidewalk chalk
Crayons and markers
High-quality drawing paper
Sketch pads for museum visits
Children's scissors
Quality paint brushes
Watercolors

<u>Nature Study and Observations</u>
Binoculars
Magnifying glass
Glass jars
Butterfly net
Flashlight
Field guides and identification books

<u>Arithmetic and Mathematics</u>
Abacus
Number line
Fact flashcards
Counting beads or tokens

Calendar
6" ruler
12" ruler
Yardstick
Meter stick
Ruler with centimeters and millimeters
Timer
Pennies, nickels, dimes, quarters, half dollars
Protractor

History and Geography
Globe with raised markings for elevations
Wall map of biblical times
Wall map of the world today
World atlas

Organization
Three-ring binders or accordion file
Three-hole punch
Divider tabs
Pocket folders
Green painter's tape for hanging posters or artwork
Sturdy backpacks or tote bags for bringing work to activities or appointments
Hand sanitizer for removing dry erase and permanent marker
Post-it notes
Clipboards

Instruction
White board or chalkboard
Individual easels or small slates
Dry-erase markers or chalk
Lesson planner
Bingo markers for academic games, reward tokens, or conduct charts

Reference Materials
Noah Webster's 1828 Dictionary
Placemats with science facts, U.S. presidents, etc.
Set of encyclopedias
Student dictionary
Student thesaurus

C. Resources for Teaching the Christian Faith

<u>EARLY CHILDHOOD/PRESCHOOL/PRIMARY</u>

A Child's Garden of Bible Stories, Concordia Publishing House (CPH): Share with your child 60 key stories of God's faithfulness, grace, and mercy. Save this book and enjoy again as an early reader, when your child begins reading!

The Story Bible, CPH: With a Lutheran emphasis on God's promises fulfilled in Christ, the child learns more than 130 elegantly-illustrated Bible stories in this book's 480 pages. Includes simple tips for art, drama, discussion, and prayer, along with the stories.

Sing the Faith CD, CPH: The catechism is set to music for early, enjoyable memorization. Each of the 67 songs is sung by children's voices and encompasses the entire Small Catechism.

My Very First Bible, CPH: With 1,888 pages, this beautifully illustrated ESV translation provides introductions to biblical books, central themes, and questions for reflective discussion.

My First Hymnal, CPH: Teach hymns with the beautiful colors, symbols, and psalms of the Church. Includes selected prayers and liturgical orders for devotional use. Add the *My First Hymnal* CD set to enjoy three audio CDs of more than 50 hymns.

My First Catechism, CPH: This illustrated version of the Small Catechism assists memory work and understanding. For ages 6 to 10, this volume prepares for closer study of the catechism in later years.

Our Faith From A to Z, CPH: Introduce your young child to the language of our faith with alphabetically-organized theological terms such as "C is for Catechism" and "K is for Kyrie." This 32-page book is a nice gift for the family of a newly baptized child.

O Lord, Open Our Lips (and all in the CD set): From a children's choir under the expert direction of the Rev. Richard and Barbara Resch, the hymns on these CDs provide Lutheran hymns sung in children's voices for each season of the Church Year.

<u>UPPER ELEMENTARY</u>

120 Bible Stories, CPH: With stories told through the words of Holy Scripture, each lesson provides memory work, discussion questions, and full-color illustrations. The book includes maps, a timeline, and a glossary.

Worshiping with Angels and Archangels, Behold the Lamb, Ordering Our Days in His Peace, CPH: Share the rich liturgy, tradition, and symbols of the Divine Service and Church Year with these books.

Luther's Small Catechism, CPH: If not yet memorized, be sure to have this memorized prior to confirmation classes!

To All Eternity: The Essential Teachings of Christianity, CPH or *Lutheranism 101 for Kids,* CPH: Teach the essentials of the faith in a simple way, before the student explores them in greater depth in confirmation class and beyond.

Hymns for All Saints CD series, CPH: With choral selections from the *Lutheran Service Book,* these CDs help teach doctrine, familiarize children with hymns as preparation for the Divine Service, and edify your children in the home or while traveling.

MIDDLE SCHOOL

Lutheran Service Book, Hymn Accompaniment Edition, CPH: For the student of piano, organ, or voice, obtain this edition to assist and encourage our future church musicians!

A Simple Way to Pray, CPH: Before too long, your middle school student will be much more independent, so teach him to pray now, that he may continue praying long after he leaves home. This brief treatise by Luther, first published in 1535, is revisited in accessible terms by the Rev. Dr. Matthew C. Harrison in an affordable booklet for devotional study.

Martin Luther: Hymns, Ballads, Chants, Truth, CPH: This four-CD set includes a 64-page booklet with each hymn text and brief explanation of the history and music with words from Martin Luther. Play these at home and in the car to prepare your high school student for carrying the music of his Christian faith with him into young adulthood. Consider creating a "Music of the Reformation" course from this set!

HIGH SCHOOL

The Lutheran Study Bible, CPH: If you cannot afford the entire Essential Lutheran Library from CPH, purchase this single volume for your high school student. Rich with notes from the Church Fathers, Lutheran reformers, theologians, and pastors, this all-in-one resource with maps and timelines assists personal study as well as engaged participation in Bible class.

Lutheran Bible Companion, CPH: With maps and more than 600 color photographs, this two-volume handbook helps the student explore the biological and geographical contexts of biblical history and literature.

The Lutheran Difference, CPH: When your high school student asks about the beliefs of friends, co-workers, or neighbors, he can study the answers from a biblical foundation. This book explores essential Lutheran teachings by providing comparisons and contrasts with other worldviews and with the beliefs of other Christian denominations.

Why I Am A Lutheran, CPH: Paired with the above resource, this book helps answer questions high schoolers raise about Lutheranism from a reliable, respected source.

The Church from Age to Age, CPH: Create a uniquely Lutheran church history course for your high school student from the maps, primary sources, index, and timeline contained in this one-volume resource.

Spirituality of the Cross, CPH: Engage your high school student in a personal, doctrinal study of the means of grace, the two kingdoms, and other aspects of confessional Lutheranism.

Heirs of the Reformation CD, CPH: Play this at home for a continual foundation, or give a set to your young driver for his car. With deeply beautiful texts and settings from Gerhardt to Gerike, this four-CD set includes varied music with soloists, choirs, and period instruments.

Concordia: The Lutheran Confessions, CPH: Read through this book in its entirety with your high school student over a period of one to three years.

RECOMMENDED FOR THE ENTIRE FAMILY

Lutheran radio – lutheranpublicradio.org and *WorldwideKFUO.org:* Free 24/7 "streaming" music and discussions

D. Homeschooling Curriculum Recommendations

These resources are among those most often recommended by Lutheran homeschoolers. For a more comprehensive list reviewed by Lutherans, see the *Curriculum Resource Guide for Classical Lutheran Education*, Swope and Heine (CCLE Press, 2015).

Consider purchasing directly ffrom the publishers listed on the next page for optimal customer service and updated editions. Other purchasing options:
- Amazon
- Christian Book Distributor
- Rainbow Resource Center

Publishers and Catalogs

- Classical Academic Press
- Christian Liberty
- Institute for Creation Research
- Answers in Genesis
- Veritas Press
- Rod and Staff
- Memoria Press
- Peace Hill Press
- CiRCE Institute
- Concordia Publishing House

Teaching Resources

Reading
Alpha-Phonics, Paradigm Company
First Start Reading and Classical Phonics, Memoria Press
Teach Your Child to Read in 100 Easy Lessons, Fireside
The Ordinary Parent's Guide to Teaching Reading, Peace Hill Press

Penmanship
New American Cursive (opt. StartWrite Software), Memoria Press
D' Nealian Handwriting, Scott Foresman
Handwriting Without Tears, HWT Company
Spencerian Penmanship, Mott Media

Recitations and Copybook
Living Memory: A Classical Memory Work Companion, Lulu.com
Recitations within Classical Core Curriculum, Memoria Press
Copybook Series, Memoria Press
Simply Classical Copybook, Memoria Press

Writing
Introduction to Composition and *Classical Composition*, Memoria Press
Institute for Excellence in Writing resources, IEW
Writing with Ease, Peace Hill Press
Writing and Rhetoric, Classical Academic Press

Spelling

Christian Liberty Academic Speller, Christian Liberty Press
Spelling Workout, Modern Curriculum Press
Spelling You See, Demme Learning

English Grammar

First Language Lessons, Peace Hill Press
Rod and Staff English Grammar
Shurley English, Shurley
Writing Road to Reading, Spalding

Latin

Prima Latina; Latina Christiana; First Form Latin, Memoria Press
Latin for Children, Classical Academic Press
Wheelock's Latin, Harper and Row Publishers, Inc.
Henle Latin, Loyola Press

Latin and Greek Roots

Rummy Roots, Eternal Hearts
Roots of English: Latin and Greek Roots for Beginners, Memoria Press
Book of Roots: Advanced Vocabulary Building From Latin Roots, Memoria Press
Vocabulary From Classical Roots, Educators Publishing Service

Greek

Elementary Greek, Christine Gatchell
Song School Greek, Classical Academic Press
Greek for Children, Classical Academic Press
Basics of Biblical Greek Grammar, Zondervan

Logic

The Fallacy Detectives, Bluedorn
Art of Argument, Argument Builder, Classical Academic Press
Traditional Logic I and II, Material Logic, Memoria Press

Rhetoric

Writing and Rhetoric, Classical Academic Press
Rhetoric and Poetics of Aristotle, various
Classical Rhetoric with Aristotle, Memoria Press
Rhetorica ad Herennium, Harvard University Press

The Mathematical Arts and Liberal Sciences

Arithmetic and Mathematics (K-12 options included here)
Ray's Arithmetic, Mott Media
Arithmetic, Rod and Staff
A Beka Traditional Math Series, A Beka Book
Saxon Math K-Calculus, Saxon Publishers
Elementary Algebra, Geometry, Mathematics: A Human Endeavor, W. H. Freeman
The Joy of Mathematics, The Teaching Company

Astronomy and Natural Science
Peterson Field Guides, Houghton Mifflin Harcourt
My Nature Journal, Memoria Press
Science and Enrichment Sets, Memoria Press
Christian Liberty Nature Readers, Christian Liberty Press
A Beka Health and A Beka Science, A Beka Book
Apologia Science, Apologia
The Book of Astronomy, Memoria Press
J. H. Tiner series, available through Memoria Press
Nature's Beautiful Order, available through Memoria Press
The Amazing Story of Creation from Science and the Bible, Institute for Creation Research

Moral and Theological Sciences
See Appendices C and G

The Great Art, Music, History, and Literature of Western Civilization

Art
Fine Arts Primer, Veritas Press
Janson History of Art, study guide, Memoria Press
The Annotated Mona Lisa, Strickland
Art Cards and *Creating Art*, Memoria Press

Drawing
Drawing with Children, available through Veritas Press
Drawing with Teens, available through Veritas Press
Draw-Write-Now, Barker Creek
Composition and Sketchbook (with *Timeline Program*), Memoria Press

Poetry
Favorite Poems Old and New, Helen Farris
Harp and Laurel Wreath, Ignatius Press
Poetry for the Grammar Stage; Poetry, Prose and Drama, Memoria Press
Linguistic Development through Poetry Memorization, Andrew Pudewa, IEW

History/Geography/Literature
The Story of the World, Peace Hill Press
Geography Songs with CD, Audio Memory
Classical Studies Series, Memoria Press
Geography I and II; Timeline Program, Memoria Press

Literature/The Great Books of Western Civilization
Literature Guides, Memoria Press
All Through the Ages: A Literature Guide through History, Nothing New Press
The Great Books, Anthony O'Hear
Teaching the Classics and other resources by Adam Andrews, Center for Lit

Music
Classical Kids: Collection, Alliance
An Introduction to the Classics, Vox Music Masters
How to Introduce Your Child to Classical Music in 52 Easy Lessons, Leslie and Robert Spencer
Discovering Music, Carol Reynolds

Online Options

- HSLDA Online Academy (formerly Patrick Henry Preparatory Academy) *academy.hslda.org*

- Memoria Press Online Academy *memoriapress.com/onlineschool*

- Wilson Hill Online Academy *wilsonhillacademy.com*

- Veritas Press Scholars Academy *veritaspress.com/online-education-vp-scholars-academy*

- The Well-Trained Mind Academy *wtmacademy.com*

- (Lutheran) Wittenberg Academy Online *wittenbergacademy.org*

- (Lutheran) Faith Lutheran in Plano, Texas *flsplano.org/academics/high-school/live-online-courses/*

E. Literature Favorites for Children and Teens

More Resources for Teaching Literature

Reading Between the Lines: A Christian's Guide to Literature, Gene Edward Veith

Teaching the Classics, Adam Andrews

Invitation to the Classics: A Guide to the Books You've Always Wanted to Read, Os Guiness

How to Read a Book, Mortimer Adler

The Well-Educated Mind, Susan Wise Bauer

The Great Books, Anthony O'Hear

Tending the Heart of Virtue: How Classic Stories Awaken a Child's Moral Imagination, Vigen Guroian

Books That Build Character: A Guide to Teaching Your Child Moral Values Through Stories, William Kilpatrick, Gregory and Suzanne M. Wolfe

Suggested Literature Lists

- *All Through the Ages: A Literature Guide through History*, Christine Miller
- Quality Literature: *ccle.org/quality-literature/*
- 1,000 Good Books: *classical-homeschooling.org/celoop/1000.html*
- "Books for Boys and Other Children Who Would Rather Make Forts All Day," *iew.com/sites/default/files/videocourse/fileattachment/TB-Resources.pdf*

A Sampling of Our Children's Favorite Literature

The Complete Tales of Beatrix Potter

Treasury for Children, James Herriot

Aesop's Fables

A Child's Garden of Verses, Robert Louis Stevenson

Fairy Tales, Hans Christian Andersen

Velveteen Rabbit, Margery Williams

Paddington Bear Series (unabridged), Michael Bond

The Pooh Series, A. A. Milne

Lassie Come-Home, Eric Knight

The Adventures of Pinocchio, Carlo Collodi

The Little House of the Prairie Series, Laura Ingalls Wilder

Charlotte's Web; The Trumpet of the Swan; Stuart Little, E. B. White

The Secret Garden; A Little Princess; Little Lord Fauntleroy, F. H. Burnett

The Story of Doctor Dolittle Series, H. Lofting

Pollyanna, Eleanor H. Porter

Heidi, Johanna Spyri

Black Beauty, Anna Sewell

The Chronicles of Narnia; The Space Trilogy, C. S. Lewis

D'Aulaires' Book of Greek Myths, Ingri and Edgar d'Aulaire

Mr. Popper's Penguins, R. and F. Atwater

Bambi: A Life in the Woods, Felix Salten

The Wind in the Willows; The Reluctant Dragon, Kenneth Grahame

Charlie and the Chocolate Factory, Roald Dahl

The Railway Children; The Story of the Treasure Seekers; Five Children and It, E. Nesbit

The Book of Virtues, William J. Bennett

Misty of Chincoteague, Marguerite Henry

The Little Lame Prince, Dina M. Mulock

The Bronze Bow, Elizabeth G. Speare

Where the Red Fern Grows; Summer of the Monkeys, W. Rawls

The Light Princess; The Princess and the Goblin; The Princess and Curdie; At the Back of the North Wind; The Golden Key, George MacDonald

The Story of Peter Pan, James M. Barrie

Little Britches Series, Ralph Moody

Hans Brinker, Mary M. Dodge

Rebecca of Sunnybrook Farm, Kate Wiggin

Trouble at Timpetill, Henry Winterfeld

My Side of the Mountain, Jean C. George

Beorn the Proud, Flame over Tara, Madeleine Polland

Black Ships Before Troy; The Wanderings of Odysseus, R. Sutcliff

Jungle Books; Captains Courageous, Rudyard Kipling

Anne of Green Gables, L. M. Montgomery

Old Yeller, Fred Gibson

Shadrach; Along Came a Dog, Meindert DeJong

The Island of the Blue Dolphins, Scott O'Dell

Call It Courage, Armstrong Sperry

The Call of the Wild; Sea Wolf; White Fang, Jack London

Robin Hood, Howard Pyle

The Swiss Family Robinson, Johann R. Wyss

The Adventures and The Memoirs of Sherlock Holmes, Sir Arthur Conan Doyle

Little Women; Little Men; Eight Cousins, Louisa May Alcott

The Three Musketeers; The Count of Monte Cristo, Alexandre Dumas

The Hobbit; The Lord of the Rings Trilogy; The Children of Hurin; Sir Gawain and The Green Knight; The Book of Lost Tales, J. R. R. Tolkien

A Wrinkle in Time, Madeline L'Engle

Treasure Island; Kidnapped; The Strange Case of Dr. Jekyll and Mr. Hyde, Robert Louis Stevenson

Romeo and Juliet; The Merchant of Venice; A Midsummer Night's Dream; Twelfth Night; Hamlet, William Shakespeare

Sense and Sensibility; Pride and Prejudice, Jane Austen

Oliver Twist; Great Expectations; A Christmas Carol, Charles Dickens

Robinson Crusoe, Daniel Defoe

Iliad, Odyssey, Homer

Aeneid, Virgil

F. Further Reading on the Family and on Education

The Classical Lutheran Education Journal, CCLE

Blogs by the CiRCE Institute

Articles by Dr. Christopher Perrin of Classical Academic Press

The Classical Teacher magazine with curriculum and articles, Memoria Press

Curriculum Resource Guide for Classical Lutheran Education, Cheryl Swope and Melinda Heine

Lutheran Education: From Wittenberg to the Future, Thomas Korcok

Simply Classical: A Beautiful Education for Any Child, Cheryl Swope

Classical Education, Gene Edward Veith and Andrew Kern

Family Vocation, Gene Edward Veith and Mary Moerbe

A Handbook on Classical Lutheran Education, Hein, Swope, Cain, Strickland

The Liberal Arts Tradition, Kevin Clark and Ravi Scott Jain

Climbing Parnassus, Tracy Lee Simmons

Johann Sturm on Education, Lewis W. Spitz

The Seven Laws of Teaching, J. M. Gregory

The Well-Trained Mind, Susan Wise Bauer and Jessie Wise

Designing Your Own Classical Curriculum, Laura Berquist

The Latin-Centered Curriculum, Andrew Campbell

Norms and Nobility, David Hicks

Wisdom and Eloquence, Robert Littlejohn and Charles T. Evans

Postmodern Times, Gene Edward Veith

Amusing Ourselves to Death, Neil Postman
The Great Tradition, ed. Richard Gamble
www.KatieLutherSisters.org
www.SisterDaughterMotherWife.com

G. Lutheran Devotional and Doctrinal Resources

Prayer
The Brotherhood Prayer Book, Emmanuel Press
The Lord Will Answer, Concordia Publishing House (CPH)
Lutheran Book of Prayer, Concordia Publishing House
Reading the Psalms with Luther, Concordia Publishing House
Treasure of Daily Prayer, , Concordia Publishing House
Evening and Morning: Music of Lutheran Daily Prayer CD, Concordia Publishing House
Meditations on Divine Mercy, Concordia Publishing House
Lutheran Service Book, Concordia Publishing House

Devotional Writings
Lutheran Spirituality: Life as God's Child, ed. Robert Baker
Christ Alone: Meditations and Sermons, Chad L. Bird
Every Day Will I Bless Thee: Meditations for the Daily Office, Burnell F. Eckardt, Jr.
Broken: 7 Rules that Every Christian Ought to Break as Often as Possible, Jonathan Fisk
Sacred Meditations, Johann Gerhard
An Explanation of the History of the Suffering and Death of our Lord Jesus Christ, Johann Gerhard
The Hammer of God, Bo Giertz
Christ Have Mercy: How to Put Your Faith in Action, Matthew C. Harrison
Visitation: Resources for the Care of Souls, Arthur A. Just and Scot A. Kinnaman
Heaven on Earth: The Gifts of Christ in the Divine Service, Arthur A. Just
Grace Upon Grace: Spirituality for Today, John Kleinig
Where God Meets Man, Gerhard O. Forde
The Defense Never Rests: A Lawyer's Quest for the Gospel, Craig A. Parton
Thy Kingdom Come: Lent and Easter Sermons, David H. Petersen
God With Us: Advent, Christmas and Epiphany Sermons, David H. Petersen.
Dying to Live: The Power of Forgiveness, Harold L. Senkbeil
Sanctification: Christ in Action, Harold L. Senkbeil

God at Work: Your Christian Vocation in All of Life, Gene Edward Veith

Good News magazine

Doctrinal and Historical Writings

Concordia: The Lutheran Confessions, A Reader's Edition of the Book of Concord, ed. Paul McCain

The Book of Concord, ed. Theodore G. Tappert

The Theology of Martin Luther, Paul Althaus

Baptized Into God's Family, A. Andrew Das

The Lutheran Difference, ed. Edward A. Engelbrecht

On Being a Theologian of the Cross: Reflections on Luther's Heidelberg Disputation, 1518, Gerhard Forde

We Believe: Essays on the Catechism, ed. Scott C. Klemsz

A Summary of Christian Doctrine, Edward W. A. Koehler

Bondage of the Will, Martin Luther

Lutheran Theology, Steven D. Paulson

Didache, John T. Pless

Handling the Word of Truth, John T. Pless

A Theology to Live By, Herman A. Preus

The Fire and the Staff, Lutheran Theology in Practice, Klemet Preus

Spirituality of the Cross: The Way of the First Evangelicals, Gene Edward Veith

Here I Stand: A Life of Martin Luther, Roland Bainton

Getting into the Story of Concord: A History of the Book of Concord, David P. Scaer

The Divine Service

Worshiping with Angels and Archangels, Concordia Publishing House

Ceremony and Celebration, Concordia Publishing House

Lutheran Service Book, Concordia Publishing House

Made in the USA
Charleston, SC
11 November 2015